THE CLASSICS OF WESTERN SPIRITUALITY

NICODEMOS
of the
HOLY MOUNTAIN
A HANDBOOK OF SPIRITUAL COUNSEL

TRANSLATION AND FOREWORD BY
PETER A. CHAMBERAS

INTRODUCTION BY
GEORGE S. BEBIS

PREFACE BY
STANLEY S. HARAKAS

PAULIST PRESS
NEW YORK • MAHWAH

Cover Art: William Bakos's interest in iconography began at the age of four. His parents, both very artistic, were instrumental in the development of his talents, but it was under the supervision of his high school art instructor, Shirley B. Bloom, that his techniques were further developed. Bakos received a bachelor of arts in 1982 from Hellenic College in Brookline, Massachusetts, and in 1985, a master of divinity from its mother school, Holy Cross Greek Orthodox School of Theology. Both his undergraduate and graduate studies were preparatory courses for entrance into the priesthood, and plans for ordination are in the future.

Library of Congress Cataloging-in-Publication Data

Nicodemus, the Hagiorite, Saint, 1748–1809.
  Nicodemos of the Holy Mountain / by Peter A. Chamberas, George S.
Bebis.
    p.   cm.—(Classics of western spirituality)
  Translation of: Symvouleftikon Encheriridion.
  Bibliography: p.
  Includes index.
  ISBN 0-8091-0419-9 : $15.95 (est.).—ISBN 0-8091-3038-6 (pbk.) :
$12.95 (est.)
    1. Spiritual life—Orthodox Eastern authors—Early works to 1800.
2. Christian ethics—Orthodox Eastern authors—Early works to 1800.
3. Man (Christian theology)—Early works to 1800.   4. Orthodox
Eastern Church—Doctrines—Early works to 1800.   I. Chamberas, Peter
A.   II. Bebis, George S.   III. Title.   IV. Series.
BX382.N53   1989
248.4'819—dc19   88-36506
                                                             CIP

Published by Paulist Press
997 Macarthur Boulevard
Mahwah, New Jersey 07430

Printed and bound in the United States of America

Contents

CONTENTS

Author of the Translation of the Volume

REV. PETER A. CHAMBERAS was born in Sparta, Greece, and received the B.A.Th. degree from Holy Cross Greek Orthodox School of Theology, Brookline, Massachusetts; the Lic.Th. degree from the School of Theology, University of Athens, Greece; and the S.T.M. degree in biblical studies from Boston University School of Theology. He studied under Professor Markos A. Siotis of Athens University and at Oxford. His doctoral thesis, "The Transfiguration of Christ," was approved for publication by the University of Athens in 1970.

Father Chamberas has taught at the Academy of St. Basil, Garrison, N.Y., and at Hellenic College and Holy Cross Greek Orthodox School of Theology, Brookline. He was ordained to the priesthood of the Greek Orthodox Church, and is currently the pastor of St. Nectarios Church in Boston.

Among his many scholarly works are the translations of "The Unity of the Church According to St. Paul," by Vasilios Ioannides, in the *Greek Theological Review*; "The Essence of Orthodox Iconography," by Constantine D. Kalokyris, and "The Distinction between Essence and Energies and Its Importance for Theology," by Christos Yannaras, in *St. Vladimir's Quarterly*.

Father Chamberas has also published "A Glossary of Greek Orthodox Theological Terms," in the *Greek Orthodox Archdiocese Yearbook*, 1969. He is now preparing the volumes *Baptism and Chrismation: Beginning Our Christian Life in the Orthodox Church* and *An Orthodox Prayer Book*.

Author of the Introduction of the Volume

DR. GEORGE S. BEBIS was born in Greece and studied for his B.A. and B.D. at Holy Cross in Brookline, Massachusetts. He received his S.T.M. from Harvard Divinity School and his Lic. of Orthodox Theology and his doctorate in theology from the University of Athens. He studied ecumenics at Bossey, Switzerland. Dr. Bebis served as a member of the Roman Catholic-Orthodox Consultation, and now serves as a member of the Anglican-Orthodox Consultation. He is a member of the American Association of University Professors, the American Society of Church History, the American Medieval Academy, the North American Patristic Association, and the Orthodox Theological Society in America. He has represented the Greek Orthodox Archdiocese of North and South America in national and international conferences.

Author of the Preface of the Volume
STANLEY S. HARAKAS is Archbishop Iakovos Professor of Ortho-
dox Theology in the field of Orthodox Christian Ethics at Holy Cross
Greek Orthodox School of Theology, Brookline, Massachusetts, and is
a priest of the Greek Orthodox church. He is the author of *Toward
Transfigured Life: The Theoria of Orthodox Christian Ethics*.

Translator's Foreword

In the traditional spirituality of Orthodox Christianity, there is a memory of the mind and there is quite another memory of the soul. The former, through an amazing intellectual process, deposits impressions and knowledge in the mind externally. The latter, however, being a spiritual and incorruptible memory, produces an untaught knowledge in the depths of the purified soul. The one knowledge begins in this world and is rational, limited and determined by the philosophical categories of human thought. The other knowledge, revealed by God who enlightens both the physical and the spiritual world, is received according to the degree of purity of the heart and the degree of love for God and man that a person has.

In *A Handbook of Spiritual Counsel*, St. Nicodemos holds that it is in the renewed and purified heart where true theology begins and where divine knowledge and teaching spring up by the grace of God. Had St. Nicodemos acquired only the external knowledge through the memory of his mind and not the purity of his heart, he would not have been able to draw out into the light of day from the depths of his soul the spiritual gifts of God, and to express them in terms that others can find beneficial. This is why Fr. Theokletos Dionysiatis, a contemporary monk of the Holy Mountain and a biographer of St. Nicodemos, observes that *A Handbook of Spiritual Counsel* is a virtual miracle and a creation *ex nihilo*. A work of such spiritual value that emanates the fragrance of the Holy Spirit is not the product of the memory of the mind alone; it is also the product of the memory of the soul imbued by God.

In the spiritual tradition of the Orthodox Church, the inner or the so-called mystical theology, the theology of the experience of holiness, is the one that comes first in importance to all other activities. This mystical union with God in the heart of the Christian believer is the

xi

goal, the destiny which one struggles to achieve through faith, prayer, love and the joyous contrition of repentance. Having learned the theory through practice, having absorbed the Orthodox Christian tradition of spirituality in his pure and holy heart, and having become a sacred vessel containing the aroma of divine knowledge, St. Nicodemos was able to pour it out abundantly into *A Handbook of Spiritual Counsel* for the benefit of all.

In rendering into English the original Greek text of this spiritual classic, I have worked from the third printed edition by Soterios N. Schoinas of Volos, Greece, dated 1958. This particular edition includes three short studies at the end, not directly related to the main subject. It also includes the biography and the liturgical hymns in honor of St. Nicodemos to be used on his feast day, July 14. All of these have been excluded from this translation for practical reasons. However, certain lengthy notations that appear as footnotes in the Greek edition of 1958 have been very carefully edited and placed appropriately in the main body of the text. This has been done not only because they are indeed substantive notes which enhance the subject matter with additional scriptual and patristic references, but also because the editor of the 1958 edition claims that these notes are indeed original additions of St. Nicodemos himself, who wrote them in by hand on an early copy of his book, belonging at first to a certain Father I. Martinos and now in the possession of the editor mentioned above.

By placing these additions into the body of the text where they rightfully belong, as afterthoughts of the author himself, it became possible to remove from the body of the text the many patristic references, and to cite them as simple footnotes. It must be noted here, however, that since most patristic references were quoted from memory by the author, as Dr. Bebis explains in the Introduction, these were translated as they appear in the original text of St. Nicodemos, and no effort was made to locate them in critical editions or translations. Consequently, most footnotes appear in their original brief form, citing simply the Church Father with a general reference to the name of his work. Biblical quotations, on the other hand, are, in most cases, taken from the Revised Standard Version with an expanded edition of the Apocrypha, and references are included in the text.

Finally, I should like to express what a spiritual delight indeed it has been for me to prepare this translation of *A Handbook of Spiritual Counsel*, and thus to help make this classic work of Orthodox Spirituality available to the English-speaking world. Of the more than one hundred writings of St. Nicodemos, this volume is only the third to appear in English translation, following the *Unseen Warfare* and *The Rudder*. From the start I have considered this project a very special privilege, and I am grateful to the Paulist Press for inviting me to be part of the team, together with my esteemed colleagues, Fr. Stanley S. Harakas and Dr. George Bebis. I should like also to express my gratitude to Nikolaos Hatzinikolaou for his graciousness in proof reading my manuscript, and to Georgia Christo of Paulist Press for her valuable collaboration.

Preface

The monk Nicodemos the Hagiorite (1749–1809), almost unknown by Western Christians, is a spiritual giant not only for the Orthodox people of Greece, but for all Orthodox Christians of every national tradition.

Nicodemos lived in the waning years of the Ottoman Empire, which from the fifteenth century had incorporated many of the Orthodox peoples within its domain. Allowed to maintain their religious and civic life as subject peoples, the Orthodox Christians of the Muslim Ottoman Empire remembered the past glories of Byzantium from within a restrictive "second-class" citizenship. Survival was the major virtue in this Muslim-dominated society, as the ranks of the "neomartyrs" witnessed. Though some modest institutions of learning existed for the Greek-speaking Christians, learning was not extensive, much ignorance prevailed, and much of the Church's life was routine and formal, and subject to manipulation by the Turkish overlord.

In such an environment the need for renewal and fresh inspiration was great. Some forces for spiritual enlightenment and growth in the Church did exist, not the least of which was the Ecumenical Patriarchate of Constantinople. Other forces, however, tended to foster nationalistic trends inspired by the Renaissance and the emerging secularist traditions, largely ignoring the Church and her spirituality. Nevertheless, in practically every generation, some personalities of intelligent faith and commitment reminded the Orthodox people of the great spiritual heritage of Orthodox Christianity that was theirs and provoked them to growth in the image and likeness of God, which was their calling as Christians.

Perhaps the greatest of these was Nicodemos, the monk of the Holy Mountain Athos. A number of aspects of his ministry to the people of his times (and to the generations that followed) justify this assessment. Possibly the most important was the comprehensiveness of his perspective on the Christian life. The Church Fathers who knew and appreciated learning, science, and culture, but who saw these as integrally related to the Christian world view and under the purview of the Holy Trinity, were one source of his inspiration.

Of course he was not and could not be a man of the twentieth century. He had the prejudices, limitations of knowledge, and misunderstandings of the age in which he lived, and these are apparent in his writings. A narrow man, however, he was not. Rather, he not only was encyclopedic in the range of his knowledge and interests, but he consistently sought to hold the knowledge of science, philosophy, and culture in close connection with the more important truths of faith and spiritual life. He embodied the best traditions of Orthodox Christianity, which may be characterized as holistic and integrative.

Nevertheless, Nicodemos' major interest was the spiritual renewal of the people of the Orthodox Church for whom he worked, wrote, and prayed. It has been said that if Nicodemos had written only the *Philokalia*, his contribution to the advancement of the spiritual life of the Orthodox people of his time would have been adequate to assure him a supreme place in the roster of spiritual leaders of modern Orthodox Christianity. This five-volume collection (in the Greek edition) is a compilation of numerous monastic writings on prayer and discipline—"*askesis*" in the practice of the Eastern Orthodox Church. These writings both expressed and nurtured Eastern Christian spirituality for a millennium and a half, and were at the root of hesychast spirituality. Nicodemos' compilation and publication of this work had immediate impact of international dimensions within the Orthodox world, and continues influencing the Orthodox to this day. (At this writing, three volumes have been translated into English.)

Nicodemos clearly believed in the power of education for the reform and renewal of the Church. He wrote about a hundred works, some of which remain unpublished. In his Introduction to this volume, Dr. Bebis describes a portion of this array of spiritual literature. Nicodemos wrote of holy men and women, with his compilations of the lives of the saints and the gathering of information regarding the lives of the New Martyrs. He defended specific dimensions of Orthodox life through his apologetical works. The ascetic life was another area of concern, cultivated especially through the *Philokalia* and the *Evergetinos*. Nicodemos was a biblical commentator, but more in the pastoral spirit of the Fathers than in the spirit of academia, with com-

·

mentaries on the psalms, the epistles of Paul, and the seven Catholic epistles among his works. Nor were poetical and liturgical works absent from his interests; he wrote books on Church feasts and liturgical hymns.

In the strict theological sense, Nicodemos' main contribution was the publication of the works of Symeon the New Theologian and the effort to publish the writings of Gregory Palamas. Works especially written to guide the practical life of the Christians of his day were sometimes modeled after Western Christian writings, which Nicodemos so thoroughly reworked and revised that many no longer consider them translations or even paraphrases, but equivalent to original works. These include *Unseen Warfare* and the *Spiritual Exercises*. Among his original works in this category are the guide for Father Confessors, the *Exomologetarion*, and his tract on frequent Holy Communion.

Through a collection of canons with his own extensive commentaries, Nicodemos sought to provide a handy reference guide to the canonical tradition of the faith; his *Pedalion (Rudder)* is still one of the Church's chief handbooks of canon law. More ethical in character are *Chrestoetheia* and the present volume, the *Symvoulevtikon Encheiridion*.

In all, his writing shows a balance of scriptural and patristic grounding, sensitivity to knowledge and science, and zeal in fervent commitment to the spiritual life. That his writings were published again and again is a sign that they both provoked and met the needs of spiritual renewal among the Orthodox Christians of the late eighteenth and early nineteenth centuries.

The occasion for the writing of the work at hand was a request from Nicodemos' cousin, Ierotheos, who had recently been ordained Bishop of Euripos, to provide him with "counsels" regarding the fulfillment of his responsibilities as a bishop. According to the preface in the third edition published in Greece by the "Hagiorite Library" of Volos, the first edition was published with the personal character of the text, as the author addressed his "counsels" directly and by name to his cousin, Bishop Ierotheos. However, in the subsequent editions these were edited out and the work now addresses the reader, who is presumed simply to be a Christian. Wherever appropriate, the clerical references remain, but the work has been understood as applicable to all Christians, both clergy and laity.

According to the Preface to the third edition, from which this translation has been taken, "the *Symvoulevtikon Encheiridion* belongs to the category of ethical and neptic writings, which deal with ethical

3

cleansing and thus prepare the soul to become receptive of the un-created energies of God, and then to union with Him, which consti-tutes the supreme desire of the God-loving soul." Nicodemos is thus within the mainstream of Orthodox ethical thinking, which invariably draws all ethical reflection and teaching from the faith tradition of Orthodoxy and works within that tradition.

As regards its substance, Nicodemos' *A Handbook of Spiritual Coun-sel* is still a valuable and timely contribution to growth in the spiritual life for the contemporary reader who yearns for purity of body and soul. Its focus—psychological, ethical, and practical—readily com-mends it to the laity. The modern reader will recognize in its pages some passages that reflect views and prejudices of another age, and will discount them.

When Bishop Ierotheos received the manuscript and read it, he wrote a letter of deep appreciation to his monastic cousin. Among the words of praise was this assessment of its value to him: "From it, I gathered much profit, not transient nor limited to the benefit of the mortal body, but everlasting and pertaining to the immortal soul. . . . You have provided me with sweet and aromatic honey, by which you sweeten not only me and those associated with me, but sweeten all persons, as well, who in the future will study its pages. For them I foresee good things, since it will become the provocation of spiritual health."

Many thanks are due to the Paulist Press and to editor John Farina for including this text in The Classics of Western Spirituality series; to Fr. Peter Chamberas whose fine translation introduces Nicodemos to the English-speaking world as an author in his own right; and to Dr. George Bebis of the faculty of Holy Cross Greek Orthodox School of Theology for his extensive introduction to the life and work of Nicode-mos. My prayer is that Ierotheos' assessment will prove valid for the readers of this translation, as it has for the generations who have read the Greek original.

Introduction

I. Background

The eighteenth and early nineteenth centuries, during which St. Nicodemos lived, found the Great Church of the East "in captivity."[1] It was a captivity under which most Orthodox peoples of the East had lived since the fourteenth century when the Turks extended their conquest from the distant deserts of Africa to the cold mountains of the Balkans and Southern Europe.

The Greek people, under the spiritual guidance and protection of the Ecumenical Patriarchate of Constantinople, endured with bravery and patience the vicissitudes of foreign domination. With remarkable faithfulness to their tradition, they managed not to succumb to external and internal pressures that could have annihilated them.

The period that covers the fall of Constantinople (1453) to the struggle for independence, which began in 1821, has begun to attract the interest of serious scholars and students of history and theology. Indeed, we now have a host of works dealing with this almost unknown and "dark" period of the Eastern Church.[2]

These studies portray a Church that, though constantly under siege, is at the same time full of dynamic spiritual strength, resourcefulness, and genuine piety grounded in a living theological tradition. Theory and praxis, faith and knowledge, conscious sharing in the mystical experience of the Church, active participation in her "mysteries" or sacraments, an impressive production of religious and theological literature, and, above all, the appearance of individuals of heroic spiritual proportions who withstood hardships and persecutions of all kinds make this period most interesting and worthy of careful study.

One cannot fully understand the state of the Orthodox Church during this period without being aware of the conditions of the Turkish

INTRODUCTION

State in which the Orthodox Church had to live and survive. On the one hand was a Christian Church accustomed to collaborating with a friendly Christian theocratic state (Byzantine); on the other hand was a young and vigorous theocratic state with a religion completely alien and hostile to Christianity, a state that diametrically opposed the precepts of Byzantine theocracy. The purpose of Byzantine theocracy was to establish the kingdom of God on earth; the Islamic theocracy visualized a new world conquered by sheer force and oppression of its opponents.

To be fair, however, we must admit that Mehemet the Conqueror, putting aside all his immediate theocratic ambitions, allowed the Church to function rather normally in the period after the fall of Constantinople (1453). For both political and religious reasons, the Turks recognized the Ecumenical Patriarch as a religious and civic leader and granted a sort of self-administration to the Church as far as its internal affairs were concerned. The teachings of the Koran consider Christianity a religion of "the book" (the Bible) and Christ a respected prophet. In addition, political interests suggested to the sultan a policy that would preserve the separation of the Eastern Church from the churches of the West, thus preventing assistance from any Western Christian country that might endanger the Ottoman Empire. The Eastern Church, therefore, remained a "Rum Millet," or a "Roman Nation," that is, a self-administered religious and civic institution with great spiritual authority on the religious, educational, family, and marital affairs of her people.

This situation was far from absolute freedom for the Greek and Balkan peoples. The Turkish State, being theocratic, considered the patriarch the leader of a minority with election subject to the approval of the sultan, its supreme political and religious leader. Misused in the hands of the Turkish government, the election and appointment of the Ecumenical Patriarch became a tragic and painful process that eventually suffered from the interference of the Catholic and Protestant powers of Europe. The dramatic case of Patriarch Cyril Lukaris in the seventeenth century is illustrative of the difficult situation the Ecumenical Patriarchate faced during this critical period of its history. The Western Christian powers engineered Lukaris' downfall by bribing the Turkish authorities. Indeed, five times Lukaris was dethroned and five times returned to his throne. Finally he was executed in a most unmerciful way.[3]

However, we cannot exonerate the mistakes and the ambitions of some of the Greek Orthodox of the time. The Phanariots, for example, who composed the Greek wealthy and educated elite of the time and who resided in the Phanar (the well-known suburb of Constantinople), where the Ecumenical Patriarchate was and is still located, about whom Arnold Toynbee writes in less than flattering terms, bear significant responsibility for the tragic situation.[4] Professor Vasilios Stefanides of the University of Athens,[5] as well as Timothy Ware,[6] point to the decay and the corruption that in many instances overcame the Orthodox Church during these dark days. Ware writes:

> But if Greek Orthodoxy was enabled to survive under the Ottomans it paid a heavy price. . . . Christians had to wear a distinctive dress and were not allowed to serve in the army. . . . They were permitted to display a little or no outward sign of their religion. . . . Intrigue, simony and corruption dominated the higher administration of the Church. Each Patriarch of Constantinople on his election required a *berat* from the Sultan, as a confirmation of his spiritual and secular authority.[7]

This is not however, the whole truth. Although some of the Phanariots became political and secularized, the majority remained steadfast in their culture. The patriarchs paid a great price for the cross they had to carry as "ethnarchs" and religious leaders of a powerless minority. Between the fifteenth and the twentieth centuries the Turks on 105 occasions drove patriarchs from the throne; there were 27 abdications, often involuntary; six patriarchs suffered violent deaths by hanging, poisoning, or drowning; only 21 of the 159 patriarchs of that period died natural deaths while in office. In the seventy-five-year period from 1625 to 1700 there were 50 patriarchs who held office an average of eighteen months each. At any given moment there were, usually, a number of patriarchs (or rather, ex-patriarchs) living in exile; they were often recalled to resume office once more. Some even occupied office on four or five distinct occasions.[8]

This lamentable situation had repercussions on the whole life of the Church. George Wheler, who visited the East during the seventeenth century, writes:

> The Authority which they [the Greek patriarchs] thus obtained by Simony, they maintain by Tyranny; for as soon as

they are promoted, they send to all their Bishops to contribute to the Sum they have disbursed for their Preferment; and such as deny, they depose, and send others to their Charge. Again the Bishops send their inferior Clergy; who are forced to do the same to the poor people, or to spare it out of their Wives and Children's mouths. But many times they engage for more than they can perform and bring the Church so much in debt to the Turk, that its ruin is daily threatened thereby.[9]

There was no alternative for either the clergy or the laity to follow. Thus, under this oppressive climate, they performed their duties to the Church and to the Greek "nation" with sacrifice and extreme devotion. This explains the great "cloud" of Christian neomartyrs, both clergy and laity, of all social classes, who died for Christ and his Church in an admirable way.

There is another question that should be addressed here before we proceed to St. Nicodemos himself: Were the Greek Orthodox clergy and people left without education during this period? The answer to this question is crucial because it will show whether the Greek people, in spite of being isolated and oppressed, remained steadfast to the roots, traditions, and faith of their ancestors.

Western scholars such as M. Crusius and P. Recaut, who visited the Orient during this period, described the Greek clergy and people in most unfavorable terms. They both lamented the low educational standard as well as the moral decay of the Greek clergy and people.[10] Steven Runciman tends to agree with them.[11] However, Timothy Ware believes that these assertions grossly exaggerate the reality:

The proportion of Greeks in the Turkish period who could read and write was probably as great as in any European nation at the same time; and in every century there were at least one or two Greek theological writers little inferior to their Latin counterparts, or to most of their Byzantine predecessors.[12]

In villages and small towns basic education was offered by priests, monks, or private teachers who taught young people in their own homes.[13] There were also local schools in Ioannina, Patmos,

INTRODUCTION

Chios, Thessalonike, Trebizond, Smyrna, Athens, Arta, Myconos, Naxos, Dimitsana (six patriarchs were among its graduates), Corfu, Zante, Jassy, Bucharest; the Greek College in Venice; and the Great School of the Nation (*He Megale Tou Genous Schole*) in Constantinople.[14] Many Greek youths traveled to the West to receive higher education in Pisa, Florence, Halle, Paris, Oxford, and Rome. There was a continuous publication of ecclesiastical and theological books, as well as works of practical theology such as ecclesiastical rhetoric.[15] In addition, books were published on mathematics, logic, physics, geography, and history. It is interesting, also, that from 1453 to the end of the nineteenth century more than 60,000 words were added to the Greek vocabulary.[16]

Theodore Papadopoulos concludes that many foreign visitors underestimated the moral stamina and the deep dedication of the Greek people to education, even in the most trying circumstances. He argues that they consciously or unconsciously compare the period of 1453–1821 with the products of the classical period and neglect, at the same time, to take into account the fruitful production of ecclesiastical and religious literature.[17] As C. M. Woodhouse pointed out, the Greek people, enjoying an education in their own language, religion, and traditions, would find it inevitable to some day seek their liberation from the Turkish yoke.[18] Runciman also recognizes the importance of tradition to the Greek people:

> Nevertheless the importance of the Greek tradition in the survival of Orthodoxy during the Ottoman period must not be forgotten. Throughout all its vicissitudes the Church was determined to keep its flock conscious of the Greek heritage. The monks might be suspicious of pagan learning and of attempts to revive the study of philosophy; but everyone who called himself a Greek, whatever his actual racial origins might be, was proud to think that he was of the same nation of Homer and Plato and Aristotle, as well as of the Eastern Fathers of the Church. This faith of the Greek genius kept hope alive; and without hope few institutions can survive. The Greeks might be languishing by the waters of Babylon; but they still had their songs to sing. It was Orthodoxy that preserved Hellenism through the dark centuries; but without the moral force of Hellenism, Orthodoxy itself might have withered.[19]

INTRODUCTION

It was in this kind of environment and within these spiritual, intellectual, and political circumstances that St. Nicodemos was born and flourished.

II. Life

St. Nicodemos[20] was born in 1749 on the island of Naxos, one of the beautiful islands of the "Kyklades" in the Aegean Sea. His baptismal name was Nicholas, and his last name was Kallivourtsis. His parents, Anthony and Anastasia, were pious people. His mother later became a nun at the Monastery of St. John Chrysostom, taking the monastic name Agathe.

From his early years young Nicholas was distinguished by his exceptional alertness, his industry, his labors and love for religious and secular learning. He was gifted "with great acuteness of mind, accurate perception, intellectual brightness,"[21] and with a vast and strong photographic memory, which helped him later in the writing of a most impressive number of books. In a letter one of his fellow-students calls young Nicholas "an excellent miracle of his times. He knew from memory whatever he read, not only the philosophical, economic, medical, astronomic and even military treatises which he has read, but also all the poets, and the historians ancient and new, Greek and Latin, as well as all the writings of the Fathers. It was enough for him to read a book once and remember it throughout his life."[22]

His first teacher in Naxos was the wise and prudent Archimandrite Chrysanthos, the brother of the New Martyr and apostle of the Greek Nation, St. Kosmas Aitolos.[23] Undoubtedly, Chrysanthos had a lasting influence on Nicholas. The love of this great Aitolian family for the Greek people and their care in preserving the flame of faith can be seen in the great missionary work of St. Nicodemos, who remained close to the heart, traditions, and language of the average Greek Orthodox of his times.

Since Naxos could not offer enough education for the impatient, brilliant young man, Nicodemos went to Smyrna to the renowned *Evangelike Schole* (Evangelical School), where he studied under the spiritual guidance of the famous master of his time, Ierotheos Voulismas. Nicodemos stayed in Smyrna for five years. There he mastered, besides the Greek language, Italian and French. He so distinguished himself in all the academic fields that he quickly became the teacher of his fellow students. Father Theokletos Dionysiatis notes that all these academic achievements did not spoil the brilliant young man. On the contrary, he served young and old with admirable humility, attracting the love and gratitude of his fellow students as well as that of his teacher Ierotheos. Ierotheos later invited him to take over the directorship of his school. "Come, my son, even now in my old age, that I might leave you as a teacher at the school, as I do not have anyone else like you in attainment."[24]

In 1770 the Russians burned the Turkish fleet at Tsesme, one of the most important ports on the west coast of Asia Minor. The Turks punished the Greek Orthodox people with extreme reprisals. The massacres and extensive persecution provoked young Nicholas to leave Smyrna for his native island of Naxos. He stayed there for five years and served as secretary and assistant to the Metropolitan of Paros and Naxos, Anthimos Vardis, who apparently developed high esteem for the purity of character and vastness of learning of this promising scholar. During this period Nicholas met the highly admired and respected priest-monks Gregory and Niphon, as well as the *gerontas*[25] Arsenios, all of whom were well versed in the Athonite way of life and practitioners of the spiritual "art" of hesychasm.[26] Apparently, "their moral excellence and their true piety influenced Nicholas immensely. They introduced him to the life of the ascetics of Mount Athos and persuaded him to follow the life of the Spirit, the life of unceasing prayer, the life of hesychasm, poverty, humility and absolute devotion to Christ."[27]

But who were these holy men, and why were they in Naxos during this time? They belonged to the group of monks known as the *Kollyvades*, a sarcastic and derisive appellation for the monks of Mount Athos who believed that *Kollyva*[28] should be sung on Saturdays, in accordance with the ancient tradition, and not on Sundays, the day dedicated to the resurrection of the Lord. Their enemies stated, wrongly, that the *Kollyvades* demanded that the Divine Liturgy should be moved to the predawn hours and the celebration of the Presanctified Liturgy should be celebrated after sunset. In addition, the *Kollyvades* were charged with insisting on the need for frequent holy communion. This was true, but it was in accordance with the ancient practice of the Church. They did not eliminate the necessary preparation of fasting and confession as they were accused of doing. They were also accused of promoting the reading of all the "mystical" or "secret" prayers of the liturgy aloud. This accusation was not true.[29]

INTRODUCTION

The controversy arose around 1754 when the monks in the skete of St. Anne on Mount Athos were building a church with the financial assistance of Orthodox Christians from all over the Balkan peninsula and especially from Smyrna. Since the monks were busy and tired from the labors of the week, they held the memorial services for the dead not on Saturdays, but at the Sunday vigil services. This innovation provoked tremendous commotion, tension, and even spiritual division among the monks and their lay followers. The controversy occupied the Orthodox Church for almost fifty years. Two synods, one on Mount Athos (1774) and one in Constantinople (1781), actually condemned the *Kollyvades*. Father Theokletos Dionysiatis, one of the contemporary spiritual fathers of Mount Athos, rejects as untrue all the accusations against the *Kollyvades* except their emphasis on frequent holy communion and on not performing the memorial services on Sundays.[30]

Most of the *Kollyvades* were men of high intellectual caliber, educated in the ancient Greek and Christian literatures and well versed in the biblical and patristic sources of the Church. Among them were St. Macarios of Corinth,[31] Christophoros of Arta, Agapios of Cyprus, Athanasios of Paros, and Neophytos the Kausokalyvites. St. Nicodemos was later added to the list of the luminaries of the *Kollyvades* movement.[32]

In any case, the controversy ended with the intervention of the Ecumenical Patriarchate. In 1772 Patriarch Theodosios II, with the consent of Sophronios, Patriarch of Jerusalem, decreed that to sing memorial services on Saturdays is not contrary to the doctrines of the Church and to perform them on Sundays does not constitute a sin. In an important encyclical letter in 1819 the ethnomartyr Patriarch Gregory V decreed that memorial services could be performed on Saturdays or Sundays or any other day of the week. As far as the frequency of holy communion, Gregory V agreed with his predecessor Theodosios II that the Orthodox Christians should receive holy communion as frequently as possible provided they prepared properly through fasting and confession. Gregory V added that those who found themselves worthy should receive holy communion without any hesitation.

Behind the *Kollyvades* movement, one could also distinguish the effort of all these enlightened men to revive the Eastern mystical tradition of the Orthodox Church. "Back to the Fathers" became a reality through the collection and edition of patristic texts. The *Kollyvades* were persecuted by their colleagues and even by some in the official Church. As a consequence of the persecution, they dispersed all over

INTRODUCTION

Greece, producing a "renaissance" of Orthodox spirituality in Greece and in the Balkans. As we said earlier, the young Nicholas met the Athonite *Kollyvades* Gregory, Niphon, and Arsenios.

The greatest of the *Kollyvades* was indisputably Macarios of Corinth. Because of the Russian-Turkish war of 1768, Macarios was forced out of, and finally lost, his episcopal throne in the great city of Corinth. With the permission of the Ecumenical Patriarchate he became a traveling bishop. Apparently Nicholas heard about him and met him on the small Greek island of Hydra. A long, devoted, and genuine friendship developed between the two, producing a collaboration that bore splendid fruits for Orthodox theology and spirituality. In Hydra, Nicholas also met Silvestros of Caesarea, a great monk and spiritual father, who cultivated in the heart of the young Nicholas the divine *eros* or love for the life of contemplation.

Thus, in 1775, at the age of twenty-six, Nicholas, with letters of recommendation from Silvestros, left for Mount Athos. There he renounced the world, was tonsured a monk, and received the *Mikron Schema* or "small habit," the second step into the monastic life of the Church. According to monastic custom, he changed his secular name from Nicholas to Nicodemos. The holy fathers of the Monastery of Dionysiou then appointed him reader of their cenobitic community. He spent his two years there studying in the library of the monastery. In 1777 Macarios of Corinth visited Mount Athos. The two men met in Karyes, the capital of the Holy Mountain, where they began to work together on the publication of the magnificent *Philokalia*. St. Macarios was at that time forty-seven years old and Nicodemos twenty-eight.

St. Nicodemos did not stay in only one monastery during his life at the Holy Mountain. First, he wanted to use all the resources the Holy Mountain provided at that time. He visited libraries, studied manuscripts, and worked on his publications constantly. Second, he aspired to a better spiritual life, an unceasing ascension toward perfection. He was seeking *hesychia* and wanted to be free of all human needs. Third, he was seeking a spiritual father in order to exercise the great virtue of *hypakoe*, that is, obedience. He hoped that through obedience he would be granted greater spiritual achievements in prayer, humility, and divine contemplation. Father Theokletos Dionysiatis calls him an eagle flying all over the spiritual mountains in order to live the experiences of divine love and be closer to his Creator—always closer and closer.[33]

INTRODUCTION

For some time St. Nicodemos remained at Karyes as a guest at the kelli (cell) of St. George, which belonged to the Monastery of Lavra and was commonly known as the Monastery of "Skourtaioi." The monks provided for him, giving him love, attention, and care, so that he could continue researching and writing his books. Then he tried to travel to Romania to meet the great Russian coenobiarch Paissy, but it apparently was not God's will for him. His boat met a violent storm on the high seas, and after reaching the island of Thassos, St. Nicodemos was forced to return to Mount Athos. After staying a short time at the Skourtaioi Monastery, he left for a skete, a small monastic place where monks lived alone with their spiritual father. At the skete of the Monastery of Pantokratoros, known today as Kapsala, he practiced *hesychia* (stillness) under the spiritual guidance of the famous *gerontas* Arsenios the Peloponnesian, whom he had met in his native Naxos.

Yet he still sought something higher. He traveled with Arsenios to the small, barren island of Skyropoula across from Euboia. There they practiced the strict ascetic life for one year. He wrote that he lived "the life of a worker and laborer; digging, sowing, harvesting, and every day doing all the other things by which the toilsome life on a barren island is characterized."[34]

In 1783 he returned to Mount Athos, received the "Great Schema," and settled close to the Monastery of Pantokratoros at the Kalyva of Theonas, taking as his disciple a co-patriot from Naxos named John, who had changed his name to Ierotheos. This monk served Nicodemos for six years.

St. Nicodemos' life is impressive in its simplicity, the hard and poor way of his living, the complete renunciation of all the pleasures of the flesh. As his spiritual brother Euthymios writes, his food consisted of rice boiled in water, honey diluted with water, olives soaked in fava beans, and bread. He rarely ate fish. He practiced *xerophagy* (the ascetic mode of eating bread, raisins, and nuts) in the true sense of the word. The neighboring monks used to bring him food or invite him to their spare table where, beginning to talk, he would forget completely the food prepared for him.[35] Those who knew him said that he lived the life of an angel. He was humble, sweet, meek, and without possessions. He spoke of himself as "a monster," "a dead dog," "a nonentity," "unwise," "uneducated."[36]

His fame spread, and many Orthodox and non-Orthodox visited him to receive advice and spiritual guidance. Apparently he was kind to all, and although V. Grumel[37] suggests that he was "anti-Western," he did not hesitate to participate in a dialogue with Roman Catholic theologians.[38] Patriarchs, metropolitans, and lay officials such as John Kapodistrias, who later became the first prime minister of Greece, visited him and supported his publications. They were amazed to see a man dressed in rags—he had only one cassock—with plain sandals; old, without teeth, exhausted from the fasting and the hardships of his strict monastic life. His eyes were full of flame and his mouth did not cease speaking the word of God. As his spiritual brother Euthymios was to say, he was ready to explain the Scriptures to everyone, and then he would bend his head to the left side and say secretly the famous Jesus Prayer, "Lord Jesus, save me." Many times he would say, "Fathers, let us go to a barren island so that we may get rid of this world."[39]

The end of his life, however, was approaching. In 1809 he stayed for a time at the "kelli" of the icon-painter Kyprianos, where he continued to work on the "Anabathmoi," or the "Degrees" of the *Octoechos*.[40] Feeling constantly weak, he returned once more to his beloved monks of the Monastery of Skourtaioi. On July 5, 1809, he suffered a stroke and was not able to speak easily thereafter. Medical doctors visited him, but they could not provide substantial help. He made a general confession and received the sacrament of holy unction. On July 13 he felt that the end was near. He had recited the Jesus Prayer all his life in his heart. Now he began to say it aloud. He asked for the sacred relics of his spiritual fathers, St. Macarios and St. Parthenios. With tears in his eyes, he asked the saints to take him to "the glory of the Lord," which they now enjoyed. The brothers remained awake all night. "Teacher, how do you feel?" they asked him. "I die, I die, I die," he said, and asked for holy communion. He crossed his hands and stretched out his legs. Early in the morning of July 14, 1809, "the spiritual sun," as one of his biographers calls him, quietly left this world. As one of his admirers said, "Fathers, it was better for a thousand Christians to die than Nicodemos."[41] He had labored in the mystical vineyards of the Lord so hard; his body could not suffer any more. Euthymios concludes his biography by saying, "The rays of his teachings are with us and they illuminate us and they illuminate the Church forever."[42]

Nicodemos' death left great sorrow among the Orthodox people in all the world. His fame, a fame of holiness, sacrifice, and creative spiritual fruits, left immense and indelible marks on the Eastern Church. The pious Orthodox people in their consciousness, and almost immediately after his death, elevated him to the state of a saint. He became known everywhere as the "Hagiorite," as representative of all the spiritual beauty and mystical virtues of the Holy Mountain. On May 31, 1955, the Holy Synod of the Ecumenical Patriarchate, with Patriarch Athenagoras presiding, approved and signed a synodical act regarding St. Nicodemos the Hagiorite. The synodical act stated that through the guidance of the Holy Spirit, and following the proper synodical examinations and deliberations, the Holy Synod decreed that St. Nicodemos the Hagiorite be enumerated among the saints of the Church and be honored with special services, hymns, and "encomia" on the fourteenth of July of each year, the anniversary of his passing from this world to everlasting life.[43]

This synodical act was the response to an official report and request submitted by the abbot of the whole monastic community of Mount Athos. The Greek people, most especially, accepted this decision with great enthusiasm.[44] A special service in his memory was written by Father Gerasimos Mikragiannanites, the greatest Greek Orthodox hymnologist of our times,[45] and churches were built in his honor on the Holy Mountain as well as in other provinces of Greece. Every year uncountable lips sing and chant the "Apolytikion," or the special dismissal hymn of St. Nicodemos:

> Adorned with the gift of wisdom, O Father, thou has appeared as a clarion of the Spirit and a teacher of virtue, O Nicodemos, who speakest of God; for to all thou has offered teaching of salvation and purity of life, revealing effulgence by means of thy writings, through whose riches thou has shone as light in the world.[46]

On February 7, 1956, the Holy Synod of the Church of Russia, under Patriarch Alexios, decided that the Russian Church would honor and celebrate the memory of St. Nicodemos on July 14 of each year.[47]

Before I close this section concerning the life of St. Nicodemos, perhaps I should mention his human weaknesses and shortcomings. He was thought to be too much of a conservative and a traditionalist, and he was accused of being strong-willed and uncompromising. He has also been charged with being a traveling monk who never found his roots and peace in a single monastic community on Mount Athos; moreover, he was accused of misleading the Orthodox people by translating and paraphrasing books from the West like *Unseen Warfare* and *Spiritual Exercises*. His emphasis on the canons has been perceived by his detractors as a superficial, pietistic trend, more Western than Orthodox in orientation. He has even been ridiculed as unclean and unbecoming in his physical appearance. Apparently St. Nicodemos was not free of the traits of fallen human nature!

History indicates, however, that St. Nicodemos' shortcomings were overcome by his excellent Christian virtues, his constant efforts toward Christian perfection, and his absolute dedication to the fundamental precepts of Orthodox doctrine and spiritual life. Notwithstanding his shortcomings, his life and his writings have been accepted by the Orthodox people as those of a true saint of the Church.

III. Writings

St. Nicodemos of the Holy Mountain is one of the most prolific writers of the post-Byzantine era. Indeed, he is probably one of the most productive writers of all time. He authored, corrected, or published (some still remain unpublished) more than one hundred works. A complete list has yet to be compiled. Father Nicodemos Paulopoulos, in a small but comprehensive book published in Greek, provides a useful account of the works of St. Nicodemos[48] as does Father Theokletos Dionysiatis.[49] In English we have lists published by Professors Cavarnos[50] and Bebis.[51] I shall present here the most important writings of St. Nicodemos.

Hagiographical Works

The most important hagiographical books of St. Nicodemos are, first, the *Neon Eklogion*, a collection of the lives of the saints,[52] and second, the *Synaxaristes*, again a collection of lives of the saints by Maurikios, deacon of the Great Church of Constantinople.[53] The latter collection is written in archaic Greek and translated by Maximos Margounios, bishop of Kythera during the sixteenth century. This translation was incomprehensible to the people and St. Nicodemos translated it into a smooth, modern Greek idiom. It was done with the encouragement of patriarchs and bishops of the Church as well as the monastic community of the Holy Mountain, all of whom saw the need to make the lives of the saints accessible to the people. St. Nicodemos succeeded completely. He worked for two full years to complete this work (1805–1807). He used to say that the collection of the lives of the saints illuminates, warms, revives, and activates the creativity of virtues in all the Church.[54] He included in this three-volume work 650 lives of saints and 59,148 names of otherwise unknown saints. His hagiological works included voluminous notes, providing detailed information about the lives of the saints and their environments. He added edifying admonitions and advice for the spiritual uplifting of his readers. In sending his work to Patriarch Gregory V for publication he asked that his *Synaxaristes* be published in "large letters," so that old people could read it, especially during the night hours.[55]

A third important hagiographical work of St. Nicodemos is his *Neon Martyrologion* or "New Martyrologium." Its introduction has been translated into English by the Reverend Nomikos M. Vaporis with excellent comments and important added information.[56] Vaporis makes the point that St. Nicodemos contributed greatly to the "religious enlightenment" of the Greek people. Some modern historians have favored the so-called secular enlightenment as having prepared the ground for the independence of the Greek people. However, it was people like St. Nicodemos, St. Kosmas the Aitolos, and Nectarios Terpos who prepared the religious awakening of the Greek people, thus cultivating their souls for the revolution against the Ottoman yoke.

St. Nicodemos' writings provided spiritual uplift and direction toward spiritual introspection, which in turn led eventually to the conviction that inner freedom is closely interrelated with political freedom and vice versa. Religious freedom and political freedom, therefore, are closely associated in the heart and mind of the Christian. Vaporis notes that "conversion to Islam meant not only an irrevocable loss for Orthodox Christianity but for Hellenism as well. It is often overlooked that except for some philhellenes, only Orthodox Christians participated in the Greek revolution."[57] The second point made by Vaporis is that in addition to the measures taken against individual Christians, tremendous pressure was exerted on the Christians as a religious group. "As the eighteenth century wore on, corruption within the Ottoman Empire increased and losses on the battlefield multiplied. Correspondingly, the lot of the individual Christian worsened."[58] Third, Vaporis points out, individual Muslims considered it an act of great piety and merit to effect a conversion, most especially of people who were distinguished in physical stature or mental and spiritual achievements.[59] A fourth point is that the Turks used economic oppression against the Christians; taxation, heavy and unbearable, often forced them to deny Christ and join the Muslim religion.[60]

It was in the context of all these pressures that St. Nicodemos writes:

> Do not allow the efforts and the love or your parents, brethren, relatives, wife, children, and belongings to defeat you. Do not allow the love of mercy, glory, and pleasure of this world, indeed, do not allow even the love for your own life, to prevent you from walking on the blessed road to martyrdom. For if you wish to lose your life for Christ, then you will find it.[61]

Then, to remind the Christians that worldly possessions are of secondary importance, he exhorts them by writing: "Your treasure is Jesus Christ. Your glory is Jesus. Your pleasure is Jesus. Your whole life is Jesus. Because by suffering for Jesus, you have Jesus. And by having Jesus, you have gained all earthly and heavenly things, you have gained everything—everything."[62]

St. Nicodemos was a practical man. He knew very well that the situation among the Christian peoples was not bright. He speaks about a situation in which "the fear of God disappeared, when faith was weakened, and when hope has diminished."[63] A contemporary scholar, Father Demetrios J. Constantelos, points to the great dangers the Church faced during the Ottoman period.[64] The triumph and progress of the Turks vis-à-vis the sufferings of the Christians could be misconstrued as evidence that God had abandoned them. Moreover, a religious syncretism began to develop, promoted by some dervishes who claimed that there was a close affinity between Islam and Christianity and thus apostasy of Christians to Islam was not bad after all. In addition, the revolutions appearing in Europe created a strong xenophobia among the Turks, and the wars between Russia and Turkey increased the anti-Christian feelings among the Turks.[65]

St. Nicodemos knew all this, and in his beautiful and instructive way justified the presence of Neo Martyrs in the Church of his time by emphasizing that martyrs appear in the Church so that the Church will be renewed, that those weak in faith will be ready to imitate their example, and that the Orthodox Christians "tyrannized under the heavy yoke of enslavement" may take courage and patience in the course of their difficult lives.[66]

INTRODUCTION

Confession of Faith

The *Confession of Faith, or Apology for His Accusers (Homologia Pisteos, etoi Apologia pros tous Autou Kategorous)* is St. Nicodemos' most important work. It was written in 1805 and published in Venice in 1819. It was clear that Nicodemos wanted to answer and confound, once and for all, the enemies who claimed that the *Kollyvades* were heretics and therefore untrustworthy. He confesses, first of all, the twelve articles of the Creed of Faith; second, he declares that he believes in the most important doctrines of the Church, especially the Holy Trinity and the Incarnation of the Word of God. He accepts the seven sacraments of the Church, and he keeps all the teachings of the Apostles, the seven ecumenical councils, the local councils, the holy canons, and all the teachings of the Fathers. In other words, St. Nicodemos writes that whatever the holy, catholic, and apostolic Church of Christ and the Eastern Church accepts and confesses, he, as a genuine son of the common spiritual mother, accepts and confesses. The work is a short, brilliant declaration of the Orthodox faith that echoes the writer's profound belief in his innocence of any heretical taint. He speaks also about his position on the frequency of holy communion and on the opinion of the *Kollyvades* that according to tradition the *mnemosyna* (Memorial Services) should be performed on Saturdays and not on Sundays. He appeals, finally, to the bishops and all the clergy to uproot hatred and envy from their hearts and to fill them with love for each other and peace for all.[67]

The Philokalia

Even if St. Nicodemos had published only the *Philokalia*, this contribution alone would have made him famous. It is a work of profound spiritual magnitude and great edifying power. The term derives from the two Greek words *philos* and *kalos*, and means "the love and attraction toward the spiritually beautiful and the virtuous." By extension, it means dedication to the ultimate Truth, the source of life and all sustenance, that is, the love of God himself, the only Way who can provide purification, illumination, salvation, and deification.

The term *philokalia* was used by early Greek authors. The first Christian authors to use the word as a title were St. Basil the Great and St. Gregory the Theologian, who collected material from the writings of Origen, the great third-century theologian of Alexandria. Thus, *philokalia* also came to mean an anthology, a collection of texts for spiritual and edifying purposes.

St. Nicodemos, a man of great spiritual acumen and vision, realized the importance of collecting patristic texts concerning the spiritual life and formation of Christians. The texts, written by great spiritual fathers of the Eastern Church between the fourth and fifteenth centuries, were found in the libraries of Mount Athos before the time of St. Nicodemos. It was ascertained that the first compilations were made by spiritual fathers of the Holy Mountain around the second part of the fourteenth century, almost immediately after peace prevailed in the Church following the hesychastic controversy.[68] The manuscripts were found in the libraries of the Holy Mountain—"dusty and moth-eaten," St. Nicodemos writes in his Prologue. Probably Macarios, bishop of Corinth and mentor and friend of St. Nicodemos, secured the texts for him. We are not in a position to know whether St. Nicodemos added or deducted from the original collection. Apparently, however, his contribution consisted in correcting the texts philologically, making a successful comparative study of the texts, providing his own input in the form of notes, writing short biographies of the authors, and adding an excellent Prologue. In 1777, after two years of work, the voluminous task was complete.

The *Philokalia* was published for the first time in Venice in 1782. The impact of the *Philokalia* was monumental. It became and still is one of the most popular religious books ever published in the Orthodox world. A second edition was published in Athens in 1893, and in 1957–1963 a third edition in five volumes was published by the Astir Publishing Company of Athens.[69]

The *Philokalia* was destined to have an immense impact on the spiritual life of the Russian people. The Russian monk Paissy Velichkovsii (1772–1794), a contemporary of St. Nicodemos, traveled to Mount Athos. He translated the *Philokalia* into Slavonic. It was first published in Moscow in 1793 under the title *Dobrotolulibe*. A second edition followed in 1822. The first Russian translation was made by Ignatii Brianchaninov (1807–1867) and the second in 1877 by the respected Bishop Theophan the Recluse, under the title *Dobrotolubiye*. All these translations were selective and partial renderings of the original text. Partial French and Roumanian translations also exist today.

The first English translation was made by E. Kadloubovsky and G. E. H. Palmer in two volumes: *Writings From the Philokalia on Prayer of the Heart* and *Early Fathers from the Philokalia*, published by Faber and

INTRODUCTION

Faber in London in the years 1951 and 1952 respectively. It was unfortunate that these useful translations were made not from the Greek original but from Theophan's Russian translation. These editions carried less than a third of the original Greek material. The English-speaking peoples owe a great debt of gratitude to G. E. H. Palmer, Philip Sherrard, and Kallistos Ware, who undertook the translation of the complete *Philokalia* into English from the original text of St. Nicodemos.[70] Although they have remained faithful to the work of St. Nicodemos, they have done a critical evaluation of the texts and corrected some errors. For example, the work *On Prayer*, originally attributed to St. Neilos, was properly ascribed to Evagrios.[71]

It is unfortunate, however, that the translators of this magnificent work did not translate the Prologue or Introduction of St. Nicodemos. It is there that we find a synoptic expression of the Orthodox world view, the ground of all Orthodox spirituality; it is there that St. Nicodemos presents a panoramic view of the history of salvation, creation, fall, and redemption. According to this perspective, the ultimate purpose of creation and the redemptive work of Christ aimed at making humanity "god," by divinizing humankind and thus defeating once and for all the deceiving power of Satan over human beings and nature. Through the sacrament of baptism, St. Nicodemos holds, we all have received the "seeds" of the perfecting grace of the Holy Spirit for our advancement in this life; unfortunately, under the pressures of our materialistic lives, because of ignorance and confusion deriving from our attachment to worldly cares, the Holy Spirit is in danger of being extinguished from our hearts. In the Fathers of the Church, however, we discover a method of unceasing watchfulness and attentiveness for the guarding of our whole human existence: the unceasing prayer to Jesus Christ our Lord. This is the famous Jesus Prayer, which, together with the fulfilling of the commandments, destroys the passions, warming and brightening the mind and heart by the fire of the Holy Spirit, for "God is fire which consumes evil." Thus mind and heart are cleansed and united together as the fruits of the Holy Spirit abound in them profusely.

According to St. Nicodemos, the spark that exists in us since baptism comes out polished by the ashes themselves, and our purification, illumination, and perfection become a reality leading us to our deification. Further, according to the way of Orthodox spirituality, the Jesus Prayer, the Prayer of the Heart, the "inner work" combined with the "outer work," that is, the keeping of the commandments and the

INTRODUCTION

practice of the moral virtues, are not only duties for those who live the monastic life. On the contrary, they have universal character. They are the duties of all Christians regardless of their calling. Of course, they presuppose a solid doctrinal basis and a sound ecclesiological or ecclesiastical framework and are practiced within the parameters of the beautiful liturgical life of the Church. The fact that a layman of the Church, John Mavrocordatos, had provided the finances for the publication of the *Philokalia* testifies to the universality of its spiritual message. St. Nicodemos' lamentation, that we have forgotten the task of our sanctification, deification, and salvation, changes into unspeakable joy with the publication of this "spiritual book," as St. Nicodemos calls his anthology. He calls it the

> treasury of watchfulness, the keeper of the mind, the mystical school of the prayer of the heart. A book which is the excellent pattern of the practical virtue and the infallible directive of contemplation, the paradise of the Fathers, the golden series of virtues. A book which is the dense teaching of Christ, the trumpet which recalls back the grace, in two words, it is the instrument itself of deification.[72]

Finally, St. Nicodemos invites his readers to read his *Philokalia:*

> Come, therefore, come and eat the bread of knowledge and wisdom, and drink the wine which spiritually delights the heart and dispels all the material and immaterial things because of deification—which is caused by the liberation of ourselves—and become inebriated with the truly alert inebriation. Come all you who are participants in the Orthodox way, together, laymen and monks, all of you who seek to find the kingdom of God which is within you, as well as the treasure which is hidden in the field of your heart. And this is the sweet Christ. Thus being freed from the imprisonment of this world and the wandering of the mind, with your heart purified from the passions, with the awesome unceasing invocation of our Lord Jesus Christ together with the collaborating virtues, which this book teaches, you will be united among yourselves, and united this way, you will all be united with God, according to the prayer of our Lord to his Father, who said, "So they may be one, as we are one" (Jn 17:11).[73]

INTRODUCTION

It goes without saying that the *Philokalia* has become one of the most widely read books in the Orthodox English-speaking world as well.

The Evergetinos

The *Evergetinos* is comprised of sayings of the Fathers. The compilation first was made by a monk named Paul, founder of the Monastery of the Most Holy Theotokos, the Mother of God, the Benefactor. Thus the book was called *Evergetinos*, that is, dedicated to the Benefactor of the Monastery, the Virgin Mary herself. St. Nicodemos edited texts of the book and published it in Venice in 1783. The last edition in Greek (1957–1966) is comprised of four large volumes. It has become popular among the monks and those who enjoy reading the moral teachings of the Fathers.

A Most Edifying Book by Our Fathers Saint Barsanouphios and Saint John

The title refers to the great ascetic Fathers who lived in Palestine during the sixth century. The original text was found on Mount Athos in the form of 836 questions and answers conveying the advice and the opinions of these two great Fathers on the spiritual life. St. Nicodemos prepared this book, with a most useful introduction, around 1797. It was published later in Venice in 1816.

Concerning Continual Communion of the Divine Mysteries

This fascinating book (*Peri tes Synechous Metalepseos ton Theion Mysterion* in Greek) caused St. Nicodemos much sorrow, but left a lasting effect on the liturgical life of the Church. The book was not authored originally by St. Nicodemos himself. Father Theokletos Dionysiatis has expressed the opinion that it came from the pen of the Hagiorite monk Neophytos, who was one of the protagonists of the *Kollyvades*.[74] Recently, the Hagiorite monk Theodore has discovered the original manuscript of Neophytos in the library of the Academy of Bucharest, Roumania, dated in 1772, as well as the first printed edition made in the more popular language, which was edited in 1777. Father Theodore has proved beyond any doubt that St. Nicodemos' edition in

INTRODUCTION

1783 was based on Neophytos' work.[75] St. Macarios encouraged his friend to undergo a revision of this splendid book, and St. Nicodemos revised, enlarged, and enriched Neophytos' original work to such an extent that it may almost be considered a new book. St. Nicodemos extended the original 173 pages to 343. He wrote two introductions and divided the book into three parts. In the first part, in nine chapters, he analyzes and interprets the Lord's Prayer (not found in Neophytos' book); in the second part, he speaks about the need for frequent holy communion; and in the third part, in the form of questions and answers, he refutes the arguments of his opponents that frequent holy communion is not proper and necessary.

It is true that according to ancient Christian tradition and practice, the Christians of the early periods received holy communion quite frequently. St. Basil the Great in his famous ninety-third letter to Patricia Caesarea speaks of receiving holy communion at least four times during every week, that is, Wednesday, Friday, Saturday, Sunday and also on any other day the memory of a saint was commemorated.[76] During the last years of the Byzantine period and afterward, the reception of holy communion among the Orthodox was restricted to three times per year, namely, Christmas, Easter, and the Koimisis of the Theotokos on August 15. The feeling of unworthiness and the emphasis on awesomeness in confronting the Holy Eucharist created an atmosphere that up to the present time causes Orthodox to hesitate to approach the Eucharistic cup. St. Nicodemos and Neophytos stress the importance of receiving holy communion frequently, for when taken with the proper physical and spiritual preparation, the sacrament purifies and sanctifies the communicant, contributes to the spiritual growth of the faithful, diverts the Christian from spiritual death and unites the believer with Christ and grants eternal life.

The sacred and Most Holy Body of our Lord, when properly and worthily received, becomes a weapon for those who fight the good fight, it becomes the cause of returning back to God for those who went astray; it strengthens the sick, it delights the healthy, it heals illnesses, it preserves health; with the Holy Communion, it is easier to correct ourselves, to become more forbearing and more patient in the pains and the sorrows, more warm in love, more sensitive to knowledge, more

willing to obedience, more sensitive and more responsive to
the energy of the [divine] charismata.[77]

St. Nicodemos bases his arguments on the Bible, the Fathers of the
Church, and the holy canons. It is an excellent book, written with the
carefulness of sound scholarship and the flaming heart of a genuinely
pious man. It is unfortunate that there is no English translation up to
now.

Unseen Warfare

The original germ of this book was not produced by the pen of St.
Nicodemos. Apparently when he was still on Naxos, where many
Roman Catholics lived, he found the well-known spiritual book of a
famous Italian priest Lorenzo Scupoli (born of a noble family in
Otranto in 1529). The title of the book was *Combattimento Spirituale* or
Spiritual Combat. The first edition, published in Venice in 1589, was
composed of only twenty-four chapters, but by 1599 it reached the
length of sixty-six chapters and its popularity grew constantly because
it was recognized as a masterpiece of spiritual guidance and assistance.
St. Nicodemos found the edition of Naples of 1599 and reworked the
whole book in a most admirable way. This shows St. Nicodemos'
openness to the good theological works coming from the West, and as
he put it himself: "We must hate and detest the misbeliefs and unlawful customs of the Latins and others who are Heterodox; but if they
have anything sound and confirmed by the Canons of the Holy Synods, this we must not hate."[78]

The famous Bishop Theophan the Recluse translated Nicodemos'
version into Russian (Moscow, 1886), and an English translation of this
Russian version has been published by E. Kadloubovsky and G. E. H.
Palmer with an excellent introduction by H. A. Hodges under the title
Unseen Warfare (London: Faber and Faber Limited, 1952). A reproduction of this English translation was published by St. Vladimir's Press
(Crestwood, New York, 1978). Hodges is aware of the original Western style of this book, but his introduction minimizes its importance.
He points out that St. Nicodemos used the edition of 1599, omitted the
1610 supplement of Scupoli, and attached to it *The Path to Paradise*,
another separate work by Scupoli. Thus he formed a new continuous
work that is redivided into two parts. The first part is taken from *The
Combat*, the second from Chapters 14–27 of *The Path*. He omitted

INTRODUCTION

Chapter 8 of *The Path* and Chapter 61 of *The Combat;* perhaps he felt that they were repetitious. He prefixed a short introduction explaining the purpose of the book, and he enriched the text by adding many footnotes that were references to the Bible and the Fathers.[79] No doubt St. Nicodemos tried to adapt Scupoli's book for his Orthodox readers. He removed references to the Latin teachings on purgatory and the Sacred Heart. He changed the term *image* to *icon* and inserted the Orthodox practice of praying the Jesus Prayer.[80] The most serious changes made by St. Nicodemos are in Chapters 21 to 24 in Scupoli's text (in the English version, Chapters 21–26). These chapters deal with the senses and the imagination. Also, St. Nicodemos made some changes in Scupoli's discussion on prayer by introducing the patristic understanding of prayer through the experience of the hesychasts, and he gives a beautiful definition of the famous *monologistos euhe*, the one-word prayer. This mental prayer, recited while controlling the breath, is composed of the words "Lord Jesus Christ, Son of God, have mercy upon me." St. Nicodemos makes clear that in this prayer the three constituent parts of the soul, the intuitive (*nous*), the discursive reason (*logos*), and the will or spirit (*thelesis, pneuma*) are united in a single act, and the soul thus united within herself is made fit for union with God.[81] The emphasis of St. Nicodemos on the Jesus Prayer and his emphasis on the Orthodox understanding of receiving holy communion (as it appears in *On the Frequency of Holy Communion*) gives an Orthodox perspective on the mystical theology of Nicodemos. The "spiritual communion" of Scupoli combined with the emphasis of St. Nicodemos on the partaking of the flesh and blood of Christ complement each other, and they make Nicodemos' teaching on the sacrament of the Eucharist more obvious and more relevant toward spiritual edification. Finally, the addition of Nicodemos' own prayers and his references to the *Philokalia* make this book "a true hymn of the mystical spirit of the Orthodox Fathers, and a clear mirror of the heart and the soul" of St. Nicodemos.[82]

The translation of *Unseen Warfare* which Theophan the Recluse made in Russian differs a great deal from the original translation from St. Nicodemos. As H. A. Hodges notes in the Introduction, Theophan himself tells us that his work was a "free rendering" rather than a "literal translation" of St. Nicodemos. In some instances Theophan omitted whole chapters and substituted his own. Hodges adds that the emphasis by Theophan on perpetual prayer, which is the abiding sense of God's presence in the soul, and the emphasis on spiritual warmth of the heart make the translation of Theophan a genuinely Orthodox work, "a worthy modern companion to the *Philokalia.*"[83]

The Spiritual Exercises

The *Spiritual Exercises*, in Greek *Pneumatika Gymnasmata*, is an adaptation of a book written originally by Pinamonti under the title *Esercizii Spirituali*. Personal enemies of St. Nicodemos like Iakovos Neasketiotis and Theodoretos maintained that this book was derived from a synonymous work of Ignatius of Loyola, the founder of the Jesuit order. Theokletos Dionysiatis, who has studied the issue carefully, believes that St. Nicodemos found on Naxos a French version of *Exercices Spirituels*.[84] What is important is that St. Nicodemos expanded the original, which was only 30 pages, to a voluminous book of 650 pages. It is composed of thirty-four meditations on various subjects concerning man's salvation and his spiritual perfection. Then there are thirty brief meditations, each one designated for a month, followed by eight exercises of self-examination. In addition, there are eight uplifting spiritual readings. As the editors of the various editions (Venice, 1800; Athens, 1869; Volos, 1950) observe, the book has been adorned, corrected, amplified, and illustrated by St. Nicodemos himself; thus one may justifiably say it is a personal achievement exhibiting St. Nicodemos' profound involvement, study, and total grasp of the mind of the Fathers. Father Theokletos Dionysiatis writes that St. Nicodemos emptied all his wisdom and love into this book. He adds, however, that the disadvantage of this massive book is precisely its size, and he suggests that it be condensed without altering the basic substance and morphology. He calls this book "a masterpiece of Orthodox spirituality, where the spiritual character of St. Nicodemos contributes to the spiritual piety of the Christian people."[85]

St. Nicodemos describes human nature as an active entity that must constantly be exercised for its spiritual perfection.

> Thus man, according to St. Gregory the Theologian, is endowed by various powers and energies; according to Nemesios he is the connecting bond between the two worlds of the visible and the invisible; he is the epilogue of all creatures according to St. Gregory Palamas; the archon, ruler, and king of all the visible creation according to the Scriptures; the temple, image, and likeness of God, according to all theolo-

gians; man is the horizon of the material and immaterial, according to St. Ignatios; the great miracle according to Hermas; the measure of all things according to Pythagoras; the miracle of miracles according to Plato; the political animal according to Aristotle; the priceless paradigm according to Theophrastos. Thus man has been created by God, not to remain unoccupied and immobile, but always to move forward, so that he may exercise, and through this exercise receive formation and perfection, which is—in this present life—the acquiring of the divine grace, and in the future life acquiring of the divine glory.[86]

In the strongest language St. Nicodemos discusses the great dramatic experience of death, which he calls "the end of deceit." This is so because daily we are deceived in this "miserable life" by the earthly things of this world, and we forget the heavenly pleasures; thus "we call the good evil and the evil good, like being in a house filled by smoke, where we cannot see clearly either the inside, or the outside of the house; so we know the present things poorly and the future worse."[87] He describes in the most beautiful language the joys of paradise, or as he puts it, "the glory of paradise where everything is perfect and eternal."[88] In precise christological language he speaks about Christ's role on earth.[89] He develops the importance of receiving holy communion.[90] He also stresses the importance of the pentecostal event through which the Holy Spirit completely changed the language, the mind, and the heart of the apostles.[91] He also emphasizes God's love toward humanity. Meditation 17 is a flaming hymn of God's love for humankind:

God loves you with the same love that he loves himself. And although through this love he does not want your good exactly as it is his own, that is for you to be God by nature, for this is impossible, he does want for you an infinite good, for he wants to make you another god, by grace through the participation in heaven . . . The eternal Father, in order to liberate you from infinite misery which you have in Hades, and in order to make you a communicant of an infinite happiness in paradise, gave to you as a gift his divine Son: "For God so loved the world that He gave His only-begotten Son."[92]

INTRODUCTION

In conclusion, this book is one of the most important Orthodox spiritual guides for the advancement toward perfection. It is unfortunate that it has not been translated into English as yet.

Anthology from the Psalms of the Prophet-King David[93]

This is a strange compilation of divergent prayers of St. Augustine, a homily for the office of the bishop, an interpretation of the Psalms of the Prophet-King David (excluding those read in the daily and nightly services) apparently made by Patriarch Gennadios Scholarios (fifteenth century), a splendid homily on repentance, and a collection of prayers of contrition of the Fathers of the Church, such as St. Basil the Great, St. John Chrysostom, St. Symeon the New Theologian, St. Ephraim, St. Isaac the Syrian, St. Theodore the Studite, and others. It is interesting that St. Nicodemos profoundly appreciated the prayers of contrition of St. Augustine and also had great respect for the office of the bishop.

Christian Morality[94]

This is a splendid book that deals with Christian "ethos," the character and the life style of the Christians. In recommending this book, Gregory V, the patriarch of Constantinople at the beginning of the nineteenth century, calls St. Nicodemos a man with "golden words." With a sense of profound faith and absolutely engulfed in the spirit of the Scriptures and the Fathers, St. Nicodemos offers us the way, the motive, and the "phronema" of the Christian life. As an excellent Christian psychologist, or rather I should say, as a Christian spiritual father, St. Nicodemos analyzes human existence and directs it to Christ as the supreme model to follow and as its ultimate sanctifier and savior. He appeals to Christians to entirely avoid all bad habits and customs; he speaks of the dangers that come from secular music, dancing, and theaters, as well as unnecessary laughter and actions that may scandalize the simple and the innocent. Christians should not scandalize their brothers and sisters; rather, they should work for the spiritual benefit and correction unto the salvation of their brothers and sisters.

In one of the most beautiful chapters of this book St. Nicodemos explains that Christians should go to church because the Church is "the table and the fountain for those who are hungry and thirsty." It is "the spiritual ark" and "courtyard," "the common healing center," "the common house of all the Christians," "the garden and the paradise," "the feast," "the spiritual harbor" of all Christians. The Church is "the Body of Christ," "the Temple of God," where all the Christians as a body pray together in the spirit of harmony, agreement, and love. In unison clergy and laity offer their prayers to the common Father, together with the angels and saints participating and living the mystery of the divine liturgy. Only in the Church of Christ can Christians avoid divisions and schisms and declare publicly the common faith, being one body, one spirit, one hope, one union in Christ.[95]

The book, which is composed of thirteen homilies, ends with lyrical descriptions of the unspeakable glory of paradise. Nicodemos writes, "such is the joy and the exaltation which the saints feel in paradise and which comes out from the blessed rejoicing of the all-holy and life-giving Trinity, that it makes them feel that 1000 years is a day. St. Augustine says that such is the beauty of the unwaning light, the sweetness of the uncreated wisdom, the pleasure of the heavenly blessedness, that if it were possible to stop there only one day, we should abandon all the years of transitory life and all the bodily pleasures just for that one day."[96] He continues:

> If you really desire, my brothers, to enjoy this blessedness, suffer with patience all the forthcoming troubles of life, and feel hatred against vain wealth, because the most unworthy slave of God is glorified more immensely than the greatest king of this world. . . . [The most important thing is to gain life everlasting which is] the kingdom of heaven, the kingdom of the kingdoms of all the ages where hills produce honey and milk, and mountains produce sweetness. It is the paradise and mansion of the blessed of whom the eternal God is life and king.[97]

Holy words from a holy man.

Exegetical Works

A man of profound biblical background, St. Nicodemos paid much attention to the exegesis and interpretation of the word of God so that it might become easily accessible and understandable to the masses. In this sense St. Nicodemos could be considered an important biblical scholar of his time. Above all, and beyond scholarly technicalities, he was interested in the spirit and the message of the Holy Scriptures. He followed his own method of interpretation, which I would call pedagogical and didactic. He interpreted the text in plain contemporary language, added his own instructive comments, and richly embellished his text with patristic references and quotations.

The first of his exegetical works to be discussed here is *The Interpretation of the 150 Psalms of the Prophet-King David*.[98] This book has become one of the most popular exegetical books among Greek Orthodox. It is very useful because of the importance of the Psalms in the liturgical life of the Orthodox Church; there is no liturgical service without the reading of Psalms. St. Nicodemos apparently knew the Hebrew language, and he was able to contribute his own spiritual insight to Zygabenos' text.[99] Although more than two centuries have passed since St. Nicodemos completed this work, the text still inspires many of the Orthodox faithful by introducing them to the beauty and the spiritual magnificence of the Psalms.

The second exegetical book of St. Nicodemos is *Paul's Fourteen Epistles Interpreted by Theophylaktos, Archbishop of Bulgaria*.[100] Theophylaktos (1030–1126) interpreted the fourteen letters of St. Paul on the basis of the exegesis made by St. John Chrysostom. It is an outstanding work and clearly shows the excellent biblical background of St. Nicodemos. Theophylaktos "paraphrases" Chrysostom closely, and the clarity of thought, the brevity of expression, the simplicity of style, and the ability to enter into the spirit of St. Paul and St. John Chrysostom are obvious. St. Nicodemos not only interpreted the already unusable dialect of Theophylaktos into contemporary language, but he also provided his own insights, interpretations, and conclusions. The patristic references, and especially the interpretive elements taken from Theophylaktos, Oikoumenios, St. Photios, and Theodoritos, cover only one-third of this three-volume work. St. Nicodemos recognizes the great importance of St. Paul's theology. He dares to say, following St. John Chrysostom, that the letters of St. Paul contain insights and mysteries greater than the Gospels, and that the Lord himself revealed and taught through Paul greater mysteries according to "Verily, verily I say to you that the one who believes in me and the works that I do, he will do them and he will do greater than this because I am going to my Father" (Jn 14:12).[101] St. Nicodemos calls these fourteen letters of St. Paul the "secure basis of the faith of the Christians, the principles of the piety according to Christ, the elements of the one, holy, catholic, and apostolic Church which extends from

East to West."[102] Moreover, St. Nicodemos calls these fourteen letters "the complementary books of the New Testament," for as the fourteen stations comprise the general art of rhetoric, as the fourteen voices comprise the universally accepted joyful art of music, these fourteen letters of the heavenly inspired Paul comprise and constitute all the Christian fullness of the ecumenical Church of Christ. These contain the exactness of high theology, the security of natural philosophy, and the straightest teaching of ethics; these are the rules of the correct dogmas, and the reproof of the spurious teachings.[103] St. Nicodemos, in order to prove the originality and uniqueness of St. Paul's theology and the great benefit derived from it, points out that it is from these letters that we learn of the existence of the spiritual world, that is, of the existence of the blessed Angels, Thrones, Dominions, Authorities, Principalities, and the rest of the orders of the bodiless angels. From these letters we learn the supernatural and heavenly powers taught by the Church—the wisdom of God in all its glory and in all its varied forms. From them we also learn that the angels are liturgical spirits sent by God to serve those who will become inheritors of redemption.[104] To make his point more clear, St. Nicodemos compares St. Paul and Christopher Columbus. St. Paul recalls for us the world beyond our senses; Christopher Columbus discovered the "new" visible world of America.[105]

St. Nicodemos wrote this work for inexperienced preachers and for simple and uneducated Christians. With great humility he compares himself to a worker who cleans the road of stones, thorns, and boulders. He stresses the fact that even the educated may benefit, even patriarchs, bishops, and priests, and all people without exception. Finally, with St. John Chrysostom, he urges the faithful to read the New Testament books constantly and to keep them as "medicines of the soul," as consolation for all difficult circumstances, and as "weapons" in the spiritual war against evil.[106]

The third important exegetical work of St. Nicodemos is the *Interpretation of the Seven Catholic Letters*.[107] This work is based mostly on the interpretive work of Hierarch Metrophanis, bishop of Smyrna in the ninth century, Theophylaktos and Oikoumenios. It was edited by St. Nicodemos' cousin Ierotheos, metropolitan of Ioannina, with the support of the former patriarch of Constantinople, Neophytos VII. St. Nicodemos used the vernacular of his time because, as in his previous exegetical works, he wanted to make biblical texts available to the great masses of Orthodox people. Writing to his cousin about his work he notes that the word of God is richly found in the seven Catholic letters of the holy apostles James, Peter, John, and Judas, and he describes the letters as a pleasant garden full of grace and refreshment.[108] In an excellent introduction addressed to all Orthodox people, he compares the apostles with clouds that send to the world the sweet water that satisfies the earth and produces the most pleasant fruits for the spiritual uplifting of the faithful.[109] This spiritual rain, which produced pleasant, sweet, and drinkable water, has been collected into the "wells" of the books of the New Testament. The wells of the catholic epistles are especially deep, both in language and in spiritual insights, and it requires a long rope to draw the water in order to satisfy the spiritual needs of the readers. Therefore, precisely because of the difficulty these beautiful New Testament books present, St. Nicodemos has tried to make their meaning accessible to the Orthodox people.

Fully aware of the profound theological and pastoral content of these seven books of the New Testament, St. Nicodemos compares them to the seven planets of the solar system and to the seven most beautiful flowers, that is, hyacinth (blue bell), violet, lily, rose, pimpernel, madder red, and narcissus. He compares them with the seven most important metals on earth: gold, silver, iron, copper, glass, tin, and lead. He also compares them with the seven most important gifts of the Holy Spirit—wisdom, prudence, knowledge, piety, counsel, power, and fear of God—which fill people with divine grace and deify them.[110] Finally, he appeals to the faithful who claim they are poor and cannot buy these books. He agrees here with St. John Chrysostom that such a pretext is vain because these books are most beneficial for the soul and its salvation. They teach the Orthodox faith and the Christian way of life, and poverty cannot be a justification for not buying them.[111] At the end of his introduction, St. Nicodemos humbly dedicates his book "to the glory of God, to the enrichment of the whole Holy Church of Christ, and for the general benefit of the nation."[112]

Another of St. Nicodemos' exegetical works is *New Ladder*.[113] It is written in a form similar to that of the *Ladder of St. John Climacus* (seventh century), which views the ladder of Jacob as the prototype of the spiritual ascent to perfection. St. Nicodemos interprets the seventy-five *Anavathmoi* or Degrees of the Orthros Service in the liturgical book, which is called the *Great Octoechos* or *Parakletike*. The *Anavathmoi* number "nine in each of the first seven modes of Byzantine chant and twelve in the eighth mode," and were probably written by St. Theodore the Studite (ninth century).[114] The work discusses doctrine, Christian morals and spiritual life in the most constructive and comprehensible way.

Yet another of the exegetical works of St. Nicodemos is the *Heortodromion*,[115] in which St. Nicodemos interprets the hymnological canons of the great feasts concerning the life of our Lord Jesus Christ and his mother, the holy virgin Mary. It is an important book for the understanding of the liturgical texts of the Church.

The last of the exegetical works of St. Nicodemos considered here is *Garden of Graces*.[116] The title refers to the multiplicity and variety of spiritual flowers—that is, divine gifts or graces—that decorate the spiritual life of the Christian.[117] The brothers of the Cell of Skoutaioi, where Nicodemos spent his last days, and who later published this book, called St. Nicodemos a holy farmer who has planted fruitful trees, and has truly developed a garden of divine graces.

Basically St. Nicodemos interprets in this book the verses of the nine odes that are chanted every day in the orthros or matins. These odes have been selected by the spirit-bearing Fathers of the Church and the sacred teachers, and there are nine because the orders of the blessed angels in the heavens are nine. In that way the Fathers wanted to show that the ecclesiastical hierarchy on earth is fully united with the heavenly hierarchy of the angels.[118] St. Nicodemos also makes the point that the first eight odes are from the Old Testament and the ninth is from the New Testament. This proves the interconnection and the absolute eternal unity of the Old Testament with the New Testament. Each one is connected to the other. Because most of the verses of the odes come from the Old Testament, and because most of the themes of the odes come from the New Testament, the holy Fathers put them together in order to show that the Old Testament preceded as an icon and a shadow, and the New Testament followed as the prototype and the truth.[119] Later, in interpreting the eleventh verse from the Ode of Moses (Dt 32:11), he says that the eagle of whom Moses speaks is Christ himself and his Church and every Christian also, and the two wings of the eagle symbolize the Old Testament and the New Testament in accordance with the saying in the book of Revelation:

> But the woman was given two great wings to fly to the place in the wilderness . . . and ascends to the heights of spiritual contemplation [theoria] and knowledge, and is illuminated in the spiritual rays of the supersubstantial sun as the genuine

children of the eagle do as they are brightened by the rays of the material sun.[120]

To illustrate the scope of this book, I will mention two examples. Interpreting the famous verse of Isaiah, "But the dead live, their bodies will rise again. They that sleep in the earth will awake and shout for joy; for thy dew is dew of sparkling light" (Is 26:19), St. Nicodemos speaks beautifully and constructively of the resurrection of the dead, which Isaiah teaches so successfully. St. Nicodemos believes in the general resurrection of both the good and the evil, the pious and the impious, because the Lord granted this grace and this gift universally to all humanity by the power of his own resurrection. Following St. Paul (1 Thes 4:13) he speaks about the "falling asleep" of the righteous, an expression that is used by the Fathers of the Church. The term "dead," which is used by Isaiah, refers most especially to the dead in the Lord, not only in the general resurrection, but also in the temporary resurrection of those who rose after the crucifixion of Christ.[121]

Continuing, St. Nicodemos interprets Isaiah's term *dew* as meaning the power and the energy of the life-giving Holy Spirit through whom the dead will rise up and receive healing, that is, strength, life, and incorruptibility. Following St. Cyril, he says that as the dew refreshes the earth and makes the seeds grow, in the same way the life-giving dew of the Holy Spirit takes away corruptibility from the dead bodies of the deceased and grants them life and incorruptibility.

The second point is found in the interpretation of the forty-eighth verse of the Virgin Mary's ode, "All generations count me blessed . . ." (Lk 1:48).[122] St. Nicodemos appeals to all Christians to bless the Theotokos so that she may bless all those who continuously and piously petition her. He explains that Mary is both grandmother and mother of Christians. She is their grandmother because her Son is called Father according to the title given him by the prophet Isaiah, "Father of the Future Age" (Is 9:6). She is the mother of all Christians because her Son himself said he is our brother. Thus every Christian must be a grandchild and child of the Virgin Mary by grace, and every Christian has the obligation to bless her as grandmother and mother according to grace and her position. She is a grandmother who exceeds the love and empathy of carnal mothers, and a mother who exceeds in affection and love all physical mothers.[123]

Finally, St. Nicodemos appended to his work various edifying texts, one written by himself on *logismoi* or recollections, a work on the

INTRODUCTION

Prayer of the Heart by Kallistos, patriarch of Constantinople, and a work on the spiritual law of the Gospels and on the importance of the "spiritual" worship of God written by the famous Gennadios Scholarios, the first ecumenical patriarch after the fall of Constantinople (1453).

Theological and Patristic Works

The man who so cherished the Fathers of the Church and was so fully dedicated to the correctness of the Orthodox faith could not help but pay ardent attention to the doctrines of Orthodoxy as he wisely expounded the Orthodox faith through the works of the Fathers. Although there is a presentation and explanation of Orthodox doctrine in all his works, and although there is no book of his that does not include patristic references, nevertheless some of his works concentrate specifically on doctrinal and patristic themes. One of these books is the *Alphabetalphabetos* or *The Alphabet* of the Orthodox faith.[124] The original text belonged to St. Meletios the Confessor, a saintly monk who lived during the years of the Emperor Michael Palaeologos during the thirteenth century. The thirteenth century was critical for the identity and the esteem of the Orthodox Church and her relations with the West. St. Nicodemos corrected the original text and added an excellent introduction and many references. The book, which is written in the form of 13,824 verses, deals with issues concerning the ascetical and the ecclesiastical life of the time, but primarily with the basic doctrines of the Church. This book was first published only recently, in 1928, by the publishing house of the famous hagioritic periodical *Athos*. I agree wholeheartedly with Father Theokletos Dionysiatis that this book has not been adequately studied and analyzed.[125]

Second, I shall mention *The Extant Works of Saint Symeon the New Theologian*.[126] A question arises immediately in dealing with this monumental work on St. Symeon the New Theologian, the famous and much respected father of Orthodox spiritual life who lived in Constantinople during the eleventh century. Did St. Nicodemos translate the text or not? There is disagreement among scholars concerning this. Father Theokletos Dionysiatis believes that St. Nicodemos paraphrased in contemporary Greek the works of St. Symeon.[127] Out of humility he did not put his name on the publication. He did this when he edited *The Philokalia*, *Evergetinos*, and *On the Frequency of Holy Communion*. Thus the book bears the name of Dionysios Zagoraios as translator.[128] Constantine Cavarnos believes that Zagoraios was the translator and Nicodemos the editor. He accepts the arguments of St. Nicodemos' earliest biographers, Euthymios and Onouphrios, who do not credit Nicodemos with this translation. Euthymios notes simply that St. Nicodemos corrected and embellished the book of St. Symeon the New Theologian.[129] Moreover, Onouphrios says that St. Nicodemos "corrected the writings of St. Symeon the New Theologian."[130] Cavarnos accepts that the introduction of the book was written by St. Nicodemos.[131] Considering the great interest and admiration of St. Nicodemos for St. Symeon the New Theologian, it is reasonable to conclude that St. Nicodemos contributed actively to all phases of this publication. We should add here that St. Nicodemos wrote a special "akolouthia," that is, all the hymns of the Vespers, Orthros, and Divine Liturgy for the feast of St. Symeon the New Theologian. He also wrote a most elegant and eloquent *Encomium* for St. Symeon the New Theologian.[132] Here St. Nicodemos describes St. Symeon as a wise man and a great theologian whom God graced, glorified, and ornamented with all the supernatural gifts while being on earth, and when he was brought into the heavens, God ornamented him with the unspeakable glory of blessedness. He asks the militant Church to co-celebrate with the triumphant Church in the heavens for the achievements of St. Symeon, for he has gone through all the ranks and orders of those who are saved and has reached all the possible perfection that a human being can reach. He writes,

All the saved ones may be divided into six ranks and orders. And the first rank is when someone for the fear of God and hell, keeps some of the divine commandments like a slave; and the second rank is when someone keeps the Master's commandments for the reward of the kingdom of the heavens, as a paid servant; the third rank is when someone keeps the Lord's commandments and only for the sake of God's love, as a friend; and the fourth and superior rank is when someone reaches the point of becoming a son or daughter of God according to grace to whom the inheritance of the kingdom of God is given according to the apostolic saying, "If a son, then an inheritor of God" (Gal 4:7). The fifth and higher rank is when someone becomes worthy to become a brother of Christ, and for this brotherhood, becomes with Christ, an inheritor of the kingdom of God, in accordance with the Apostles' saying, "The inheritors of God, but also co-inheritors with Christ" (Rom 8:17). Most high of all the ranks is when someone becomes worthy to become mother of Christ in accordance with the word of Christ Himself, who said, "Here are my mother and my brothers. Whoever does the will of my heavenly Father is my brother, my sister, my mother" (Mt 12:49–50).[133]

With excellent and painstaking analysis, and with able scriptural and patristic support, St. Nicodemos presents the life of St. Symeon going through these steps, ranks, or orders of perfection. He stresses, for instance, the fact that because Symeon kept all the commandments of God as a friend of God, God revealed to him all the heavenly and mystical things that can only be revealed to friends of God. He was full of divine love, and his heart had been stricken with the sweet arrows of the love of Jesus. "Thus he only understood Jesus; he only desired Jesus; he studied only Jesus; Jesus was the ultimate object of his mind; Jesus was the *joy* of his tongue; Jesus was the sweet occupation and talking of his heart; Jesus was his breath."[134] Precisely because of this divine love, St. Nicodemos writes, the gift of theology has been granted to him beyond and above other saints and theologians of our Church, and thus he is known to us today as St. Symeon the New Theologian. He was a man of love and a man of theology. "Because these two gifts, that is, divine love and theology, have the habit for one to give birth to the other and vice versa, again, one is born of the other."[135] Here St. Nicodemos makes the point that as the love became warmer in the heart of St. Symeon, his theology increased, and as his theology increased, his love also increased; thus love and theology became the two basic characteristics of his spiritual perfection.

St. Nicodemos also stressed the fact that St. Symeon became a mother to Christ, bearing Christ himself within.[136] In other words, Christ was formed within him, according to Paul's saying, "For my children, for whom I am in travail until Christ is formed in you" (Gal 4:19). Where is Christ formed? St. Nicodemos asks. Not in the face or the chest but in the heart, and not bodily, but in a bodiless way as is fit to God. As a pregnant woman realizes her condition because of the movements of the fetus, in the same way those who have formed Christ in themselves know his inner movements, that is, his radiance and enlightenment, and they realize that Christ lives in them. Precisely because of this spiritual formation of Christ in him, and because Christ spiritually became his mother, St. Symeon became worthy to be illumi-

nated with the spiritual and supernatural illumination of the Holy
Spirit, and to receive in his heart the true illumination of the divine
grace. His sacred face radiated and shone like a second sun.[137] He has
become a teacher and an example for us, both for monks, and for
Christians who live in the world, so both of us should benefit from his
commemoration, and both of us should try to receive the Holy Spirit
as St. Symeon did.[138] We should read the life of St. Symeon, which is

> the depository of virtues, the healing of the passions, the
> restoration of the divine grace, the trumpet of deification, the
> guidance of perfection, the height of theology, the depth of
> economy, the width of creation, the length of providence, the
> heirloom of the ascetic philosophy, the school of the mental
> prayer, the treasury of the mystical dogmas.[139]

No heart can remain unmoved with these words of St. Nicodemos.
    The final writing of great patristic significance is the edition of the
works of St. Gregory Palamas. It is, however, a sad story. St. Nicodemos, at the exhortation of his friend Athanasios Parios, a leading
Kollyvades Father, and Leontios, metropolitan of Heliopolis, undertook
the effort of collecting and editing all of the works of St. Gregory
Palamas. St. Nicodemos was not only a great admirer of St. Gregory
Palamas, but also a fervent student of his works, and most important,
an ardent practitioner of the celebrated hesychastic theology. For St.
Nicodemos, the Jesus Prayer and all the spiritual requirements of the
ascetic theology of Palamas became the main substance of Christian
growth toward perfection and illumination. Therefore, with great care
and through extensive research in the libraries of Mt. Athos and other
parts of Greece, he prepared all the existing works of St. Gregory
Palamas in three volumes and sent them to Vienna for publication.
The volumes were lost in Vienna. We do not know for sure how this
happened. It is said that the Greek press to which Nicodemos sent his
work was destroyed by the Austrian authorities because it was involved in the preparation and printing of revolutionary material related
to the Greek struggle for independence.[140] St. Nicodemos lamented his
loss, and he never forgot it. However, his introduction has survived,[141]
and some of the manuscripts of St. Nicodemos may have survived
also.[142] The introduction was written in archaic Greek and does not
appeal to the general reader. The spontaneous spark of St. Nicodemos'
pen is missing. He expresses once more his high esteem for St. Greg-

ory Palamas who, he says, is not at all deficient in comparison with the great and glorious Fathers and theologians of the Church. He makes the point that the writings of St. Gregory Palamas illuminate the readers and transfigure them toward theosis.[143]

Pastoral Books

A man who grasped both the letter and the spirit of the canons of the Church, St. Nicodemos was also a pastor par excellence. He excelled as a spiritual father, confessor, and counselor. Three books that can be included among his pastoral and canonical works are *The Manual of Confession*, *The Rudder*, and *A Handbook of Spiritual Counsel*.

There is no doubt that *The Manual of Confession*[144] is one of the most impressive of the books of St. Nicodemos, an edifying and helpful spiritual book. It is original in its conception and original in its implementation. We know that St. Nicodemos was one of the best-known spiritual fathers of his time. The powerful and the weak, the rich and the poor, the educated and the illiterate, came from all over the Orthodox world to confess their sins and receive forgiveness, advice, consolation, and restoration of their spirits and their bodies to the spiritual life of the Orthodox Church. Father Theokletos Dionysiatis calls St. Nicodemos a great psychologist, a brilliant interpreter of the "epitimia" (penances), the paternal herald of repentance, the physician of monks, laity, and clergy. He calls him both brother and father, as well as son, and describes him as sweet and serious, philanthropic and strict, a lenient literalist, a profound reader of the secret wounds of the soul who was always loving and discrete in the interest of the sinful human soul. St. Nicodemos was scolding, condescending, and forgiving—binding and loosing, as necessary. He combined in himself the spiritual father and the legal mind of the Church, always associating his vast learning with his profound love for God and man.[145]

The Manual of Confession is composed of three parts. The first part deals with the requirements for a spiritual father and confessor. The second part is comprised of thirty-eight canons of St. John the Faster and his seventeen penances.[146] St. Nicodemos offers his own insight and his rich spiritual experience as father confessor. His interpretation is not only linguistically brilliant, not only rich with a vast number of references to the Scriptures, the Fathers, and the canons of the Church, but also full of his own understanding of the problems of the daily life of Christians, whether clergy, monks, or laity. The third and final part of the book is composed of paternal advice to penitents and includes an excellent homily on repentance.

A few things should be said about St. Nicodemos' understanding of the special preparation and the spiritual requirements of the father confessor. First of all, he asks the spiritual father to excel in virtue and holiness above all the other people and even his fellow priests. He should have healed and constrained his own human passions, and he should live a spiritual life completely governed by the grace and discretion of the Holy Spirit.[147] He prefers spiritual fathers to be married, financially independent, and of mature age.[148] Of course, the father confessor must have a special "laying on of hands" by his bishop, and a written permission in order to exercise his duties.[149] Then St. Nicodemos gives detailed instructions how, where, and to whom the confessor can exercise his duty. He advises, for instance, that a spiritual father not ask curious questions, not ask names, but use great skill and prudence in extracting the sinful confession of the penitent.[150] He must act with special care toward those who have committed carnal sins in order to convince them that their sins are detrimental to both their physical and spiritual health.[151] He gives special directions for the confessions of clergy and monks, and finally he offers a long list of penances for individual cases. He gives special emphasis to the penance of abstaining from holy communion. Although he concedes that it is strict and unbearable, he believes that it makes repentance more secure and more effective.[152] In the case of sick or elderly people who have committed serious sins but are unable to perform the required physical penances, he advises prayer, the reading of spiritual books, almsgiving, but not permission for receiving holy communion.[153] He concludes that a spiritual father is obligated by the divine ecclesiastical canons not to reveal through word of mouth, letter, or sign of the eye, or through any other way, the sins that have been revealed to him. The punishment is defrocking by the ecclesiastical authorities.[154] Of course, St. Nicodemos advises the spiritual father to be knowledgeable of Scripture, dogma, and the canons of the Church, and to know on the basis of the Ten Commandments the nature of sin, as well as the character of these sins. In Nicodemos' view some sins are forgivable; some are mortal by nature and by character.[155] He especially stresses the importance of the human mind and human thoughts in committing sinful acts. As the most important "medicine" he suggests the Jesus Prayer and continuous resistance and complete contempt toward all evil and sinful thoughts.[156]

INTRODUCTION

The third part, which is written for the penitent, gives a series of spiritual counsels for all Christians in order to avoid sinful deeds. St. Nicodemos suggests avoidance of all the causes of sins, frequent confession, remembrance of death, remembrance of hell and paradise, and especially remembrance of Christ's crucifixion for our own personal redemption. [157]

In his beautiful homily on repentance he says that the inner sorrow and pain of the heart are substantial and necessary components of the sacrament of confession and repentance. [158] This sorrow and repentance must be constant and continuous throughout our lives on earth. [159] Then he asks the sinner to cut off all the roots of sin and to plant in the heart all the Christian virtues, which are the best guarantees of not sinning again. [160] God, he concludes, will not call us on the day of our death and last judgment in order to ask us whether we theologized, or performed miracles, or have seen the divine light; rather, God will ask us why we did not repent and why we did not feel sorrow for our sins. Therefore, St. Nicodemos teaches that we—all sinners—must examine ourselves every day and every hour to determine whether we have truly repented. If we have not done that, we must say to ourselves that we have lost that day. We must heal our passions and wounds of sin, and then we shall be able to keep all the commandments of the Lord and progress in all virtues. The kingdom of God is not a hospital or a clinic that accepts the sick and those who are in misery; it is a mansion and a palace that accepts the healthy and the strong. [161] An English translation of this book would be most beneficial.

The second book that belongs to this section is *The Rudder* (Pedalion). It is a book of monumental proportions; the English translation is 1,034 pages. No such work existed before, for the canons were scattered in an unmeasurable number of manuscripts, unavailable to the clergy and laity because the language was no longer understood by them. When he was approximately thirty-nine years old, St. Nicodemos collected the most important canons of the church, and after painstaking and ceaseless work for two to three years, he produced one of the most important books of the Orthodox Church. His unmatchable memory, his patience, his profound respect for the tradition of the Church, and his own love for the Church of Christ, the people of God, inspired him to complete this incomparable work. The Greek title, *Pedalion*, refers to the metaphorical ship that symbolizes the Catholic Church of Christ. The full title of the book is *The Rudder of the Orthodox Christians or All the Sacred and Divine Canons of the Holy and Renowned*

43

Apostles, of the Holy Councils, Ecumenical as well as Regional, and of Individual Divine Fathers as Embodied in the Original Greek Text for the Sake of Authenticity, and Explained in the Vernacular by Way of Rendering Them More Intelligible to the Less Educated.[162] The publication names as its authors first Agapios the Peloponnesian and then Nicodemos the Hagiorite. Agapios, a teacher by profession and a monk, was an assistant to St. Nicodemos and undoubtedly contributed extensively to the success of this great enterprise, but there is no question that the work was a product of the pen and the pain of St. Nicodemos himself. Out of his great humility, once more, he allowed the honor of authorship to one of his friends and assistants. The Ecumenical Patriarchate wholeheartedly approved the publication of *The Rudder*.

A strange story is associated with the first publication of this book. The technical matters concerning the publication were entrusted to a monk named Theodoretos from the city of Ioannina. He was a hard-working man, who used to travel throughout the monasteries of Mt. Athos collecting manuscripts and speaking about his own personal "mystical" experiences.[163] When he supervised the publication of *The Rudder*, he inserted into the work his own personal opinions and interpretations, which were completely alien to the teaching of the Orthodox Church. Fortunately, the patriarch of Constantinople, Neophytos VII, in an encyclical letter (August, 1802) asked that all of Theodoretos' interpolations be omitted; he also pointed out the seven most important deviations of Theodoretos. This patriarchal letter is now inserted in all publications of *The Rudder*, including the English translation. Nicodemos was greatly saddened by this episode, but, as one of his biographers writes, he accepted with great humility this betrayal by one of his "pseudo-brothers."[164]

The universal acceptance by Orthodox churches all over the world witnesses the great success of this book. A Russian translation has been made, and D. Cummings' English translation, done faithfully from the fifth edition and published by John Nicolaides in Athens in 1908 is indeed useful.[165] Cummings has done good work, but he added a long prologue by Apostolos Makrakis, a famous and controversial Greek lay theologian of the last century. He also added in many instances Makrakis' personal comments on the interpretations of St. Nicodemos.

In summary, the contents of *The Rudder* are as follows: (1) a personal dedication of Agapios and Nicodemos to the "most affectionate mother of all Orthodox Christians, the Holy Great Church of Christ";

INTRODUCTION

(2) the Patriarchal Letter of Neophytos VII with the approval for the publication and the warning against the interpolations by Theodoretos; (3) a brotherly salutation of the authors to all readers; (4) prolegomena in general to the sacred canons; (5) the eighty-five canons of the Holy Apostles; (6) prolegomena and canons of the seven ecumenical councils; (7) the canons of the regional synods; (8) prolegomena and the canons of the holy Fathers of the Church; (9) a chapter with accurate canonical instructions concerning marriages; (10) forms of some letters; and (11) a description of the Orthodox Church building.

From this description one can understand the breadth, the vastness, the immensity, and the spiritual profundity of this magnificent work. Half of the text is composed by St. Nicodemos himself. To the original text of the canons, he adds his own interpretation (*hermenia*) in the vernacular, and then he adds the "harmony" (*symphonia*) or concord. Here he harmonizes all the information, of which he had a great command, and adds his own personal understanding and experience.

St. Nicodemos and his assistant, Agapios, realized the great impact this book would have on the life of the Church, and in their dedication to the Mother Church, they write:

> Indeed, this canonical handbook is a sort of rudder and spiritual compass; since it alone, in truth, points accurately and undeviatingly to the Pole—that is to say, heaven itself. With it, as with a rudder, the Church of Christ can very surely and very safely steer her course on her voyage to that really calm harbor of that blissful and wantless destination.[166]

An icon at the beginning of the book depicts this ecclesiological reality by saying that the keel of the ship

> represents the Orthodox Faith in the Holy Trinity. Its beams and planks, the dogmas and traditions of the faith. Its mast represents the Cross; its sail and rigging represent Hope and Love. The master of the vessel is our Lord Jesus Christ, whose hand is on the helm. The mates and sailors are the Apostles, and the successors of the Apostles, and all clergymen, secretaries, and notaries, and occasional teachers. The passengers comprise all Orthodox Christians. The sea symbolizes the present life. A gentle and zephyr-like breeze signifies whiffs and graces of the Holy Spirit wafting the vessel on its course.

INTRODUCTION

Winds, on the other hand, are temptations baffling it. Its rudder, whereby it is steered straightforwardly to the heavenly harbor is the present handbook of the sacred canons.[167]

Precisely because of the great importance of the canons for the life of the Church, to "benefit both the erudite and learned, and the simple and unlearned as well,"[168] and to avoid "death-dealing fruit," "perdition of souls," "miscorrecting the sinners," St. Nicodemos decided to produce this monumental work. In a careful and scholarly way, St. Nicodemos describes the methodology he followed. He offers a list of his sources, which a contemporary scholar would admire. Then he argues that just as the all-efficient Holy Trinity created this first and material world with various natural canons (or laws) of the elements, which resulted in the orderliness and the coherence of the universe, so in like manner the same Holy Trinity, having constructed this second and supersensible world of the Catholic Church, with sacred and divine canons has bound her together and has consolidated her. As the material creation needs laws in order not to fall into dissolution, in the same way the Church needs the canons, so that order will prevail.[169] In the words of St. Nicodemos himself, "As a result of these sacred canons, the earthly ecclesiastical hierarchy becomes an imitation and expression of the heavenly hierarchy."[170] Therefore, he appeals to the Orthodox people "to accept this necessary scripture which comes next after the Holy Scriptures."[171] In other words, a "single melody" and a "perfect harmony" between heaven and earth is achieved through the canons of the Church, which are based equally on scriptural and patristic grounds and which lead us "to the great light of full knowledge" (Is 42:7; Mt 4:16). Thus the canons become a means to our salvation.[172]

In order to understand the spirit and method by which St. Nicodemos approached the interpretation of the canons, a few examples will help. Speaking, for instance, on the sixty-ninth apostolic canon, which postulates fasting during Lent and every Wednesday and Friday, he makes the point that we do not fast in order to mourn the cross of Christ; rather, we fast because Christ himself fasted, because of our sins, because the apostles ordered it, and the Fathers recommended it, and because it is to the best and greatest benefit of our souls. At the same time, he is fully aware of the main details concerning fasting; for instance, that we do not fast on Pentecost Wednesday and Friday because of the joy of the descent of the Holy Spirit and because the Holy Spirit is co-essential with the Son.[173] Speaking about kneeling or genuflection, he refers to the canons of the ecumenical councils and of individual Fathers, which do not allow genuflection during the paschal period and on Sundays, and he even makes the point that the genuflection on Pentecost Sunday actually takes place at the vesper service, which belongs to the next day, that is, Monday.[174] In interpreting the sixty-eighth apostolic canon, which forbids reordination, he makes the point that the sacrament not only leaves an indelible imprint on the human soul (an explanation that does not satisfy St. Nicodemos). "But to me," St. Nicodemos continues, "on the other hand, it seems that the sole reason why these two mysteries [baptism and ordination] alone are incapable of being celebrated a second time in the life of one and the same individual as a recipient thereof, is because they are carried out in the type or form of the Lord's death, which occurred but once and can never occur a second time."[175] In conjunction with this point, St. Nicodemos made clear that two liturgies should not be celebrated on one and the same day and on the same altar table precisely "because of the fact that the unique death of Christ cannot occur a second time."[176] Nicodemos based his conclusion on the local synod held in the time of the Emperor Herakleios in the city of Antisiodore in 613. He draws the same conclusion in his *Exomologetarion*, where he refers to the eleventh canon of the same synod.[177]

These examples show how informative and practical *The Rudder* is for contemporary Christians. The vast amount of information and the penetrating spirit of St. Nicodemos make this book indispensable for any serious student of the life of the Church.

The last book in this section is *A Handbook of Spiritual Counsel*.[178] The subtitle is "The Guarding of the Five Senses and the Imagination of the Mind and Heart. The Cultivation of the Natural Delights of the Mind." This book has been translated from the original Greek by Peter A. Chamberas and is published in the present volume. It is an astonishing book because St. Nicodemos wrote it when he was in self-exile on the small, barren island south of Mt. Athos known as Skyropoula, and he carried no books at all with him. Thus this book is a blessed fruit of the heart, mind, and memory of St. Nicodemos. It not only shows how knowledgeable he was in both the secular and sacred learning of his times, but how he also transformed the life of the spirit into a way of life and the way of life into the way of the spirit. It is true that only a pure heart completely liberated from worldly cares has the ability to enter into the refreshing waters of Christian theology, to ascend the steps of perfection, and to transmit its divine experiences to all of us.

This book was written at the request of his cousin, Ierotheos, bishop of Euripos, and St. Nicodemos did it with extreme carefulness and loving affection. Bishop Ierotheos in his letter to St. Nicodemos writes that he is fully aware of the temptations and the spiritual toils he is facing, and he says that he is not ashamed to ask his cousin for advice. St. Nicodemos obliged, and in order, as he says, to avoid disobedience, he wrote this book as a small spiritual offering to his cousin. On receiving this book, Ierotheos expressed admiration, and he prophesied that generations to come would benefit "from the fragrance of scriptural and patristic meadows" as well as from the taste "of the sweet and beautifully-smelling honey" contained in this work.[179]

The book begins with a preface in which St. Nicodemos speaks about the election of bishops only from the ranks of the monks. He makes the point that bishops in earlier times were "theokletoi" or "demokletoi," that is, that they were chosen by God himself and the people of God.[180] Then in twelve chapters he speaks about the guarding of the five senses, as well as of the imagination, the mind, and the heart; he also develops the theme of the cultivation of the natural delights or pleasures of the human mind. The book includes an anatomical description of the heart, and the miracle of the eclipse of the sun during the crucifixion of our Lord Jesus Christ. It concludes with a note of defense for his teaching on the virgin Mary, the mother of God, which he included in *Unseen Warfare*. The reader of this volume will see and feel the impact of St. Nicodemos' theology and practical spiritual experience. A few comments beforehand are necessary, however.

St. Nicodemos bases his spiritual counsel on a sound scriptural and patristic anthropology. Following St. Gregory the Theologian and St. Gregory Palamas, he rejects Democritos' declaration that man was created by God as a microcosm within the greater world of nature. Rather, he holds that man was created as a macrocosm, that is, a greater world within the smaller universe. Even compared with the angels, man is a greater world because he is composed both of the invisible and the visible worlds, whereas the angels are composed only of the invisible world. Immediately, St. Nicodemos describes the human body as a palace and the mind as a king who dwells in it, which shows the balance and correct understanding of both components of human existence, the physical and the spiritual. Naturally, the human

INTRODUCTION

mind has a special purpose, and whereas the body is inclined to material things for its nourishment, growth, life, and pleasure, the rational soul leads and rules the body and the senses. The five senses of the body serve as openings to the world around us, and through them the mind can receive spiritual nurture and pleasure.[181]

St. Nicodemos speaks in the second chapter about the enslavement of the mind to the physical pleasures and the role of the senses in this dreadful bondage. When the mind is free through spiritual nourishment—the reading of Sacred Scripture, the acquirement of virtues, the doing of the commandments of the Lord, the practice of prayer—all these bring the senses back to the spiritual pleasures. Thus an interaction is achieved between soul and body, and the soul draws the body together toward their divine Creator.[182]

From chapters three to seven St. Nicodemos analyzes the methodology of guarding the five senses—vision, hearing, smell, taste, and touch—against all the external temptations and dangers. Even a contemporary anthropologist and psychologist would envy the systematic study and the depth of St. Nicodemos' analyses. He emphasizes, for instance, the importance of the eyes in committing sins, the great dangers that impress upon our souls, and how clergymen and laymen alike should guard their sight from all the external temptations that lead to lust and downfall.[183] He stresses the dangers a Christian faces from hedonistic melodies and how fragrances are alien to the life of the Christian. He makes the point that ascetics who do not wash themselves exude a pleasant and fragrant odor. Speaking on the sense of smell, he strongly advises against smoking, which can destroy both body and soul in a devastating way. Sumptuous meals are alien to the Christian way of life because they also harm the health of the soul and body, and in the last analysis the abundance of food creates a fat body that becomes susceptible to sexual temptations; the mind loses its clarity; the divine illuminations depart from the heart; moreover, a fat person is led to death more quickly than a thin and ascetic one.[184]

All these ideas are relevant to our times, which stress so persistently and incorrectly the senses and their satisfaction in our daily life. Our senses are attracted by the sirens of consumerism, quick sensual satisfaction, and false materialistic promises. Under these continuous attacks our senses lose their orientation, and instead of becoming instruments for our salvation, they become organs for our spiritual and physical destruction. St. Nicodemos realizes the failings of our fallen nature and warns us of the tremendous destructive power our senses can hold over us. He recognizes that the senses have a place in the life of the Christian, of any Christian, if and when they are used properly and correctly. This is why he warns us that the human body is inclined to "worldly cares" or "pseudo-good."[185] The human body with the senses is naturally inclined to the pleasures derived from physical things, or it merely marvels and enjoys the corruptible creation around it and remains unconcerned for the spiritual glory of God. Again and again, St. Nicodemos stresses the importance of a balanced coexistence of body and soul, of material and immaterial, rational and irrational, each one having been created for the glory of God and the salvation of humankind. He makes very clear that God intends for the rational to rule over the irrational and the greater to rule over the lesser, which ought to obey its directives.[186] Thus, the "hegemonic mind" leads the human body and its senses and controls them, leads them and guides them toward wisdom, goodness, power, truth, sweetness, and all the other activities and perfections of the Creator that can be discerned in creation and in the Bible.[187] Moreover, according to St. Nicodemos, as an instrument of the Holy Spirit the body has the ability, through the senses, to use all created things and all of Holy Scripture to rise step by step from the seen to the unseen, from the effects to the causes, and from the images and types to the originals. In other words, through our mind and our senses, we can rise from created things to the Creator, from the words of the Holy Scriptures to God himself, in accordance with the following saying of the prophet Isaiah: "Come, let us go up to the mountain of the Lord, to the house of the God of Jacob; that he may teach us his ways, and that we may walk in his paths" (Is 2:3). This is the beautiful ultimate goal of the senses according to St. Nicodemos, and he calls them doors or portals through which we can perceive the Creator by observing the created, and by watching over ourselves vigilantly so that we may always delight in these spiritual things, stretching both our mind and appetite toward them.[188]

In an original and provocative chapter, he speaks on the imagination, which he calls the "internal sense of the soul." He makes clear that the imagination is more refined than sense perception and is the "map of the ruling mind upon which everything is recorded; it is the broad board on which things are painted; it is the wax upon which things are imprinted." The imagination then takes into its possession all the passionate impressions of the senses and through them causes passion and agitation to the soul. Thus it is easier to sin through the imagination, and therefore a passionate imagination has a greater authority over humankind than the senses themselves. The devil also tempts the human imagination quite frequently, but the Lord himself who was completely free of the power of Satan was completely independent of all the temptations because he did not have imaginings, that is, passionate and fruitless thoughts.[189]

Then St. Nicodemos goes a bit further and discusses the mind and the heart. The heart, which is the "mystical and hidden chamber of the mind," must be kept under continuous vigilance for all the external temptations, and mental prayer is one of the most important ways to guard the purity of the heart. In a remarkable section he speaks about the fruits of this spiritual prayer and how human nature as a whole is purified of the evil passions and made capable of receiving the supernatural grace of God.[190]

More specifically, these fruits are complete liberation of the human heart from the "beautiful" things of this world and from the physical pleasures of the senses. The delusion of the imagination that activates evil and shameful thoughts fades away. Silence prevails along with humility, contrition, tears, purity, spiritual exercises, and, above all, the presence in ourselves of the grace and energy of God.[191] St. Nicodemos makes it clear that to enjoy these spiritual fruits, we must keep our hearts constantly vigilant. All our senses must be cleansed. For if one sense only or one power of the soul is polluted, the pollution is sent directly to the heart, and thus the whole human person is polluted. The heart contains and holds the inner senses and is the root of all good and evil things. If the root is holy, so are the branches holy. If it is evil, so are the branches evil. Constant vigilance therefore is required. Thus through these spiritual works we will establish the whole of our inner self to be a temple and a dwelling place of the Holy Spirit while our heart, most especially, will be a holy altar, indeed a sacred sanctuary of our Lord Jesus Christ himself.[192]

In the eleventh chapter he speaks about the spiritual delights and pleasures of the mind, which have six main sources: (1) doing the divine commandments; (2) acquiring the Christian virtues; (3) reading the Sacred Scriptures; (4) contemplating the beauty of creation; (5) the knowledge of the Incarnation of Christ; (6) the contemplation upon God himself.[193] One cannot but be moved by the great faith and the intensity of the spiritual life of St. Nicodemos when he writes that these spiritual pleasures of the mind refine the whole body internally and externally; they enhance it, beautify it, strengthen it, and transfigure it to higher plateaus of divine blessedness and glorification. Indeed, it is a delight and pleasure to go through the pages of this magnificent spiritual book. In it St. Nicodemos incorporates all his scriptural and patristic acumen and becomes himself a new Father of the Church.[194]

IV. Some Conclusions

This short introduction has covered the life and the most important works of St. Nicodemos the Hagiorite. His liturgical works (a full list is given by Father Nicodemos Paulopoulos[195]) and his unpublished letters, hymnological collections, and homilies[196] have barely been touched upon. I have tried to offer the English reader some taste of his thought, theology, contemplative life, and spiritual wisdom. It is unfortunate that most of his works have not been known in the West. Without any doubt, however, he can be included among the most brilliant and productive theologians of recent times. A man of vast knowledge, he did not shun secular knowledge. He knew very well the ancient Greek philosophers, whom he quoted unhesitatingly, as well as the contemporary thinkers of his time like John Locke, Spinoza, and Voltaire; at the same time he always put secular knowledge in the proper perspective. The Western Enlightenment as well as the Greek secularism of his times did not influence St. Nicodemos. He appreciated the importance of mathematics and the physical sciences, but he pointed out that they are important for those who have not reached the stage of passionlessness. For him, the most important thing is the "eternal philosophy" or the "philosophy according to Christ."[197] Thus, St. Nicodemos is primarily a theologian who has fully and thoroughly encompassed and unified in his writings the message of the Scriptures and the tradition of the Fathers. A man of the spirit, he taught and lived the spiritual life of the Church totally and uncompromisingly. The centrality of his spiritual life was the continuous effort for his final goal, that is, union with God. He put in proper perspective the Christian virtues, which all people—clergy, monks, and laity—must attain so that they, through this "practical philosophy," will reach the true life of contemplation and immerse themselves in the ocean of the divine energies of God. By emphasizing the centrality of the heart in the spiritual life, he brought out the experience of the Fathers of the Church, who teach that only a pure heart, completely liberated from evil passions, can become the throne of God. Also, he emphasized the "circular movement" of the mind, which returns to the heart through the Jesus Prayer. He writes:

> Let me say it more clearly. Let your inner understanding say only the Jesus Prayer; let your mind pay attention through its spiritual vision and hearing to the words of the prayer only and especially to the meaning of the words, without any forms or shapes and without imagining any other perceptible or intelligible thing, internal or external, even if it is good. Because God transcends all beings both visible and invisible, the human mind seeking to be united with him through prayer, must go out of all things that are perceptible or intelligible in order to achieve this divine union.[198]

Committed fully to the life of the Holy Spirit, St. Nicodemos understands that we should exercise every effort to acquire the gifts of the Holy Spirit by cleansing our heart and making it

> a temple and dwelling place worthy of being inhabited by the Holy Spirit. How? Through inner attention and the return of the mind to the heart, followed by the practice of sacred mental prayer in the heart saying, "Lord Jesus Christ, Son of God, have mercy upon me." When you prepare your heart, my beloved, then the all-holy, all-good, and most man-loving Spirit comes and dwells in you perceptibly, actively, manifestly. Then, my brother, you receive from the Holy Spirit whatever you longed for. Do you love the gift of wisdom? You will receive it. Do you want to partake of the gift of the Apostles? You will acquire it. Do you aspire after the gift of martyrdom? You will receive it, if it is to your interest. Do you love joy? Do you love faith? Do you love love? Do you love the gifts of discernment (*diakrisis*), insight (*diorasis*), foreknowledge (*proorasis*), prophecy? The Holy Spirit will give you all these things.[199]

Moreover, this famous "Jesus Prayer" requires absolute humility, silence, and cutting oneself off from everything that would cause agitation and obstruction to the prayer. Then one continually repeats mentally the Prayer of the Heart, "Lord Jesus Christ, Son of God, have mercy upon me," and focuses his or her attention on the heart. The mental recitation of this prayer requires that a person not breathe continually, but hold the breath until his inner consciousness has a chance to say the prayer once. Then the person breathes out. This holding of the breath produces pain in the heart, because it does not receive natural oxygen. But through this slight suffering, the heart is refined, becomes warmer, soft, sensitive, humble, and more capable of contrition and tears. This controlling of the breathing also unites all the powers of the soul to return to the mind and through the mind to God, and a full union of man and God is accomplished.[200]

Psychologically speaking, the human heart is liberated from the burden of guilt and builds freely his dependence on the Creator. Theologically, it continually creates a new person and thus, in the final analysis, finds its ultimate destination in the bosom of its Creator where it finds freedom, rest, and spiritual fulfillment. It should be added that the prayer is not a technical method through which external "union" with God is achieved. It is, rather, a long process, initiated by God the Almighty, a gift from God granted to those who really fight and struggle constantly for it. St. Nicodemos knew and practiced this mental prayer with watchfulness and love. Even in the last moments of his earthly life he recited the Jesus Prayer.

Together with this contemplative theology of the Spirit, St. Nicodemos did not fail to stress the importance of the liturgical life of both the collective and private forms of prayer. A liturgist himself, he introduced a liturgical renewal in the Orthodox Church by emphasizing the importance of the frequency of holy communion and the need for participation in the liturgical life of the Church.[201]

Was Nicodemos an original thinker in the contemporary scholarly sense of the term? I believe he was. He did not merely digest and assimilate the theology of the Church in a superficial and external way, but he made Christian theology, the experience of the Scriptures and the Fathers, a new reality, a new experience, a new message. Precisely here lies the great contribution of St. Nicodemos: He rethought, relived, and reexperienced the eternally new and refreshing message of Christ and his Church. Thus he was original, in the sense that he captured the essence of the Christian message of salvation and made it approachable and accessible for our times; and he was contemporary, because he never lost sight of the perennial problems of humankind, which has gone astray from God throughout all the periods of human history. Moreover, with his message to the Orthodox people of his times, he is considered a man who prepared the spiritual and national liberation of the contemporary Greek nation.

Was he strict, and does this bear a message for the men and women of the twentieth and twenty-first centuries? Yes, he was strict. He had to be. A man who grasped the patristic tradition could not but set high standards for achieving the illuminating heights of the glory of God. Only high standards for spiritual achievement can motivate and inspire men and women to transcend their human weaknesses and ascend Mount Tabor in order to participate in the transfiguration of Christ. We need such a transfiguration today. Strictness together with his loving fatherly care, his spiritual and intellectual prowess, his saintly humility, his prayerful life and earthly humanity make him close to us today. Indeed, all of us need models such as St. Nicodemos. In the chaos created by contemporary secularism, St. Nicodemos may become the example who will offer us relief, strength, and above all direction to greener and more beautiful spiritual pastures.

Notes

1. Steven Runciman, *The Great Church in Captivity* (Cambridge: University Press, 1968).
2. These works include, among others, Runciman, *Great Church in Captivity;* Theodore Papadopoulos, *The History of the Greek Church and People under the Turkish Domination* (Brussels, 1952); Charles A. Frazee, *The Orthodox Church and Independent Greece, 1821–1852* (Cambridge: University Press, 1969); and Timothy Ware, *Eustratios Argenti* (Oxford: Clarendon Press, 1964).
3. G. A. Hadjiantoniou, *Protestant Patriarch: The Life of Cyril Lukaris (1572–1638)* (London, 1961).
4. Arnold Toynbee, *A Study of History* (New York: Oxford University Press, 1957), pp. 155–59.
5. Vasilios Stefanides, "Ekklesiastike Historia" (Athens, 1948), p. 635.
6. Timothy Ware, *Eustratios Argenti* (Oxford: Clarendon Press, 1964).
7. Ibid., pp. 3ff.
8. B. J. Kidd, *The Churches of the Eastern Christendom* (London, 1927).
9. George Wheler, *A Journey to Greece* (London, 1682). Cited by Philip Sherrard, *The Greek East and the Latin West* (New York: Oxford University Press, 1959), pp. 102–07.

10. M. Crusius, *Germanograecia* (Basel, 1585); and P. Recaut, *The Present State of the Greek and the Armenian Churches* (London, 1679).

11. Runciman, *Great Church in Captivity*, pp. 208ff.

12. Ware, *Eustratios Argenti*, p. 6.

13. Nikou Zanaropoulou, *"He Paideia Sten Tourkokratia"* (Education in the Turkish Period), ed. Pournara (Thessalonike: 1983), pp. 37ff.

14. Ware, *Eustratios Argenti*, pp. 6ff.

15. Constantinou Kourkoula, *"He Theoria tou Kerygmatos kata tous Chronous Tis Tourkokratias"* (The Theory of Preaching During the Turkish Years) (Athens: 1957).

16. S. Koumanoudis, *"Synagoge Neon Lexeon Hypo Ton Logion Plastheison Apo Tis Aloseos Mehri Ton Kath Emas Chronon"* (The Collection of New Words by Scholars From the Fall of Constantinople to Our Own Times), Vols. I and II (Athens: 1900).

17. Papadopoulous, *History of the Greek Church*, pp. 123ff.

18. C. M. Woodhouse, *The Greek War of Independence* (New York: Russell and Russell, 1952), p. 31.

19. Runciman, *Great Church*, p. 410.

20. The earliest biography of St. Nicodemos was written four years after his death by his spiritual brother Euthymios: *"Bios kai Politeia kai Agones tou Hosiologiotatou kai Makaritou kai Aoidimou Nicodemou Monachou"* (The Life, Conduct and Struggles of the Most Holy and Most Learned Monk Nicodemos of Blessed Memory) in the periodical *Gregory Palamas* (1920), p. 640. See also a new edition by Monk Nicodemos Bilalis, *Prototypos Bios tou Agiou Nicodemou tou Hagioreitou*, 5th ed. (Athens: 1985). There is also a "Life" written by Athanasios Parios, which is unpublished, and another by Onouphrios Iviritis, *"Bios en Synopsei tou Makaritou kai Aoidimou Didaskalou Nicodemou Hagioreitou"* (A Condensed Life of the Late Teacher Nicodemos the Hagiorite of Blessed Memory) in St. Nicodemos' *Paul's Fourteen Epistles* (Venice: 1819), p. xi.

    Father Theokletos Dionysiatis, a monk of Mount Athos, published an excellent account of St. Nicodemos' life and works: Theokletos Dionysiatis, *Agios Nicodemos, O Hagioretis: O Bios Kai Ta Erga Tou*, ed. Papademetriou (Athens: 1959).

    Constantine Cavarnos, a former professor at Holy Cross Greek Orthodox School of Theology, published in English a comprehensive biography of St. Nicodemos, in which he included an English translation of Father Gerasimos Microgiannanitis' "Life" of St. Nicodemos, *St. Nicodemos, the Hagiorite*, in the series Modern Orthodox Saints, No. 3 (Belmont, Mass.: Institute for Byzantine and Modern Greek Studies (IBMGS), 1974).

There is also my own monograph on St. Nicodemos, in the series Post-Byzantine Ecclesiastical Personalities by Michael Vaporis (Brookline, Mass.: Holy Cross Orthodox Press, 1978).

21. Micragiannanitis, "Life," in Cavarnos, *St. Nicodemos*, pp. 66–67.

22. Dionysiatis, *Agios Nicodemos*, pp. 30–31.

23. For this great apostle of the Greek Nation, see Constantine Cavarnos, *St. Cosmas Aitolos*, in Modern Orthodox Saints, No. 1 (Belmont, Mass.: IBMGS, 1971); and Nomikos M. Vaporis, *Father Kosmas, The Apostle of the Poor* (Brookline, Mass.: Holy Cross Press, 1977).

24. Dionysiatis, *Agios Nicodemos*, p. 34.

25. *Geron* and *gerontas* means "old man" or "elder." In the Orthodox monastic language it refers to a spiritual father who has distinguished himself by his devotion to Orthodox doctrine and canons and has, therefore, the gift to guide his spiritual children toward spiritual perfection.

26. *Hesychasm*, from the Greek term *hesychia*, means "quietness or tranquility of the heart." It is a long and difficult process that leads toward spiritual perfection. For the accomplishment of *hesychia*, special training is required under a skillful spiritual father. Although it is an ancient monastic virtue, it has become known outside Mount Athos through the teachings of St. Gregory Palamas. See John Meyendorff, ed., *Gregory Palamas: The Triads* (New York: Paulist Press, 1983).

27. Bebis, *Saint Nicodemos*, in the *Post-Byzantine Ecclesiastical Personalities Series*, p. 3.

28. Boiled wheat and the associated memorial service. Wheat or the biblical *sitos* symbolizes the human nature according to the saying of the Lord in John 12:24.

29. Dionysiatis, *Agios Nicodemos*, pp. 40ff.

30. Ibid., p. 41. For a good discussion of the *Kollyvades*, see B. Veritis, "To Anamorphotikon Kinema Ton Kollyvadon kai oi dyo Alexandroi tis Skiathou" (The Reforming Movement of the *Kollyvades* and the Two Alexanders of Skiathos), *Aktines*, 1943, pp. 99–100.

31. Constantine Cavarnos, *St. Macarios of Corinth*, in Modern Orthodox Saints, Vol. 2 (Belmont, Mass.: IBMGS, 1972).

32. For more on the *Kollyvades*, see Charilaos S. Tzogas, *He Peri Mnemosynon Eris en Hagio Orei Kata Ton IH Aiona* (The Dispute on

the Memorial Services on the Holy Mountain during the 18th Century) (Thessalonike: 1969); and Konstantinos P. Papoulides, *To Kinema Ton Kollyvadon* (The *Kollyvades* Movement) (Athens: 1971). See also reviews of these books by Nomikos Vaporis in *Greek Orthodox Theological Review* 19 (1974): 203–08. See also, Cavarnos, *St. Macarios of Corinth*, pp. 15ff.

33. Dionysiatis, *Agios Nicodemos*, pp. 121–25.
34. Microgiannanitis' "Life" in Cavarnos, *St. Nicodemos the Hagiorite*, pp. 79–80.
35. Bilalis, *Prototypos Bios*, pp. 12–13.
36. Microgiannanitis, "Life," p. 93.
37. V. Grumel, "Nicode 1 'Agiorite,' " in *Dictionnaire Catholique*, p. 486. See also the discussion of this subject in Dionysiatis, p. 287.
38. Dionysiatis, *Agios Nicodemos*, p. 287.
39. Bilalis, *Prototypos Bios*, p. 15.
40. The book of the eight tones used in the liturgical services of the Orthodox Church.
41. Bilalis, *Prototypos Bios*, p. 17.
42. Ibid.
43. Bebis, *Saint Nicodemos*, p. 1.
44. Ibid.
45. Gerasimos Mikrogiannanites, *Akolouthia tou hosiou kai theophorou patros hemon kai didaskalou Nicodemou tou Hagioreitou* (Service for the Holy and God-bearing Father of Ours and Teacher Nicodemos of the Holy Mountain), ed. Geron Ananias of the Skourtaion Monastery, 2nd ed. (1965), pp. 3–4.
46. Cavarnos, *St. Nicodemos the Hagiorite*, p. 63.
47. The relics of St. Nicodemos and especially his sacred skull are kept on Mount Athos. The skull is to be housed in a church that is to be built in his name.
48. Nicodemos Paulopoulos, *Ta Erga Tou Agiou Nicodemou*, in the series published by the Church of Greece, *150th Anniversary of the Greek Independence* (Athens: 1976).
49. Dionysiatis, *Agios Nicodemos*.
50. Cavarnos, *St. Nicodemos the Hagiorite*.
51. Bebis, *Saint Nicodemos*.
52. Published in Venice, 1803; Constantinople, 1863; Athens, 1974.
53. Published in Venice, 1819; Constantinople, 1824; Zante, 1868; Athens, 1868 and 1973.
54. Dionysiatis, *Agios Nicodemos*, p. 301.

55. Ibid., p. 303.
56. Nomikos Vaporis, "The Price of Faith: Some Reflections on Nico-
    demos Hagiorites and His Struggle against Islam, Together with a
    Translation of the 'Introduction' to His 'New Martyrologion,' " *The
    Greek Orthodox Theological Review* 23, nos. 3 and 4 (Fall–Winter
    1978): 185–215. In the same issue, see Demetrios J. Constantelos,
    "The 'Neomartyrs' as Evidence for Methods and Motives Leading
    to Conversion and Martyrdom in the Ottoman Empire," pp. 216–
    34. The "New Martyrologium" was published in Venice, 1799;
    Athens, 1856 and 1861.
57. Vaporis, "Price of Faith," p. 187.
58. Ibid., p. 188.
59. Ibid.
60. Ibid., pp. 188–90.
61. Ibid., p. 208.
62. Ibid.
63. Ibid., p. 193.
64. Constantelos, "The 'Neomartyrs,' " pp. 216–34. Constantelos dis-
    cusses all the conditions under which the Orthodox lived under
    the Turks and rejects the theory, presented by early and new
    scholars, that the Orthodox enjoyed tolerance under the Turks.
    He offers a large bibliography for the specialist on this subject.
65. Ibid., pp. 117–18.
66. Vaporis, "Price of Faith," p. 194.
67. Dionysiatis, *Agios Nicodemos*, pp. 342ff.
68. Ibid., p. 99.
69. The *Philokalia* (Astir) has gone through four editions.
70. Faber and Faber, London and Boston. At this writing three vol-
    umes have been published: the first in 1979, the second in 1981,
    and the third in 1984.
71. Cf. the first volume of this English translation, pp. 11, 30.
72. *Philokalia ton Ieron Neptikon* (Athens: Astir, 1957). Cf. pp. XIXff.
    as well as p. XXIII.
73. Ibid., p. XXIV. An excellent review of the *Philokalia* by Theodore
    Stylianopoulos appears in *Greek Orthodox Theological Review* 26, No.
    3. Father Stylianopoulos raises the issue of the omission by the
    translators of St. Nicodemos' introduction and refers to Professor
    Tachiaos' work in discovering the original manuscripts in the librar-
    ies of Mount Athos. Both Tachiaos and Stylianopoulos stress the
    contribution of St. Macarios to the publication of the *Philokalia*.

Professor Christou, in his series Greek Fathers of the Church (published by "Perivoli tis Panagias"), has begun the publication of the *Philokalia* in both original Greek and modern Greek.

74. Dionysiatis, *Agios Nicodemos*, p. 110.
75. Monk Theodore the Hagiorite, *Peri synechous metalepseos* (*On Continuous Communion*), ed. by "Tinos" (Athens, date not given). Father Theodore offers an ample history of the problem of the original text of Neophytos with a complete bibliography and discussions on this issue by both Orthodox and non-Orthodox scholars.
76. See *St. Basil: Letters*, Vol. I, in the series The Fathers of the Church, Vol. 13 (Washington, D.C.: The Catholic University of America Press, 1965), pp. 208–09. St. Basil points out that it is an "excellent and advantageous practice" to partake daily of the holy body and blood of Christ.
77. Constantine Doukakis and Antonios Georgiou, eds., *Peri tes synechous metalepseos ton Theion Mysterion* (Athens: 1887), pp. 103ff.
78. Denis, *Heortodromion*, 1836, p. 584; cf. Cavarnos, *St. Nicodemos the Hagiorite*, p. 31.
79. E. Kadloubovsky and G. E. H. Palmer, *Unseen Warfare*, Intro. by H. A. Hodges (London: Faber and Faber Ltd., 1952), p. 45. A reproduction of this English translation was published by St. Vladimir's Press (Crestwood, N.Y., 1978).
80. Ibid., pp. 47ff.
81. Ibid., pp. 53–54.
82. Dionysiatis, *Agios Nicodemos*, p. 196. For the original texts of this prayer, see the edition of *Aoratos Polemos* (Athens: Prometheus, 1922), pp. 254ff.
83. Kadloubovsky and Palmer, *Unseen Warfare*, pp. 60ff. and 67.
84. Dionysiatis, *Agios Nicodemos*, pp. 197ff.
85. Ibid., pp. 197–202.
86. From St. Nicodemos' own introduction. *Gymnasmata Pneumatika*, 4th ed. (Volos: Shoinas Publishing House, 1950), p. 7.
87. Ibid., Meditation 8, p. 51.
88. Ibid., Meditation 18, pp. 138ff.
89. Ibid., Meditations 23, 24, 25, pp. 182ff.
90. Ibid., Meditation 26, pp. 213ff.
91. Ibid., Meditation 33, pp. 286ff.
92. Ibid., pp. 130–31.
93. Constantinople, 1799; Athens, 1864.

94. Venice, 1803; Hermoupolis, Syros, 1838; Chios, 1887; Volos, 1957.
95. *Christoetheia ton Christianon* (Christian Morality) (Volos: Agioreitikes Bibliothekes, 1957), pp. 292ff.
96. Ibid., p. 400.
97. Ibid., pp. 401–02.
98. *Hermenia Euthymiou Zygabenou eis tous 150 Psalmous tou Prophetanaktos David.* Euthymios Zygabenos was a famous monk and scholar of the eleventh to twelfth centuries who translated the Psalms into the language of his times. St. Nicodemos translated the text into the Greek of his period, added an excellent introduction, and supplemented the text with many footnotes and comments. Nicodemos' own personal contribution comprises almost half of this two-volume work published in Constantinople, 1819–1821.
99. Dionysiatis, *Agios Nicodemos*, p. 274.
100. *Paul's Fourteen Epistles Interpreted by Theophylaktos, Archbishop of Bulgaria* (Paulou hai Deka Tessares Epistolai Hermeneuthesai hypo Theogphylaktou Archiepiskopou Boulgarias), three vols. (Venice, 1819). This work was published posthumously.
101. Ibid. Reprint, Athens, 1971; Introduction, p. 16.
102. Ibid., p. 14.
103. Ibid.
104. Col 1:16; Eph 1:20, 3:10.
105. *Paul's Fourteen Epistles*, pp. 15–16.
106. Ibid., p. 19.
107. *Interpretation of the Seven Catholic Letters* (Hermeneia eis tas Hepta Epistolas) (Venice: 1806).
108. Ibid., p. 9.
109. Ibid., p. 13. The simile of the apostles and the clouds is taken from Isaiah 60:8.
110. Ibid., p. 18.
111. Ibid., pp. 18–19.
112. Ibid., p. 20.
113. *New Ladder* (Nea Klimax) (Constantinople, 1844; Volos, 1956).
114. Cavarnos, *St. Nicodemos the Hagiorite*, p. 53.
115. *Heortodromion*, two vols. (Venice, 1836; Athens, 1916).
116. *Garden of Graces* (Kepos Chariton) (Venice, 1819; Volos, 1958).
117. Cf. the edition of *Garden of Graces* in Greek (Volos: Hagioreitike Bibliotheke, 1958), p. 14.

INTRODUCTION

118. *Kepos Chariton,* Introduction by St. Nicodemos, p. 11.
119. Ibid., p. 12.
120. Ibid., p. 20.
121. Ibid., pp. 48ff.
122. This is sung in the ninth ode of the Orthros Service.
123. Op. cit., p. 28.
124. The Greek alphabet is comprised of twenty-four letters.
125. Dionysiatis, *Agios Nicodemos,* p. 180.
126. *The Extant Works of Saint Symeon the New Theologian* (Tou Hosiou Symeon tou Neou Theologou ta Heuriskomena) (Syros, 1790, 1886; Athens, 1959).
127. Dionysiatis, *Agios Nicodemos,* pp. 175ff.
128. Zagoraios was a respected monk who lived on Piperi, a small island south of Athos. Aside from his devotional and ascetic life, he was a well-known copyist and calligrapher.
129. Bilalis, *Prototypos Bios,* p. 10.
130. Iviritis, *Bios en Synopsei,* p. XI.
131. Cavarnos, *St. Nicodemos the Hagiorite,* pp. 25–28.
132. Cf. the most recent edition in Greek, *Akolouthia kai Engkomion tou Osiou kai Theophorou Patros emon Symeon tou Neou Theologou,* sung on October 12, from the hand of St. Nicodemos the Hagiorite.
    Deacon Symeon P. Koutsas (Athens: Monastery of the Holy Trinity on the Island of Hydra, 1975). Deacon Koutsas thinks that the writing of the "akolouthia" and the "encomium" coincide with the preparation for publication of St. Symeon's works in 1790, pp. 37–38.
133. Ibid., p. 84.
134. Ibid., pp. 90–91.
135. Ibid., pp. 94–95.
136. This is in accordance with Christ's saying: "My mother and my brothers—they are those who hear the word of God and do it" (Lk 8:21).
137. Koutsas, *Akolouthia,* pp. 103–07.
138. Ibid., pp. 108–11.
139. Ibid., pp. 112–13.
140. Dionysiatis, *Agios Nicodemos,* p. 210.
141. Published in the *Ekklesiastike Aletheia* (Ecclesiastical Truth), Constantinople 4, no. 7 (November 22, 1883): 93–100.
142. Dionysiatis, *Agios Nicodemos,* pp. 210–12.
143. *Ekklesiastike Aletheia,* pp. 95–96.

144. *The Manual of Confession* (Exomologetarion) (Venice: 1974, 1804, 1893). Reprinted at least eight times. I use the edition of "O Agios Nikodemos Publishing House," Athens (no date given). It has been reproduced on the basis of the Venice edition of 1868.
145. Dionysiatis, *Agios Nicodemos*, pp. 181–83.
146. St. John the Faster was Patriarch of Alexandria during the sixth century. He was famous for his strict spiritual life, the miracles of God worked through him, and his deep understanding of human nature.
147. *The Manual of Confession*, p. 11.
148. Ibid., pp. 12–13.
149. Ibid., p. 53.
150. Ibid., pp. 58ff.
151. Ibid., pp. 70ff.
152. Ibid., pp. 88–89.
153. Ibid., p. 90.
154. Ibid., pp. 94–95.
155. Ibid., pp. 13ff.
156. Ibid., pp. 36ff.
157. Ibid., pp. 206ff.
158. Ibid., p. 250.
159. Ibid., pp. 260ff.
160. Ibid., p. 267.
161. Ibid., pp. 281–82.
162. The full work was published for the first time in Leipzig in 1800. Other editions followed, e.g., Athens, 1841; Zante, 1864; Athens 1886, 1908, 1957, 1970.
163. For more information about Theodoretos, see Dionysiatis, *Agios Nicodemos*, pp. 264–68.
164. Bilalis, *Prototypos Bios*, p. 12.
165. D. Cummings, trans., *The Rudder* (Chicago: Orthodox Christian Educational Society, 1957).
166. Ibid., p. x.
167. Ibid., p. vi.
168. Ibid., p. xiv.
169. Ibid., p. lx.
170. Ibid.
171. Ibid., p. lxiii.
172. Ibid., pp. li, liii.
173. Ibid., pp. 122ff.

174. Ibid., pp. 196ff., 395.
175. Ibid., p. 120.
176. Ibid.
177. *Exomologetarion*, p. 113. Unfortunately, we do not have the minutes of the synod in order to verify the historical background of this canon. We may, however, trust the excellent memory of St. Nicodemos. He insists on this point because even in his time Orthodox priests violated this canon.
178. *Handbook of Spiritual Counsel* (Symvoulevtikon Encheiridion) (Vienna, 1801; Athens, 1885; Volos, 1958).
179. See the Greek edition (Volos: Agioreitike Bibliotheke, 1958) where the correspondence of the two cousins is published, pp. 17ff.
180. Ibid., pp. 26–30.
181. *A Handbook of Spiritual Counsel*, Chamberas, trans., ch. 1.
182. Ibid., ch. 2.
183. Ibid., ch. 3.
184. Ibid., ch. 6.
185. Ibid., ch. 1.
186. Ibid., ch. 1.
187. Ibid., ch. 1.
188. Ibid., ch. 1.
189. Ibid., ch. 9.
190. Ibid., ch. 10.
191. Ibid., ch. 10.
192. Ibid., ch. 10.
193. Ibid., ch. 11.
194. This book ends with a small note on the Virgin Mary in which he makes the point that Mary was a direct instrument and co-existing cause of the mystery of the Incarnation, and that she was before all other creatures and all other creations, predestined and created for him. Cf. *Symvoulevtikon Encheiridion* (n. 178), pp. 201ff.
195. Paulopoulos, *Ta Erga Tou Agiou Nicodemou*, p. 184ff.; see also Cavarnos, *St. Nicodemos the Hagiorite*, pp. 96ff.
196. V. Bilalis, *Osios Nikodemos* (Athens, 1969), p. 22.
197. "St. Nicodemos the Hagiorite and Contemporary Greek Enlightenment," in Greek, *Orthodoxos Typos* 24, no. 614 (July 6, 1984): 3; also, 24, no. 615 (July 13, 1984): 3.

198. Chamberas, *A Handbook of Spiritual Counsel*, "When the mind is in the heart it must be praying," ch. 10.
199. Cavarnos, *St. Nicodemos the Hagiorite*, p. 145.
200. Chamberas, *A Handbook*, ch. 10.
201. For a discussion of St. Nicodemos' spiritual life and his contribution to the liturgical life in the Church, see Nicolaos Gr. Zacharopoulos, *St. Nicodemos as a Teacher of the Spiritual Life*, in Greek with an English summary, in *Theologikon Symposion*, Charisterion to Professor Panagiotis K. Christou (Thessalonike, 1967), pp. 465–86.

CHAPTER ONE

The Attributes of
the Mind and the Body

Why the Senses Were Created and Why Man Is a Macrocosmos in a Microcosmos

You must remember, dear reader, that God first created the invisible world and then the visible, "in order to reveal a greater wisdom and the manifold purposes of nature," as St. Gregory the Theologian noted.[1] God also created last of all man with an invisible soul and a visible body. He, therefore, has created man to be a *cosmos*, a world unto himself, but not a *microcosmos* within the greater one, as the philosopher Democritos declared and as other philosophers have upheld. Such philosophers considered man to be a *microcosmos*, minimizing and restricting his value and perfection within this visible world. God, on the contrary, has placed man to be a sort of *macrocosmos*—a "greater world" within the small one. He is indeed a greater world by virtue of the multitude of powers that he possesses, especially the powers of reason, of spirit, and of will, which this great and visible world does not have. This is why St. Gregory the Theologian again stated that "God has placed this second *cosmos* (i.e., man) to be upon earth as a great world within the small one. Even when man is compared with the invisible world of the angels, again he is and is called a "great world," while the invisible world is by comparison small. Man includes in his world both the visible and the invisible, while the angelic world does not include the elements of the visible world. St. Gregory Palamas[2] has noted that this cosmos (i.e., man) adorns both of these worlds, the visible and the invisible. Nemesios has also concluded that man as *cosmos* draws the two ends of the upper and the lower world together and thus reveals that the Creator of both is one.

THE ATTRIBUTES OF THE MIND AND THE BODY

The Body Is Like a Royal Palace and the Mind as a King Who Dwells Therein

In order to have greater understanding of this matter, let me use the following example: The body is likened to a royal palace built by the superb architectural skill of an omniscient Creator. This palace includes the "upper room" which is the head, the innermost chamber which is the heart; the messengers which are the thoughts; the passageways which are the tubelike nerves; and the doors of this palace are the five senses. The soul (or rather the mind, for a soul that is purified becomes all mind, according to St. Kallistos), must be understood as a sort of king who is upheld by the three more general powers, that of the spirit, of the mind, and of the will. This "king" is found in all the parts of the body. St. John Damascene stated that the soul is found in the whole body as fire is found in the whole of a red-hot iron. He wrote that "the whole soul is joined to the whole body and not a part to a part; nor is the soul contained by the body, but rather it contains the body as fire contains iron."³ Now, in an extraordinary manner, this king has the brain as the organ of his mental activity; his power to reason and to will and in fact his very essence is found in the heart, as we shall see in the chapters ahead. This king also possesses a map, the compass of his imagination, to write down all that enters his mind from outside through the portals of the senses.

The Mind Before and After Holy Baptism

Have you envisioned these matters with your imagination? Notice now, as some have said, how this king, that is the mind, is simple, pure, integral, and rational light according to its nature, just as soon as it is poured into the body with its perfect organization. Before Holy Baptism, the mind, being covered by the darkness of original sin, does not see clearly. But after Holy Baptism the mind becomes all light, reflecting the supernatural light of divine grace. As St. John Chrysostom said, the mind shines brighter than the rays of the sun, as long as it remains above the darkness of willful sinfulness. For this is how that good and eloquent tongue has interpreted that apostolic word: "And we, who with unveiled faces all reflect the Lord's glory, are being transformed into his likeness with ever-increasing glory" (2 Cor 3:18). Interpreting this passage, St. Chrysostom wrote:

THE ATTRIBUTES OF THE MIND AND THE BODY

What is the reflection of the Lord's glory and the transforma-
tion into his likeness? This was more clearly indicated whenever he revealed the grace of the miracles. And yet this is no
more difficult to see now for one who has eyes of faith. For
no sooner are we baptized than the soul shines brighter than
the sun, being purified by the Holy Spirit. And not only do
we see the glory of God but we also receive from it a certain
splendor just as a clear piece of silver in the rays of the sun
reflects those very rays it receives. But what a pity! It is only
right to sigh here bitterly! For this glory which is ineffable
and awesome remains within us only one or two days.[4] For
we extinguish it, being led astray by the winter of worldly
cares, the dense clouds of which block out its rays. For the
cares pertaining to living are indeed a heavy winter and even
more sullen than winter.[5]

The Natural Attributes of the Mind and of the Body. The Body Is Ruled by the Mind

The natural and essential attribute of the mind, because it is mind, is to
be always preoccupied with the spiritual matters related to it: because
it is immaterial with the immaterial; because it is immortal with the
immortal. In one word, the mind is to be preoccupied with what is
truly good and to have only these good things for nourishment,
growth, and pleasure. By contrast, the natural attribute of the body,
because it is body, is to be inclined always to the bodily things: because
it is physical to the physical; because it is material to the material. And
in one word, the body is inclined to what is only pseudo-good and has
these things for nourishment, growth, life, and pleasure. This is why
St. Gregory of Nyssa said: "In human nature pleasure has a dual
character. In the soul it is activated by dispassion and in the body by
passion. The one which our free will chooses will dominate over the
other."[6] Even though the body, inasmuch as it is a body, is naturally
inclined to the pleasure derived from physical things, it is nevertheless
led, governed, and controlled by the mind (soul) when reason is whole
and complete. For according to St. John Damascene, the difference
between a rational and an irrational soul is this: The irrational soul is
led and ruled by the body and the senses, while the rational soul leads
and rules the body and the senses. It has been thus determined by God

69

for the rational to rule over the irrational, and the better to rule over the worse, and to subdue the latter's instinctive moves. This is why when the body has a desire, it does not directly rush into action to satisfy the desire, but is obstructed by the hegemonious mind. These are the words of St. John Damascene: "The irrational creatures are not autonomous; they do not lead but rather are led by nature. This is why they do not object to physical desire, but rush to action just as soon as they feel desirous. Man however being rational leads nature rather than being led by it. Thus when he would desire something, he has the authority either to overrule that desire or to follow it."[7]

The Initial Purpose of the Senses

Because this mind of ours is enclosed within the "palace" of the body, as if in a dark prison, God has chosen to create the five senses of the body to serve as so many openings to the world around us. I am talking about the eyes, the ears, the nostrils, the mouth, and the common sense of touch, through which the mind can generally receive unto itself primarily spiritual nurture and pleasure. And first of all the mind can come to sense and to understand this visible creation around us, as well as the Holy Scriptures. Second, through this sense perception the mind is guided through rational thought to acquire wisdom, goodness, power, grace, truth, sweetness, and all the other activities and perfections of the Creator that can be discerned in creation and in the Bible. Third, the mind can move with the wings of thought to go beyond these activities and perfections to the knowledge and vision of God himself, the Creator of the world, the giver of Sacred Scripture and the possessor of such perfections. And as for creation the wise Solomon said: "From the greatness and beauty of created things comes a corresponding perception of their Creator" (Wis 13:5). St. Paul also spoke about this: "Ever since the creation of the world his invisible nature, namely, his eternal power and deity, has been clearly perceived in the things that have been made" (Rom 1:20). St. Peter too had this to say about the Sacred Scriptures: "No prophecy ever came by the impulse of man, but men moved by the Holy Spirit spoke from God" (2 Pt 1:21). St. Paul too said: "We impart this in words not taught by human wisdom but taught by the Holy Spirit" (1 Cor 2:13).

Would you like now to test what I have said with two of the senses?

70

THE ATTRIBUTES OF THE MIND AND THE BODY

Through the Vision of Creation the Mind Rises to the Knowledge and the Love of the Creator

The eyes, for example, are lifted up to look at the sky. The image of the sky is impressed upon the so-called retina of the eyes. And as soon as this image appears there, the message is received in a flash by the express carriers of the spirits that transmit it with incredible speed through the channels of the nerves to the brain, which is the source of the entire nervous system. And as soon as the contact is made there, the mind is immediately aroused to see the sky. After this perception the mind, by exercising its rational thought, can wonder at the order, the size, the beauty, the light, and all the other attributes of the sky. And in all of these, the contemplative man can see the wisdom, the creativity, the power, and the beauty of him who created it. He can thus reason and say: If the sky which is created is so beautiful, so full of light, how much more beautiful and more luminous is the Creator of the sky? On this point St. Dionysios said: "For essentially the effects are present, standing clearly before their causes."[8] And so the mind climbs as high as it possibly can to the knowledge of the Creator, and with this knowledge the mind excites the heart and the will to love this Creator.

St. Basil encouraged us to think such thoughts and through them to rise from the visible to the invisible and from the ephemeral to the eternal. He wrote: "If these ephemeral things are so wonderful, how much more are the eternal? And if the visible are so good, how much more good are the invisible? If the magnitude of heaven goes beyond the ability of human reason to measure, which mind can discern the nature of divine things? If the physical sun that is subject to corruption is so beneficial, so great, so quick to move and establish the orderly seasons, and if one does not tire looking upon it, how much more beautiful is the Sun of Righteousness? And if it is a loss even for a blind man not to see the sun, how much greater is the loss for the sinner who is deprived of the true light?"[9] This is why the wise Theodore of Jerusalem also said: "To meditate upon the nature of created beings is a most purifying experience, one that delivers us from any violent feeling against them and any deception pertaining to them. It is also most effective in leading us back to the origin of all things, namely, from the good and marvelous and great to the best and most marvelous and greatest. Or, rather, the experience of meditating on the nature of created things offers us an insight into what is actually beyond beauty, beyond marvel and beyond size."[10] Even Solomon, criticizing the Greeks who were idolaters, wrote: "If they were pleased by the beauty of created things and took them to be gods, let them also know how much better than these is their ruler. For indeed the originator of beauty created them. If then they were impressed by the power and energy of created beings, let them also understand through these how much greater is He who has created them" (Wis 13:3–4).

The Mind Can Rise through the Holy Scriptures to Know and to Love Him Who Spoke the Scriptures

And now let us consider the ears. Certain words from Holy Scripture are spoken. The words strike the air and cause a wave motion. As the air waves are raised one after the other, they fall upon the ear and its cone. From there they enter the auditory canal of the ear and strike the eardrum. When the eardrum is struck the air in the chamber behind the ear drum is set in motion and this in turn disturbs all the parts of the so-called cochlea of the ear. The acoustic nerve which has its source in the brain is also struck, and thus the mind is aroused to hear the words spoken. After this initial hearing, the mind begins to distinguish the grace, the truth, the wisdom, and the other virtues of that spoken message. And so meditation follows. If the words, which are effects and energies, are so true and so wise and so graceful, how much more true and wise and graceful is God, who spoke and produced these words? As Aristotle said: "For every reason that makes a thing great, there is another reason that makes another thing greater." Through this manner then the mind climbs up to the knowledge of God, who both inspired and spoke the Holy Scriptures. Similar to this analogy of knowledge, the mind also fires the will to love God, for as Theodore of Jerusalem again wrote: "The degree of knowledge determines the degree of will."[11] The mind can work in a similar manner through the sense of smell, the sense of taste, and the sense of touch.

In a word then, the mind can through the senses use all created things and all of Holy Scriptures as certain steps to rise from the sensory to the rational, from the effects to the causes, and from the images and types to the depicted original prototypes. And so it is, for, according to Dionysios Areopagite, "The visible things are types and images of the invisible, the perceptible of the intelligible, and the divisible and variable of the indivisible and unified. Even the very creation of the visible world has revealed the invisible things of God."[12] Through such a method the mind rises from the created things to the Creator, and from the Sacred Scriptures to him who spoke them. In all of its activities and in all of its perceptions, the mind seems to be saying those words of the Prophet Isaiah: "Come, let us go up to the mountain of the Lord, to the house of the God of Jacob; that he may teach us his ways and that we may walk in his paths" (Is 2:3).

This then is the reason why and the purpose for which God created the portals of the senses: That the mind may be, as St. Gregory the Theologian said, "an overseer of the visible creation and an initiant of the mysteries of the invisible world."[13] The mind can, through the senses, see the Creator in the creation, as the sun is seen reflected in the water. Theodore of Jerusalem philosophized: "Sense perception is needed because through it we can understand the Creator by observing the created. We see Him in creation as we see the sun in the waters, since images of the first cause of all are to be found in created things, according to their capacity to reflect it."[14] In short then, this is the reason for the senses: so that the mind may proceed through them to its rational food, to its sumptuous fare, to its delight.

In this analogy let us be reminded of those animals who "carry-their-own-house," such as snails, turtles, and others like them who go out of themselves to seek their natural food. But here again Theodore of Jerusalem reminded us: "This then is the real struggle. To watch over ourselves vigilantly so that we may always delight in the spiritual things, stretching both our mind and our appetite toward them. We must never be distracted by sense perception to look upon something and to admire it only as a thing in itself."[15]

It is Wrong and Unnatural to Look upon Nature, to Read the Scriptures and Not to Rise to the Knowledge and Love of God

Now there are of course those who do not use the senses and the subsequent meditation on creation and Holy Scripture to rise through them to the knowledge and love of God, who both spoke the Scriptures and created the world. On the contrary, such people use this sense perception simply for human aggrandizement, for the marvel and mere pleasure of the corruptible beauty in creatures, and for other bodily purposes. Or, at least, they simply remain on the level of the limited purposes of the creatures and of the Scriptures. They thus neglect to proceed further, to rise to the catholic and comprehensive view of things, to God's wisdom through which all things are known and in which all the reasons for each creature are to be found, according to St. Maximos. "The Lord by wisdom founded the earth. . . . When he established the heavens, I was there" (Prv 3:19, 27). St. Basil the Great too had something to say on this point: "There are indeed certain reasons why the primordial wisdom of God was laid as a foundation to nature at the time of creation."[16] Now, those who do not rise—through the reason endowed in nature and in the Holy Scriptures—to the hypostatic Logos of God, those who do not love Him "through whom all things were made" (Jn 1:3), as most of the worldly philosophers do not, all of these people act contrary to the Creator's purpose in nature and in Holy Scripture. And according to the wise and most insightful Kallistos, the thought of such people has lost its natural tendency and has become unnatural. This has occurred because they use the means as ends in themselves, and the causes as results, and they love the gifts more than the Giver and the creatures more than the Creator, as St. Augustine has said.[17] Since creation was not created for itself, but for the vision and glory of its Creator, it is not proper that it should be seen and admired for its own sake, but rather for the sake of its Creator. It is the same with the mirror which one does not look at for its own sake, but for the sake of the one reflected in it.

We may add, finally, that the secondary goal and purpose for the creation of the senses is so that the material body may be able to enjoy through them material nourishment, growth, and life. Truly, I do not know what to marvel at most: the "palace" that is so intricately constructed or the "king" who dwells therein. But of these two, I must certainly marvel most at the master artist and Creator who with infinite wisdom not only created both of them, but also united the mind and the body in such perfect harmony.

Notes

1. Homily on the Nativity and on Pascha.
2. Homily 1, On the Presentation of the Theotokos.
3. Treatise on the Orthodox Faith, Book 1, ch. 1.
4. The saint made this remark because in his time most persons were still being baptized as adults, and many of them fell into deliberate sins shortly after their baptism.
5. Homily 7, On 2 Corinthians.

6. Homily 10, On the Song of Songs.
7. Treatise on the Orthodox Faith, Book 2, ch. 44.
8. Divine Names, ch. 2.
9. Homily 6 on the Hexaemeron.
10. Philokalia, p. 283.
11. Ibid.
12. Philokalia.
13. Epistle to Titus.
14. Homily on Pascha, p. 286.
15. Ibid.
16. Ibid.
17. Encheiridion, ch. 26.

CHAPTER TWO

Concerning the Mind

Why the Mind Is Enslaved to Physical Pleasures

There are two reasons why the mind was enslaved to physical pleasures. The first and main reason is the fact that after the disobedience
of Adam, his body received the whole of its existence and constitution
from physical pleasure that is impassionate and irrational. Henceforth,
man is sown with physical pleasure; he is conceived with physical
pleasure and he grows and matures in the womb until the time of birth
with physical pleasure. This is what the Prophet David was referring
to when he wrote: "Behold, I was brought forth in iniquity, and in sin
did my mother conceive me" (Ps 51:5). The second reason, which
follows the first, is the fact that even after birth man is nurtured with
physical pleasure. Throughout the early years of childhood (and to a
greater degree even during the nine months of pregnancy), the power
to reason is not developed and the mind is unable to utilize the senses of
the body in order to activate its own energy and be preoccupied with
its own rationality and spiritual delight. Consequently, only the body
utilizes these senses, and not merely for its necessary nourishment, but
also for its impassionate pleasure. And to make things worse, the body
even draws the mind itself, being still imperfect and indiscreet, to the
same physical pleasure, thereby enslaving the mind to physical pleasure. The saintly Theodore of Jerusalem spoke to this point in his most
philosophical treatise:

> Because the mind is prepossessed by sense perception, we
> have the duality of desire and anger. These are irrational
> tendencies and under the influence of nature and not of rea-
> son, becoming a habit in the soul that penetrates all the parts
> of our being and is difficult to uproot. Thus the order is

76

reversed. In other words, the physical senses are complete and strong while the mind is not yet active. In fact the mind is observed to be imperfect although it is actually powerful. Consequently, the mind can be charmed to consider these physical things as good, in the very same way that they are considered by the bodily senses. Thus the faculty of reason, which is intended to rule, is made subservient to the senses and we have the better being enslaved by the worse. This is why evil is older than virtue.[1]

St. Gregory of Nyssa seems to be in agreement with Theodore of Jerusalem: "The faculty of bodily sense comes into active being simultaneously with the first birth, while the mind must await until the appropriate age to start up. . . . Because of this the senses rule over the mind even when it is somewhat developed. . . . This is why it is so difficult for us to acquire the understanding of what is truly good, for we first receive the experience of the criteria of the physical senses and thus perceive good on the basis of what is easy and pleasing."[2]

How bitter, tiresome, and painful this early use of the senses becomes later for the unfortunate mind! During the childhood period of about fifteen years, when the mind is in a sort of stupor and led by the senses, the irrational and instinctive senses receive their fill of physical pleasure, as they are indulged without the restraints of reason. During this early stage the mind is unable to activate its own powers through the bodily organs that are not yet appropriately developed to receive it. Moreover, the senses have already become accustomed to the habit of physical pleasures by the time the faculty of reason has matured. If the passions deprived of reasonable controls direct the senses toward sin, who will then be able, tell me, to easily restrain them?

For example, once the eyes become accustomed to looking passionately upon the mature beauty of living bodies; once the eardrums are accustomed to the pleasing sounds of certain songs; once the sense of smell is delighted by the fragrances of myrrh and aromatic things; once the tongue and the mouth taste or rather become accustomed to the rich and tasty foods; and finally, once the sense of touch is accustomed to fine and soft clothing—who will be able after that, even if one is most eloquent and persuasive, to convince people that what they have up to now enjoyed is not a true and rational pleasure, but on the contrary an irrational and temporal one? Who will put a muzzle on the senses that silently contradict, disagree, and assert that the only pleasure that is to be recognized is the one they have experienced and not any other that is immaterial and spiritual? Will the mind do that? Unfortunately, while the mind knows that such pleasures are appropriate to irrational animals and not to itself, it cannot bring about this change. Remember that the mind too, together with the senses, enjoyed during those early years the same pleasures, and because of its simplicity and immaturity was attracted by these pleasures and considered them to be good. Thus the mind appears to be in a state of narcosis or rather bound by the five senses as by five steel cables. In this condition the mind suffers and is troubled because it sees that while it is really the ruler of the body, it has become its slave. And yet, whether it wants to or not, the mind tends to join the senses in enjoying physical pleasures. Who then will be able to convince these physical senses to change this situation? Can the constitution of our imagination and inner understanding do this? But even this faculty of ours is painted over and filled with passionate images and idols which have over the years been impressed upon it. Thus it rather serves to excite through the memory both the mind and the senses to enjoy the same pleasures. Who then can help? Can the heart help? Unfortunately, even the heart is filled with desires and drives that have been accumulated there over many years. This causes the heart to force the mind, the imagination, and the senses and the entire body to enjoy the same physical pleasures. Not only this, but the devil himself, who rules over the carnal pleasures, in turn excites the mind and the heart and the senses even more. The holy Fathers have said that the devil, though bodiless, finds his pleasure in enjoying the bodily pleasures of men. And, metaphorically speaking, these are but the dirt and dust that he was condemned to eat through the serpent: "And dust you shall eat all the days of your life" (Gn 3:14). St. Gregory the Sinaite wrote on this point: "Humanly speaking, because the devils lost their angelic joy and were deprived of divine pleasure, they have acquired a sort of materialistic nature through their physical passions and suffer to eat, as we do, the dust of the earth."[3]

How the Mind Is Freed from Physical Pleasure

After this period of childhood and the full development of reason, the mind may learn on its own or may learn by hearing Holy Scripture and the holy Fathers that its natural and appropriate pleasure is something altogether different. What happens then? The mind, being by nature rational and prudent and loving whatever is good, cannot suffer to see the senses of its body so enslaved to their pleasurable objects. The mind cannot continue to be a co-prisoner with the senses and a contradiction: the king becoming a slave; the ruler becoming the ruled; he who by nature is self-ruled and in authority becoming the obedient subject. The mind, finally, cannot bear to receive such harm that will gradually bring it to annihilation and to hell.

It is to this end then that the mind undertakes its entire struggle. At first it seeks to show that it was created by God to be the ruler and the king of the body. That is to say, it seeks through the assistance of divine grace and all of its courage, all of its will, and all of its knowledge to uproot out of the senses of its body those longstanding and entrenched habits which they have acquired among physical things. And it does this in order to free them from the bitter tyranny of the death-bearing pleasures they have experienced. Moreover, the mind seeks to subdue with ease the physical things to its own will. This struggle is truly a mighty one because the mind comes to the knowledge of truth at a late point in life. For if the soul had not been overcome by anyone, our task would have been simply to keep it pure. But because it has now forged itself into a strong link with passions and tendencies, we all know how very difficult this struggle is to break this bond, to liberate the soul from the worship of matter and to have it acquire the habit of virtue. And how is this done? How indeed are the senses liberated from physical passions and in turn placed under the obedience of the mind?

When a certain king plans to subdue easily an enemy city that is fortified by strong walls, he cuts off the food supplies to those people in the city and thus causes them such hardship that they in time decide to surrender themselves. The mind uses the same strategy in subduing the senses. Little by little the mind deprives every sensory faculty of its customary bodily and pleasurable passions. It no longer permits them to indulge themselves and thus easily and in a short period of time brings them under its control. All the time that this method is being utilized to control the passions, the mind does not stand idle. Not at all. By receiving a certain ease and freedom from bodily concerns, the mind turns to its own natural and spiritual nourishment which is the reading of Sacred Scripture, the acquirement of virtues, the doing of the commandments of the Lord, the practice of prayer, the understanding of the purposes of the physical and spiritual creations, and all the other spiritual and divine thoughts and deeds which are to be found in the writings of the holy Fathers, especially those who are called the *neptic* Fathers in the anthologies of *Philokalia* and *Evergetinos*, and St. John Climacus and St. Symeon the New Theologian and others.[4]

As the Senses Attracted Originally the Mind to Physical Pleasures, the Mind Now Attempts to Bring the Senses Back to the Spiritual Pleasures

In addition to its own efforts to nourish itself spiritually, the mind also attempts as much as possible to bring back the senses toward the mind so that they too may enjoy with it spiritual pleasures and thus become accustomed gradually to prefer them. This is how it happened before with the mind when it became accustomed through the senses to prefer physical pleasures. At first, generally speaking, the body attempted through the senses and the physical pleasures to make the mind and the spirit of man into flesh. On the contrary now, the mind seeks purposely through the enjoyment of the immaterial and spiritual realities to uplift the body also from its physical heaviness, and in a sense to make it into spirit, as St. Maximos has witnessed in many of his writings. Here is one example:

> When desire is added to the sense perception, it becomes a passion of pleasure procuring for itself a specific image. When the sense is moved by desire it again makes the perception it receives into a passion of pleasure. When the soul is attracted against its very nature toward matter through the body, it insinuates upon itself the earthly form. Knowing this, the saints seek to move toward God through the natural tendency of the soul, while at the same time they try appropriately to familiarize the body with God through the practice of the virtues, hoping thus to beautify the body with divine outward appearances.[5]

St. Gregory the Theologian too spoke about this important point, saying that this is the reason why the soul was joined to the body: to be for the body what God is for the soul, that is, to instruct and guide the body and to bring it home to God.

CONCERNING THE MIND

The soul was joined to the body perhaps for other reasons which only God who joined them knows and anyone who has through God understood these mysteries. As far as I am able to know together with those who are with me, there are two reasons why the soul was joined to the body. One reason is that by struggling against the lower things, the soul may inherit the heavenly glory. . . . The other reason is so that by drawing the lesser unto itself and to a degree releasing it from its material thickness, the soul may draw the body upward toward God. Thus, that which God is to the soul, the soul becomes to the body, instructing and guiding through itself its fellow servant, the material body, to become familiar with God.[6]

There is an interaction and mutual influence of the soul toward the body and vice versa the body toward the soul, according to the metaphysicians. The attributes of each communicate with each other because of the ineffable and natural bond which unites the soul and the body, even though the exact reason for this union remains essentially unknown to all philosophers and theologians.

The Fall of Adam. The Reason for the Lord's Coming. The Ascetics

This then is the nature of that most renowned fall of our forefather Adam. He rejected the spiritual nourishment and pleasure and lowered himself to the pleasures of the bodily senses, according to virtually the entire tradition of the holy Fathers. From this original fall of Adam, we too have inherited that primordial drive toward the material. This is why Theodore of Jerusalem wrote: "Adam, by using the senses wrongly, marvelled at the physical beauty and considered the fruit to be beautiful to the sight and good for eating. By tasting of this fruit, he gave up the enjoyment of spiritual things."[7] "When the woman saw that the fruit of the tree was good for food and pleasing to the eye, and also desirable for gaining wisdom, she took some and ate it. She also gave some to her husband, who was with her, and he ate it" (Gn 3:6). According to St. Maximos, that tree of the knowledge of good and evil is the passionate perception of the visible creation. "The tree of the knowledge of good and evil is the visible creation, for participation in it produces naturally both pleasure and suffering. . . .

The tree of the knowledge of good and evil is also the sense of the body, in which the activity of irrationality clearly abides, and which man has experienced. Although man received the divine commandment, he was in practice unable to keep it."[8] This is also confirmed by Niketas Stethatos and others. St. John Damascene especially wrote:

> The tree of the knowledge of good and evil can be understood as the visible and pleasurable food which appears to be sweet but which in reality brings the partaker to a union with evil. For God said, 'You must not eat from the tree of the knowledge of good and evil, for when you eat of it you will surely die.' Naturally, physical food requires continual replenishment for it is subject to corruption. He then who partakes of physical food finds it problematic to attain incorruptibility.[9]

For as soon as the senses know and experience the good, that is, sensible pleasure, they also necessarily experience evil, for the sister of pleasure is suffering. This is why in general all the sensible pleasures are customarily called painful pleasures.[10]

In connection with this subject St. John Chrysostom wrote: "What is easier than eating? And yet I hear many saying that even eating is a wearisome toil."[11] In agreement with the above St. Gregory of Nyssa also wrote: "In the fruit of the forbidden tree there are two opposite elements comingled. God said that those who partake of it will die, just as one does who suffers the evil effects of poison that has been mixed with honey. By the same token, as far as the pleasing of senses is concerned, it seems good, but as far as the destruction of the partaker is concerned, it is the ultimate evil."[12] For this same reason, we have read in the history of the Romans that they worshiped two deities—joy and sorrow—at one and the same time. Even though they had dedicated to each a separate temple, they used to offer sacrifice simultaneously to both. This way they indicated enigmatically how very close joy and sorrow are united, just as pleasure and suffering are. When one deity gives joy the other creates fear, and when one harms and grieves us, the other gives us hope.

From this point of view the reason for the coming of the New Adam, Jesus Christ, can be said to be our liberation from seeking and loving only the visible things, and at the same time our exaltation to love and enjoy the spiritual realities, thus indicating our true transference to what is indeed better. Those who wanted to achieve this very goal with ease, that is, the cutting off of worldly pleasures and the enjoyment of the spiritual ones, were the true philosophers and ascetics who abandoned the inhabited places where there are always so many causes for sinful attacks and went to live in deserts and caves. Not finding there the usual causes of worldly pleasures, they were more readily able to subdue the senses and in relatively short periods of time were able to rise up to the sweetest enjoyment of the spiritual and divine realities.

The Natural and Unnatural Pleasure of the Mind

I beseech you to do this, this very same thing. You have come to know precisely on your own, being prudent, and through Holy Scripture, being a lover of learning, that the natural pleasure of the mind is to always be preoccupied with and nourished by the beauty of spiritual realities. St. Maximos wrote: "Intelligible things are food for the mind." You have also come to know that the tendency of the mind toward the pleasures of sensible things is contrary to the nature of the mind; it is a tendency that is forced, passionate, corruptive, and entirely foreign to the mind. St. Isaac wrote that "when the mind is attracted by the physical things, it partakes of the nourishment of the beasts and becomes, so to speak, beastly." According to St. Kallistos, only the spiritual pleasure can be properly called pleasure and be primarily pleasure because during the course of enjoying it and after the enjoyment, it still brings us joy. On the contrary the sensible pleasure according to the flesh cannot be properly called nor in fact be a pleasure. Physical pleasure uses the name of pleasure falsely, for in the enjoyment of it and afterwards it brings sorrow to the heart. Again, St. Kallistos wrote:

> This is what should properly be called pleasure, namely that which by nature and reason cannot be condemned and which lasts and is ever more active, bringing joy and gladness to the heart even after it is fulfilled. Anyone therefore who would desire, let him seek the pure pleasure that is not mixed with sorrow, the intelligible and spiritual pleasure. For this is indeed the true and main pleasure of the heart. . . . Carnal pleasure that is not of the mind and the spirit is even wrongly called a pleasure, for it is induced and as soon as it is done it

creates a bitter regret. It is clearly a lie to call it a pleasure, for it is a spurious and counterfeit pleasure.[13]

St. John Chrysostom wrote: "The pleasures are harsh executioners of the body, in fact they are worse than that, for they strain and force the body with bonds not made by hand."[14] It seems to me too that pleasure is like a rough file smeared with oil, which when the cat licks it up, it also licks with it the blood of its own tongue. Or it is like a fly in the honey that tastes a certain sweetness but is at the same time entrapped in the honey and dies. Pleasure is also a bait that is superficially sweet, but when swallowed brings about a painful death. This is why the wise Solomon wrote: "The lips of an adulteress drip honey, and her speech is smoother than oil, but in the end she is bitter as gall" (Prv 5:3).

For a long period of time now your senses have become accustomed to charge after physical pleasure. They have been drawing with them your mind, not permitting it to be nourished by thoughts that are natural, proper, and related to it. You have not been able to enjoy the appropriate spiritual growth in life and pleasure. What must you do? I have reminded you by what I have so far written that it is necessary to seek as much as possible to govern with great prudence your five senses. To those which are essential, that is those which sustain the body, give them what they need. Those which are not essential but only create pleasure must be cut off. In this will you prove yourself to be lord of your passions: when you will be able through your entire courage to liberate your senses from the corruptive, painful, and false pleasures, and when at the same time you will liberate your hegemonious mind from their distracting attempts, leaving it thus free to return to the desirable beauty of intelligible things which are really and truly good.

According to St. Basil the Great, it is truly inappropriate for man to allow the senses to be filled with sensible things and at the same time to block the mind from its own proper activity among the intelligible things. He wrote: "I consider it inappropriate to allow the senses unhindered to be filled with their own matter, while the mind alone is shut out of its own proper activity. For as the sense is to physical things so is the mind to intelligible things."[15] Our senses then have in a way become hooked to the physical pleasures, not only during the early years of our youthful life, as we have indicated thus far, but also during the later years. Our own mind and that of the entire human race has also been hooked upon the bait of the same physical pleasures. Consequently, we have been shamefully deprived and have all lost that blessed and true pleasure of ours. By the same token, if these senses of ours are not freed from the physical pleasures, the mind itself will not be able to be freed from them and to return to its natural pleasure. It is impossible for this to happen in any other way. It is indeed impossible.

Notes

1. This treatise had been erroneously associated with the name of Theodore of Edessa, but it is really the work of Theodore of Jerusalem. The whole of this treatise is found only in a manuscript from which this quotation is taken.
2. Homily 8, On Ecclesiastes.
3. St. Gregory the Sinaite, ch. 123.
4. These spiritual activities are discussed fully in Chapter 11.
5. Centuries on Gnosis 7, ch. 72.
6. Apology.
7. Philokalia, p. 285.
8. Centuries on Theology 4, ch. 32.
9. On the Orthodox Faith, Book 2, ch. 28.
10. There is a play on the Greek words ἡδονή (pleasure) and ὀδύνη (pain, suffering), which are combined in the phrase ἐνώδυναι ἡδοναί (painful pleasures).
11. Homily 13, On Hebrews.
12. On the Creation of Man, ch. 20.
13. St. Kallistos's work is found in manuscript form, ch. 111, 112.
14. Homily on Thecla the Protomartyr.
15. Apologetic Letter to the Caesareans.

CHAPTER THREE

Guarding the Sense of Vision

Our Eyes and Our Vision

In order for the subject under discussion to continue in a rational and cohesive order, let me now comment for you what are the pleasurable objects of each one of the senses, and how you must guard your mind from them. And here is the first sense which we meet, that of sight.

Sight is the most regal of the senses, according to the naturalists; sight is dependent upon the psychic spirit and related to the mind, according to the theologians;[1] sight is the most knowledgeable of the other senses and therefore the most dependable, according to the metaphysicians. According to the popular proverb, "The eyes are more trustworthy than the ears." According to the word of the Lord, "The eye is the lamp of the body" (Mt 6:23). According to the astronomers, the eyes are the two stars of the face. According to the moral philosophers the eyes are the two first thieves of sin. A certain wise man has called the eyes two braids of the soul which it spreads out like the tentacles of an octopus to receive from afar whatever is desirable to it. Or, if I may say with St. Basil the Great, the eyes are the two "bodiless arms" with which the soul may reach out and touch from afar the visible things it loves. For whatever we cannot touch with our hands, these we can touch and enjoy with our eyes. The sense of sight, after all, is a touch more refined than the touch of the hands, but less refined than the touch of the imagination and of the mind. St. Basil wrote: "Vision can deceive the soul toward a certain pleasure through the touch of some object by means of the rays of the eyes that act as bodiless arms. With these the soul can touch from afar whatever it desires. And the things that the hands of the body do not have under their authority to touch, these can nevertheless be embraced by the rays of the eyes passionately."[2] This is why St. Gregory the Theologian also said: "The lamps of the eyes touch the untouchable."

It is from these eyes then that we must cut off the vision of those beautiful bodies which tempt the soul to shameful and inappropriate desires. You have heard the great Father St. Basil who said: "Do not play host with your eyes to the displays of wonder workers, or to the visions of bodies that place one at the center of passionate pleasure."[3] You have also heard the wise Solomon: "Let your eyes look directly forward, and your gaze be straight before you" (Prv 4:25). Listen also to Job who said: "I have made a covenant with my eyes; how then could I look upon a virgin?" (Jb 31:1).

I beseech you then to place all of your attention upon this sense of sight. First of all, this sense is like a thief, as we said, or rather as a chief among thieves. The eyes can distract the mind very quickly and cause it in a flash to slip into the place of sin. The eyes look upon something passionately; they fondly dwell upon the idol of beauty; in an instant it is impressed upon the mind; the soul is pleased by the sight of the idol; the mind transmits its appetite and desire to the heart, and the sin is committed without a witness, according to St. Basil.[4] This then is what the Lord meant when he said: "Anyone who looks at a woman lustfully has already committed adultery with her in his heart" (Mt 5:28). This is why Solomon reminded us: "Let not the desire of beauty overcome you, neither be enmeshed through your eyes" (Prv 6:25–LXX). St. Gregory the Theologian, going still further, would have us avoid even a careless glance. He added this thought to the saying in Proverbs: "Be not captivated by your eyes, and if at all possible, not even by a careless glance."[5] In seeking to interpret this, the commentator Niketas Stethatos wrote the following: " 'Do not be captivated by your eyes' implies not only a curious and lingering look, but, if possible, not even a cursory look that comes upon you by chance, thereby protecting yourselves even from a careless glance that may mislead your vision. Because this is so very difficult to avoid, he added the phrase 'if possible.' The sense of sight then is simply to see, but on either side of this seeing there is also the condition of curious sight and the condition of oversight—the former being excessive and the latter lacking."

GUARDING THE SENSE OF VISION

What Must One Do When Captivated by the Eyes?

If ever this thief comes and captivates you, fight against him and do not allow any idol of Aphrodite, that is, of any shameful desire, to be impressed upon your soul. How? By taking refuge in God through prayer, which is the most secure way. "Deliverance comes only from the Lord" (Ps 3:8). Another way is to turn your imagination to another spiritual thought so that one imagination wipes out another and one idol destroys another. According to the popular proverb, "One peg drives out the other." This is what St. Gregory the Theologian meant when he wrote: "A vision caught me, but was checked; I set up no image of sin. Was an image set up? Yet, the experience of sin was avoided."[6] Do you hear what he is saying? The image of sin stood before him but was not impressed upon his imagination. Thus he was directly freed from the experience, that is, from the assent or the act of sin. If then the devil does not cease to tempt you with that image that has been impressed upon your imagination, St. Chrysostom and St. Syngletiki advise you to use this method in order to be delivered from his wiles: With your mind gouge out the eyes of that image, tear its flesh and cut away its lips from the cheeks. Remove, moreover, the beautiful skin that appears externally and meditate on how what is hidden underneath is so disgusting that no man can bear to look upon it without hate and abhorrence. It is after all no more than a skinned skull and an odious bone filled with blood and fearful to behold. Here is what St. Chrysostom said: "Do not therefore pay attention to the external flower here, but proceed further through your mind. Unfold that fine skin with your imagination and consider what lies beneath it."[7] The most wise St. Syngletik said this:

> If ever by thought an inappropriate fantasy comes to us, it must be expelled by reason. Thus, shut your eyes to this image. Remove from it the flesh of the cheeks, cut away the lips and imagine then a mass of bones which is deformed. Think then what the desired image really is. This way our thought will be relieved of any vain deceits, for the desired image is nothing more than blood mixed with phlegm. . . . From this point on the mind notes nothing about the once desired image, but foul-smelling and decaying ulcers, and soon imagines it lying dead next to the inner eyes. Thus it is possible for one to escape from sensual thought.[8]

GUARDING THE SENSE OF VISION

Why Sight Impresses Its Images More Deeply Than the Other Senses

Guard your sight well then for it is more refined and knowledgeable.[9] Being more knowledgeable, sight is because of this more beloved by the mind. And because sight is more beloved, the mind makes a deeper impression with its image upon the compass of imagination. And because they are deeper they are also more difficult to wipe out. The theologians and all the ascetic Fathers commonly agree that the sense of sight sees the visible objects as they really are.[10]

We can see this confirmed through our own experience, namely, that the other images that we have come to receive through our other senses, we can wipe out much more easily. But those images which we have impressed upon our imagination through our eyes, and curious eyes at that, we either cannot wipe them out at all or we can only after much time and great effort. Whether we are awake or asleep, they do not omit to attack us. In most cases they do not cease to bother us. In short, we grow old with them and we die with them.

A Hierarch and All Who Practice Virginity Ought to Avoid Conversations with Women

Be careful about this, too, I beseech you ardently, most dear friend. Guard yourself well from idle and curious observations upon beautiful faces that you may not be overcome by the desire of beauty. Be informed also that you are in great danger, especially if you are a young person, a hierarch, or anyone among the clergy. For it is virtually impossible to avoid meeting such persons, who drop into the heart the arrows of desire even when seen from afar. If it is at all possible, seek never to meet such persons, and never come into conversation with them, even when the conversation may be about confession, for the holy Fathers discourage even this.

I remember that the Seventh Ecumenical Council declared through the Eighteenth Canon that if the hierarch is in a country town and women are there, it is proper for them to go away directly as long as the hierarch is present. The canons further declare the following about these matters:

> Any bishop, who acquires a bond servant or a free woman in his home or in a monastery to serve there, must be rebuked.

89

If the situation persists he must be deposed. . . . If it so
happens and there are women present in a certain place and
the bishop or the abbot decides to go for a walk in that place,
the women ought not to attempt to do any work while the
bishop or the abbot is there. They should stay off to the side
until the bishop departs so that everything may be blameless.

How Should One Behave in Talking with a Woman?

We may conclude that the above canon forbids the bishop to look upon
women altogether. If this too, is not possible, then when you speak, let
your eyes look downward, and let the presence of God be impressed
upon them, or, what is more secure, let them be closed altogether. At
the same time think of the Psalm: "I have set the Lord always before
me. Because he is at my right hand, I will not be shaken" (Ps 16:8).
And be not alone, but have with you one or two other persons so that
no room is given to your enemy attacking you.

Once, Isidore the elder left his skete to go to Alexandria to meet
the patriarch Theophilos. When he returned the other fathers gathered
around and asked him questions. "How is the world, Father? What are
men doing out there in the world?" He responded. "I saw no man's
natural face except the patriarch's." Then they again asked him. "Have
all men disappeared or are they destroyed, Father?" He again answered. "No, but I forced myself not to look upon the face of any
person." They all marveled at the strict discipline of Father Isidore.[11]

From this story you can learn how evil it is to allow the eyes to
wander. From such idle wandering of the eyes one receives nothing
but pleasures and destructive passions. This is why St. Symeon the
New Theologian instructed that one should not attach his eyes upon
women and young persons, but should avoid this even with venerable
white-haired men. Guard yourself from these then and ask the Lord as
did the wise Sirach: "Lord, Father and God of my life, let me not lift
up my eyes, and take away desire from me" (23, 4–5). Especially be
careful to avoid looking upon the persons that may have brought upon
your heart a certain passion or desire. By seeing them you are attacked
by the devil in two ways: from within by the passion and the previous
desire and from without by the present vision of those persons.

GUARDING THE SENSE OF VISION

Some Examples of Those Who Have Not Guarded Their Eyes

Again I must tell you to guard yourself well against these things, dear friend, for as St. Paul said, "It is no trouble for me to write the same things to you again, and it is a safeguard for you" (Phil 3:1). Guard your deceiving eyes that would steal the pleasures of others. Have great concern for these portals the eyes. Most robbers enter through these portals to overthrow the castle of the soul. Had the forefathers guarded their eyes, they would not have been exiled far from God and Paradise. "The woman saw that the fruit of the tree was good . . ." (Gn 3:6). Do you hear what the text says? She saw, she desired, she received, she ate, she died. Had the sons of God, that is of Seth, guarded their eyes, they would not have been destroyed by the flood. "The sons of God saw that the daughters of men were beautiful and they married any of them they chose" (Gn 6:2). Again, had the Sodomites guarded their eyes to avoid looking upon the two angels, they would not have been destroyed by fire (Gn 19:lf.). When Shechem, son of Hamon the Hivite, saw Dinah, the daughter of Jacob, and desired her, he and all his people were destroyed by her brothers (Gn 34:2f.). David saw Bathsheba bathing and he fell into the dual pit of adultery and murder (2 Sm 11:1f.). After this when he repented and learned to call upon God to turn his eyes away from vain beauty, he wrote: "Turn my eyes away from seeing vain things" (Ps 118:37 LXX).

From Looking, Lusting Is Born, and from No-looking, No-lusting Is Born

This proverbial saying is self-evident and generally accepted by all without contradiction. It says that intense looking upon someone or something incites the passion of lusting, while on the contrary, not to see is not to lust. This is what is meant by the saying of Sirach: "A wife's harlotry shows in her lustful eyes, and she is known by her eyelids" (Sir 26:9). By knowing this rule, many among the Greeks too were enabled by avoiding the indulgence of the eyes to acquire the virtue of chastity. According to St. Basil, Alexander the Great chose not to even look upon the daughters of Darius who were known for their great beauty.[12] Also, Cyrus and Cambysis chose to deface the appearance of two women who differed greatly in beauty from the others, namely Panthia the wife of Avradatus,[13] and the priestess of

Artemis. The attempt of Soreites is also rather witty and mentioned in the *Gerontikon* by a certain father. Here is the reasoning of Soreites plainly: "What has not been seen cannot be received by the understanding; what is not received by the understanding does not excite the imagination. What does not excite the imagination does not excite the passion either. When the passion is not excited there is serenity within. What is not seen, therefore, produces serenity within." Even wittier is what one of the wise men has said: "He who would impose the eyes upon a foreign beauty no longer possesses a 'daughter' in the pupil of his eye but rather a prostitute." In this he agrees with St. Isidore, who wrote: "Not only the body must be untouched, but also the glances of the eyes. For this is the reason why we call them κόρας—they must be virgins."[14] Nature itself has provided so that their eyes are protected by the eyelids as virgins within their chambers. Thus when they venture out of their proper quarters they may be modest as they look upon any persons they meet, as St. Isidore himself noted. St. John Climacus, too, said it well: "Let us flee and avoid seeing and hearing the fruits of those things which we have resolved not to taste any longer, for I wonder if we can consider ourselves stronger than the prophet David who prayed for this."[15]

Hierarchs and Priests Who Use Mirrors Fall into Certain Evil Temptations

Since we are talking about the eyes, let me add here something about an irrational passion and vain preoccupation which certain effeminate people have in decorating their homes with large and luxurious mirrors. They wish in this manner to bring gladness to their eyes, which raises up in their heart the always sought after passion. And they do this vain thing as if it were not enough for them to simply enjoy the pleasure which nature and God's providence has established to console the eyes through so many beautiful sights; they need to add for themselves this technical pleasure. I beseech you, dear friend, to avoid such vanity and condemnable pleasure. Have nothing to do with such mirrors. And if you happen to have them, please have them taken away as altogether improper for the Christian way of life. The use of such mirrors not only brings about many condemnable extremes, but also causes many individuals to fall into improper and ridiculous self-eroticisms that have become proverbial from ancient times. Thus historians can rightly condemn that emancipated slave who sought many pleasures and indulgences to please his eyes and who covered with many luxurious mirrors all the walls of his house in order to see in them himself and all his shameful deeds. Narcissus, who saw himself in the clear water of the spring, fell in love with himself, becoming both lover and beloved in himself. Deceived by his eyes, he thought his own face to be that of another. This is not so amazing, for Narcissus was beautiful and he was attracted to this beautiful idol. There is another more monstrous example in the deformed and disgusting old woman with rotten teeth named Ache, who often looked into the mirror to see her deformed and shriveled face, and who imagined herself to be not merely an idea but a goddess of beauty. She so loved herself that she became both an idol unto herself and a worshiper of herself. She became so enamored of her idol and so deranged of mind that she would embrace it jealously without having any such companion. Such are some of the ridiculous and irrational results of the extreme and thoughtless use of mirrors.[16]

But what will you say to all of this? If you do not permit me to look upon the faces of men and women, if you do not permit me to look into mirrors, what have I left to console and please my eyes with? Dear friend, you have many things worthy of observation to bring joy to your eyes. Look up there at the suspended, sapphirelike, and most pleasant face of the most expansive heavens that are a throne and a visible mirror of the invisible God. Look at the most bright and golden sun, the center of the planets, the king of stars, the sleepless eye and the unwaning taper of the world. Look also at the luminous and silvery moon with its monthly phases. Look at the harmonious dances of the night lights and sparkling stars. Look also down here below at the majestic mountains and the flower-decorated fields, the green and verdant valleys, the cool meadows and gardens, the many-colored herbs, the azure and peaceful surface of the sea reflecting the rays of the sun. All these are objects to see and mirrors which do not merely console and please the eyes, but which actually nourish them most sumptuously. All of the innumerable beauties of nature are most pleasing and marvelous to behold. If you need to add to these natural beauties some more technical ones, then look at the holy icons, at the harmony and symmetry of the sacred churches; look at the beauty of the sacred monuments. Hold all of these as a consolation to your eyes. But when you look upon these remember to rise up to a vision of the Creator who so wisely created them and beautified them.[17]

GUARDING THE SENSE OF VISION

Some Thoughts about Sleep. There Are Three Classes of People That Do Not Sleep at Night

Those shameful images from which we guard ourselves so that they are not imprinted upon our mind while our eyes are opened will often be impressed upon us by the enemy even when our eyes are closed, that is, when we are asleep. St. Gregory the Theologian has said: "A sleepy man becomes a finder of dreams, for sleep is the initiator of apparitions and not of realities."[18] It is therefore necessary to govern well even this need of your body and to sleep moderately. Know well that too much sleep exhausts the members of the body, softens the mind, weighs down the head, and gives license to the ancient "painter" (as one of the Fathers calls him), who copies all the evil things and imprints his improper paintings upon the imagination. Thus through these we are often polluted through nocturnal influences. Moreover, too much sleep also brings harm to the health of the body, according to the doctors. Plato used to say that they who sleep are no different from those who are not living. A certain Father has said that there are two teachings about death: One is the death before time was made for us, and the other is the death after sleep was made for us. Homer said of Agamemnon that he who has the responsibility for the people must not sleep through the whole night.[19] For as the proverb says, "The vigilant eye can look into and examine the thoughts."

St. Gregory the Sinaite has noted that beginners in the ascetic life keep a vigil from the evening to midnight and then sleep till morning.[20] Those who are in the middle of the way sleep from the evening to midnight and then they keep a vigil from midnight until morning. (This is more difficult as we know from experience.) Those who are perfect keep a full vigil throughout the evening and night. However, it seems to me that you, my dear friend, will find it beneficial to divide your night into three parts: The first part you should spend in studying the Sacred Scriptures and (especially if you are a priest or hierarch) the synodical canons, as I have said and will say again in the pages ahead. The second part should be spent with your daily affairs. And the third part of the night you should give as a sort of tax to our tax-collector and sharer of our life, that is, to sleep. I remember reading about such an ordering of time that was kept by Julian the Apostate. A light and healthy sleep follows naturally the moderate filling of the stomach. On the contrary, a troubled sleep follows after too much eating, as Sirach noted: "Healthy sleep depends on moderate eating; he rises early, and feels fit. The distress of sleeplessness and of nausea and colic are with the glutton" (Sir 31:20). So much for the guarding of the eyes.

Notes

1. St. Mark of Ephesus, ch. 48, said this about the sensible light: "The power to see is not foreign to the immaterial soul, for it is dependent upon the psychic soul as those who are experts on these matters tell us."
2. Homily on Virginity.
3. Address to the Young Men.
4. Homily on Be Attentive to Thyself.
5. Homily on The New Lord's Day.
6. From his tetrastich Iambic Poetry.
7. Homily 7 on 2 Corinthians.
8. Quoted by St. Athanasios in his biography of St. Syngletike.
9. It is truly paradoxical and because of the hyperbole virtually incredible how nature has endowed the eyes of certain men with such fine light. We read in the histories how Strabo the geographer, during the African War, could see from the cape of Sicily the harbor of Carthage and the ships coming out of it. Also King Tiberius could see in the dark as the nocturnal animals that see with the light that is reflected from their eyes.
10. St. Isaac the Syrian, Homily 17, has called the vision of physical things through the senses an hypostatic vision, especially the vision of the eyes, which again he has essentially called a vision in the thickness of substance. See Homily 84.
11. The story is related in the *Gerontikon*.
12. Address to the Young Men.
13. I cannot keep silent here about what happened to this most beautiful Panthia, as St. Isidore Pelousioties has related it. Cyrus, being prudent and knowing how vulnerable he was to beautiful women, did not even allow himself to look upon her. Thus he not only avoided the passion of lust, he also became more prudent and famous. By contrast, Araspus was a fool in boasting that he could look upon the beauty of a woman and not desire her. He looked upon her and was so overcome with lustful passion that he stopped at nothing to fulfill his desire, but did not succeed. Cyrus the king had to undergo many difficulties before he could free this man from such shameful and uncontrolled passion. So we have in these

two men what is written in Proverbs: "A wise man fears the Lord and shuns evil, but a fool is hotheaded and reckless" (Prv 14:16). From this story, St. Isidore was led to write this interesting dilemma: "Either look but do not lust, or lust but do not look. If the first case seems difficult for some and impossible for others, the second case should be practiced. Security is better than confused ambition" (Epistle to Andromachios, No. 1454).

14. There is here a play on the word κόρη, which means both daughter and the pupil of the eye. St. Isidore, Epistle to the Presbyter Paul, No. 1273.

15. Homily 15.

16. Plato used to say that one should look into a mirror only when he happens to be angry. By seeing the wrath in his face, the disorderly movements of his hands, and the unnatural motion of his body, he may be put to shame by himself and despise this irrational and maniac passion.

17. From among the ancient philosophers Anaxagoras had observed the beauty and orderly movement of the heavenly bodies and when asked for what reason he had been born, he answered that he had been born in order to look upon the sky. When deprived of his possessions and criticized for allowing others to take his goods, he said that he had a fatherland in heaven, pointing to the sky with his finger. Anaxagoras was indeed the first among the ancient philosophers who knew the real cause of the heavens and the rest of creation, namely, the divine mind. Aristotle (Metaphysics a, b,) knew about the Creator of heaven by observing the beauty of heaven, and would have loved to say the words of our David about the heavens: "The heavens declare the glory of God" (Ps 19:1). From among our contemporaries there was once a certain God-fearing man who was walking in the spring among the valleys and meadows. Seeing the different and multicolored flowers upon them as another heaven with stars, he began to strike at them with his staff and to say: "Do not shout so loud!" He of course was meditating upon the great voice each flower raised up to heaven to proclaim through its striking beauty how much more beautiful is their Creator (In Procopius, vol. 1).

18. In the distychs of his Iambic Poetry.

19. Οὐ χρή παννύχιον εὕδειν βουληφόρον ἄνδρα ᾧ λαοί τ'ἐπιτετράφαται καί τόσσα μέμηλεν.

20. St. Gregory the Sinaite, ch. 101.

CHAPTER FOUR

Guarding the Sense of Hearing

Three Evils Are Born from Hedonistic Melodies

The second sense is that of hearing and one must be careful to guard it from corrupt melodies, which are composed for pleasure and which pour out the sweet honey of sound unto the ears. It seems to me that there are three evils that come from such melodies. First, these hedonistic and worldly songs tend to weaken the manly and proud bearing of the soul so that it becomes effeminate and lethargic as it listens to these sweet sounds. Secondly, these sensual songs tend to fill up the mind with the many passionate images which they describe. Thirdly, let us suppose that even if the persons doing the singing are not seen—and especially when these may be women—, nevertheless the songs themselves are capable of impressing the imagination, moving the desire of the heart and drawing out an assent from the soul. This is why St. Basil taught us: "Do not submit your souls to corrupt melodies that come to us through the ears. Many passions that enslave us have been caused to grow in our natures by this sort of music."[1] St. Gregory the Theologian in one of his paschal homilies said: "Let us not have the flute played to our hearing." And in his Iambic Poetry he wrote: "Block your ears with wax, and foolish words hear not, nor pleasant songs or thrilling melodies."

It may appear to us like a myth (even though I now hear that seamen of today do this) when we hear that the cunning Odysseus of old shut the ears with wax to avoid hearing the sweet and hypnotic voices of the Sirens. It is true however that metaphorically speaking one who is prudent must block his hearing from receiving such effeminate melodies which eat away at the soul like the deadly Sirens of the passions. This is the reason why Xenocrates instructed the young to wear a sort of covering over their ears in order to protect their ears from hearing hedonistic and improper conversations.

At this point I recall an improper custom that is connected with worldly weddings. After the couple has been blessed and the people have sat at table, the bishop or priest being present, it is customary during the course of the meal for musicians to come and play musical instruments and sing songs. I regard this custom improper and unbecoming for Christian people. This is why from earlier times certain regional synods have decreed certain canons[2] against such practices, emphasizing at the same time that Christians ought to celebrate their weddings soberly and piously, avoiding everything that does not befit their way of life. In keeping with these canons, the clergy are to encourage the people to avoid extreme worldly manifestations at the wedding feasts. In fact they are required to depart from such feasts when the people refuse to heed their pious counsel.

After the hedonistic sounds of human voices and musical instruments, one must also guard his ears against similar sounds from birds, such as parrots, nightingales, finches, canaries, and other song birds. The same holds true with the barking of small dogs, which are often cared for at great expense in the homes not only of the laity but also of the clergy. I hope and pray that you will avoid the vanity of such things and if you now have such animals in your home, please see to it that they are taken away. It is truly improper and scandalous for Christians to see and hear in the home of the bishop or priest the sights and sounds of dogs and birds, where in fact they ought to see and hear only what is modest and reverent. People who keep such animals at home often become so attached to them that they love and care for them much more than they do for rational human beings like themselves. This extreme situation is confirmed by the Emperor Honorius, who was more concerned about the well-being of his parrot called "Rome" than for the actual city of Rome itself, as reported by the historians. Moreover, various ambassadors of foreign countries living in Rome kept dogs and cared for them as if they were their very children. This prompted Caesar to ask the humorous but ironic question: "In their countries do the wifes bear children or not?" Man in his irrationality reaches the point of keeping even poisonous and deadly serpents.

There is also the bizarre practice of becoming attached to certain trees and plants. Historians refer to a certain Roman emperor who became very fond of a certain myrrh-bearing Arabian tree, which he kept in a special room by the sea. He not only cared for it and nourished it, but he also hung garlands of flowers over it. A similar story is told of Xerxes the king of Persia who so loved a certain oak tree that he used to decorate it like a bride with fine garments, ornaments, and jewelry. He even placed royal crowns on its branches and watered it with precious perfumes and waters. One might say that the decorator of this tree was actually more insensible than the tree itself that he was decorating!

The Problem of Slander

You must definitely shut your ears to slanderous remarks against other persons, as is commanded by God: "You shall not utter a false report" (Ex 23:1). You must be especially careful to oppose the slanders leveled against the clergy. St. Paul when writing to Timothy said: "Never admit any charge against an elder except on the evidence of two or three witnesses" (1 Tm 5:19). Open therefore only one of your ears to hear the words of slander according to the example of Alexander the Macedonian. Do not by any means allow yourself to open both ears to the slanderers and to draw your conclusions and decisions on the basis of what they alone have to say, and thereby judging the case *in absentia* without the presence of the person slandered to defend himself. Oftentimes many unjust and irrational decisions have followed from such slanderous accusations. St. Basil noted that each slanderer is unjust to three different persons: to himself for lying, to the hearers who may be misled and deceived, and to the person slandered for destroying his good reputation and honor. "For this very reason then I beseech your love in Christ not to accept the slanders presented onesidedly as at all true. For, as it is written, the law does not judge anyone unless the judge listens and finds out what indeed the defendant has done. It is therefore necessary not to keep silent before such slanders, not that we will avenge ourselves through controversy, but rather because by not conceding (to the slander) we do not promote falsehood and do not allow those deceived to fall into harm. He who slanders does harm to three persons at the same time. First of all he is unjust to the person he has slandered; he also harms those persons who have to listen to his slander; finally the slanderer harms himself."[3]

You must read the life of St. John the Merciful, for there you will find many examples why you must not listen readily to slanderous remarks nor be ready to condemn those who are so slandered.

GUARDING THE SENSE OF HEARING

It goes without saying, of course, that while one must avoid the many abuses of hearing, one must also be more inclined to utilize this important sense of hearing for the many positive ways available to us in our Christian way of life: to listen to the word of God, to attend and participate in the worship services of the Church, to sing hymns of praise and thanksgiving to God, to listen with compassion and understanding to the concerns of your fellow human beings, and to do so many other positive things with our wonderful sense of hearing.

Notes

1. Address to the Young Men.
2. The Synod of Laodicia, Canons 53, 54.
3. Homily 3, On Envy and Malice.

CHAPTER FIVE

Guarding the Sense of Smell

What Are Some Negative Results of Fragrances

The third sense in line is that of smell, and this too must be guarded and kept pure. For example, one must not be carried away by the fragrances of myrrhs and perfumes, for they not only weaken the manly character of the soul and give it an effeminate air, they also may incite the soul toward fornications and other moral licentiousnesses. It is already well established that the external assaults upon the senses bring about a corresponding tendency and change in the body, and by the same token the changes in the body affect corresponding changes in the soul. Veros the eparch of Sicily, who in his character and behavior resembled a wild boar, confirms this fact. For as he was given up to the fragrances, he was also similarly given up to licentiousness. We read about this person in history books that he was no eparch, but rather a slave to hedonistic pleasures. In fact he was so enslaved to the fragrance of roses that he never wanted to be without them. To achieve this he devised a net filled with roses to be placed before him at all times so that he could readily and continuously smell that captivating fragrance. Something similar is done by those who keep horses when they suspend bags filled with barley before them. Much like these dumb animals then, this hopeless eparch walked the streets of Sicily like another wild boar of May. The truly very refined fragrance of roses harmonized very badly with the nostrils of such a vile and foul-smelling animal.

This foolish and senseless habit of Veros was outdone by Marcus Aurelius, who was so immersed in the habit of pleasing his senses that he would literally fill up a pool of rose water and would swim in it with joy and pleasure. Moreover, he also had the habit of using most precious and sweet-smelling myrrh in his lamps so that as they burned he would again be pleased by their fragrance. The hedonistic desire to please the sense of smell can reach such bizarre foolishness. Not far from this particular foolishness is also the habit of those who attempt to please all their senses through the use of fragrances in general. They like to add fragrant substances to everything—their foods, their drinks, their clothes, their mattresses, and so forth. They do not at all realize, the poor souls, that this living body of ours is a veritable container of smells, but after death it becomes food for worms and foul smelling. This is why St. Gregory the Theologian said: "Do not allow your sense of smell to be effeminated; do not honor the luxury of perfumes."[1]

What Experience Is Gained by Those Who Use the Fragrances

The Prophet Amos leveled a very severe criticism against those who were using such fragrances: "Woe to those . . . who drink wine in bowls, and anoint themselves with the finest oils, but are not grieved over the ruin of Joseph" (6:6). The Prophet Isaiah also pronounced a curse upon the prominent daughters of Zion who were haughty and who dressed themselves with fine clothing and anointed themselves with a variety of precious perfumes. "The Lord will smite . . . the heads of the daughters of Zion. . . . Instead of perfumes there will be rottenness . . . and instead of a rich robe, a girding of sack cloth; instead of beauty, shame" (3:17f.). Wanting to avoid this curse, the great St. Arsenios trained himself to endure humbly even the foul smells. He would never change the water in which he soaked the palms of date trees and the young shoots which he braided into baskets, so that after a long time the water became very foul smelling. When asked why he did this, he answered that with this rule he wanted to repay for all the myrrh and perfumes which he had enjoyed in the world and among the kingdoms. See also the Sixteenth Canon of the Seventh Ecumenical Council which decreed that bishops and clergy who use perfumes must correct this improper habit. However, if they persist in using perfumes, they must be given a penance.[2]

If you really want your body, my brother, to be fragrant and to exude a pleasant odor, do not remain idle. Do each day fifty or even one hundred prostrations and as many reverences as you can. Naturally the activity of the body creates heat, which evaporates certain unnecessary liquids of the body and digests others and thereby makes the body thin. It is these liquids of the body that produce the heavy and unpleasant odor of the body. So when the body is dried out and made thin, it becomes more vital, well managed, and consequently pleasant smelling. According to natural scientists, dryness is the most effective way to produce a pleasant odor. This is why, as we have read in history books, the body of King Alexander had a pleasant odor because of the natural dryness and warmth which it possessed. Similarly fragrant was the body of the wise Ioannis Tzetzos and of all his generation, as he himself wrote in his commentary to the poet Hesiod. This is again the reason why the bodies of virtually all the craftsmen and laborers and especially of the ascetic monks do not exude any heavy odor, but rather exude a pleasant and fragrant odor. St. Isaac also wrote about this and said: "The odor of an anachorite [an ascetic monk living all alone] is most sweet, and to encounter him brings joy to the heart of those who have discernment."

All Clergy without Exception Ought Not to Smoke

Here, dear reader, I want to remind you of a bad habit not only among lay people, but also among the clergy and even the bishops. I am referring to the use of that plant called nicotine, which was discovered in some region of North America known as Anthea and which was introduced to Catherine the Queen of France by the ambassador of Portugal as a sort of miracle of the new world. This is why it was given the exalted name of a "royal plant." Of course, this is nothing other than what is commonly known as tobacco. I hope, therefore, that you will never imitate those who wrongfully use this tobacco and that you will never privately or before other persons smoke tobacco or place some of it into your nostrils as snuff. First of all, the use of tobacco is contrary to the virtuous way of life. Secondly, it is inappropriate to the high character of the priesthood. Thirdly, it is contrary to good health habits. The habit of smoking is contrary to the virtuous way of life. The true boundary of virtuous living, according to the teaching of *Galation*,[3] is trespassed when we do something that may naturally harm the senses or the imagination of noble persons and call forth an abhorrence. Who then cannot see that the use of tobacco crosses over this boundary of virtuous habits and introduces barbarous habits, rustic habits, habits that are abhorrent to those who see and who hear and imagine what is done by those who use tobacco? Proper behavior

requires that a person turn away when cleaning his nose into his handkerchief. The smoke which is inhaled through the nostrils causes the
nose to excrete that abhorrent mucus that is then collected in the
handkerchief in the presence of others. Proper manners further direct
that when a person has to sneeze before others, he must try to block it,
if at all possible, or at least to cover it with his handkerchief so that the
nose does not bellow like a horn trumpet and cause alarm and abhorrence. Now, those who would place and stuff into their nose this
tobacco powder only vex the organ of smell and bring upon themselves
the need to sneeze. A good sneeze usually creates such a violent and
terrible shaking of the head that it invokes from people standing by a
call for divine intercession with such expressions as these: "Health to
you," "Be saved," "May God help you" ("God bless you"). The most
terrible thing, however, is for a person to put into his mouth a pipe
made from an animal horn or from some type of wood and from that
pipe to inhale the smoke of burning tobacco through his larynx and
then to exhale that abhorrent smoke through the mouth and the nostrils like some smoking chimney or like the horses of Diomedes, or the
bulls of Jason that exhaled fiery smoke through their mouth and nostrils. Can one find a more abhorrent and abominable habit than this?

Smoking is also an inappropriate habit and unbecoming to the
spiritual character of the priesthood. The hierarch is a type of God, an
icon of Christ Jesus. Therefore all of his habits must be Christlike,
solemn, habits that bring not scandals, but benefits to the people.
What solemnity is there in the use of that horrible tobacco plant? Or of
what benefit is it? On the contrary, what a scandal it is to the pious
Christians, when they see their hierarch or priest holding between his
teeth that strange-looking object—the pipe—in which the tobacco is
burning! Indeed, how scandalous it is to see a clergyman exhaling from
his nose and mouth that foul-smelling smoke, and to have his house
filled with that dark cloud of unpleasant smoke! The hierarch and all
the clergy are obliged by their very nature to exude a spiritual fragrance from all of their senses so that they may transmit this fragrance
upon all those who approach them—Christians as well as unbelievers,
as St. Paul wrote: "For we are the aroma of Christ to God among those
who are being saved and among those who are perishing" (2 Cor 2:15).
When the clergy draw into their body both through their mouth and
their nose that most foul smelling smoke, that many cannot bear and
faint, how can they then be, according to the very nature of their
calling, an aroma and a fragrance of Christian life for those who are

around them? This is the reason why in that most pious Kingdom of Russia there is an untransgressed law that forbids all the orders of clergy and monks from using publicly tobacco through the nose or the mouth. Anyone so doing is considered by all to be a transgressor worthy of aversion.

Finally, the excessive use of tobacco is also harmful to the health of the body. Many who were chronic users of tobacco were found after death to have their lungs blackened and burned, as well as their brain. Inasmuch as the brain receives continuously the inhaled smoke, it consequently uses up not only the excess fluid but also the natural and essential one. Thus, it is difficult to find even one among those who use tobacco regularly who does not admit that its use is more of an evil than a necessity, and who does not condemn himself for using it. Even the moral philosophers, without exception, condemn the regular use of tobacco in public as something abhorrent and boorish.[4]

Notes

1. Homily on Pascha.
2. We read in certain history books that in India near the sources of the River Ganges there lived certain people who possessed such a refined nature and who were so temperate that they could be nourished by the fragrance of flowers which they received as food. This is not incredible. The body is in fact nourished and is influenced by every pleasant object of each and every sense. Consequently the body is also nourished by the pleasurable objects of the sense of smell, which are the perfumes and the fragrances of flowers. What is amazing is that many ill persons, especially women, faint and swoon from certain fragrances, especially if they are very strong and heavy. When the soul and the heart are given up to the inhalation of that fragrant air and the lungs are filled with it, the person experiences a sort of inebriation that chokes him, being unable to breathe any other clear air. We who are Christians, however, and especially the clergy and monks who, in obedience to Christ, have agreed not to comfort our bodies but rather to put them under stress, we must put away even these fragrances since they act as a benevolent and nourishing influence upon our bodies. This is why the wise Nikephoros Vlemides in his Homily on Virtue has instructed us in this way: "Do not go near the fragrances of roses, royal myrrhs, etc. for such things are unneces-

sary and only serve to excite irrational desires; they are inappropriate for those who have denied them and worthy of condemnation."

3. *Galation* was the name given to that small book which was written by Ioannis Delagazis, the Florentine philosopher. It received this name because it provided the true "milk" that everyone needs to partake, if one wants to enter into the way of life of the nobility. It served as a mirror of all the virtuous habits and manners and as a great condemnation of all the evil ones. All of Italy accepted this book with great acclaim and, like the Canon of Polycheitus, all the nobles and teachers and tutors of royal children learned from it all the virtuous habits and manners. It seems to me that from this book the so-called *Chrestoetheia* was translated into Latin and then from this Latin it was later translated back into Greek.

4. Even if someone were to suggest that the general use of tobacco as a common habit among so many people has made it into a virtue, we will rebut and say that this is not at all true. In fact, this common habit has made many other acknowledged evils to be considered as virtues, such as, for example, the habit of coarse jesting and ribaldry. And yet right reason and the law of Christ condemn these, nevertheless, as evils, even though they may be generally favored because of irrational and evil habits.

CHAPTER SIX

Guarding the Sense of
Taste and the Tongue

The Effects of Various Foods

The fourth sense is that of taste and generally speaking that of the mouth. Here, indeed, we find a great marketplace! This sense is like that great chasm that was suddenly opened in Rome and was so deep that no matter how much earth and debris was thrown into it, it simply disappeared and was never filled up, as the historians have written. Also this sense of the mouth is like a gulf so wide that it can contain all the edible provisions which the earth and sea produce. According to St. Gregory of Nyssa, the mouth is like a large broken earthen jar that is always filled and yet always remains empty. In a word, it is an insatiable Hades. Even though the sense of taste is fourth in line, I consider it to be first in terms of power. Be careful therefore to shut out of this door of your senses the negative effects of so many varieties of foods. Avoid then the sumptuous meals. Avoid the bewitching artistry of the chefs. Avoid wantonness and wastefulness in food. For what else were these delicacies invented? Certainly, you cannot say that they serve some need or function of the body, but only that cursed pleasure of taste in the mouth. What indeed are the effects of such a variety of foods? Nothing good, of course, comes of them, except passions and evils to the soul and to the body. Greedy licking, satiety, and gluttony are the first offsprings. If we go deeper we find drunkenness, rapacity, obesity, gout in the feet and in the hands, and even paralysis. If we go even deeper than this we can also find fornication, homosexuality, and virtually all of the carnal and irrational passions that come under the influence of the stomach. These then are the evil by-products of irrational indulgence in the delicate and tasty things of the mouth.

This is why St. Gregory of Nyssa has spoken about the sense of taste in the following manner: "One may say that it is the preoccupation with the pleasures of eating that brings forth each of the many evils. For who has not taken notice that the root of virtually all of life's faults lies in one's inordinate preoccupation with food. From such preoccupations comes sumptuousness, drunkenness, gluttony, riotous living, overabundance, satiety, revelry and the irrational and beastly tendency toward dishonorable passions."[1] This is also seen with the Sodomites who had fallen into those abominable passions, because they spent their time eating sumptuously, as the Prophet Ezekiel wrote: "Behold, this was the guilt of your sister Sodom: She and her daughters had pride, surfeit of food, and prosperous ease, but did not aid the poor and needy" (Ez 16:49). In Exodus, too, it is written that it was after the Israelites had eaten and drunk that they rose up to play: "The people sat down to eat and drink, and rose up to play" (Ex 32:6). What this play means is made clear by the Fathers and by St. Paul, who identified revelry and drunkenness, that is, sumptuous eating and drinking, with licentiousness and fornications. "Let us conduct ourselves becomingly as in the day, not in reveling and drunkenness, not in debauchery and licentiousness, not in quarreling and jealousy" (Rom 13:13). It is appropriate to recall here the saying of one of the saintly elders who said that if Nebuzaradan, the captain of the bodyguard and the chief chef of Nebuchadnezzar, had not gone to Jerusalem, perhaps the Temple of the Lord would not have been burned. "If the pleasure of gluttony had not entered into the soul, the mind would not have fallen to attack by the enemy."[2]

Sumptuous Eating Deprives One of Piety and Harms Especially Young People

Why do I talk about these physical evils only? Sumptuous eating deprives us of piety as well. It is written about the Israelites and in particular: "Jeshurun waxed fat, and kicked; [you waxed fat, you grew thick, you became sleek;] then he forsook God who made him, and scoffed at the rock of his salvation" (Dt 32:15). Now what about those persons whom St. Paul considered to be enemies of the cross of Christ, who were they? "Their end is destruction, their god is the belly, and they glory in their shame, with minds set on earthly things" (Phil 3:19). The same is true in our own time among people who, for the sake of satisfying their desire for food, have become catholics, and of course all the naturalists and the atheists.[3] Sumptuous eating is harmful to all without exception, but especially to the young. The natural reason for this is obvious. The natural warmth of the young person is enhanced when it receives the fatty matter of various foods. The heavy foods consumed draw out the heavy excretions of digestion in the stomach. These in turn are converted into substances and blood and eventually into fatty tissue. The abundance of food creates a fat body that is susceptible to the forceful temptations of one's sexuality. Thus treated and exposed the poor body becomes a flaming fire, a Babylonian furnace. If the young body is a wild and untamed animal even when it lacks essential nourishment, imagine what it is like when it is well fed! All young people know this because they experience these passions on a daily basis. This is why St. Gregory the Theologian said: "Its own evil is sufficient for the body. Why add to the existing fire any additional fuel, or any more nourishment to the beast? It will only become more difficult to control and more violent (forceful) than the mind."[4] Solomon too said: "It is not fitting for a fool to live in luxury" (Prv 19:10). In interpreting this passage, St. Basil considered the body of a young person to be "a fool." "What is more senseless than the body of a young person prone to easy temptations?" he asked.

Now if you cannot avoid these fatty foods completely, then set a discipline for yourself to eat only once a day, as many spiritual persons, hierarchs, and even worldly leaders do. In this manner the body is kept lighter and healthier and the mind is clearer and more capable of advancing upon divine thoughts. Even then, it is important not to overeat.

The Three Degrees of Eating

According to St. Gregory the Sinaite there are three degrees in eating: temperance, sufficiency, and satiety. Temperance is when someone wants to eat some more food but abstains, rising from the table still somewhat hungry. Sufficiency is when someone eats what is needed and sufficient for normal nourishment. Satiety is when someone eats more than enough and is more than satisfied. Now if you cannot keep the first two degrees and you proceed to the third, then, at least, do not become a glutton, remembering the words of the Lord: "Woe to you that are full now, for you shall hunger" (Lk 6:25). Remember also that rich man who ate in this present life sumptuously every day, but who was deprived of the desired bosom of Abraham in the next life, simply because of this sumptuous eating. Remember how he longed to refresh his tongue with a drop of water. St. Basil not only did not forgive the young people who ate to satiety but also those who ate until satisfied; he preferred that all eat temperately. He said, "Nothing subdues and controls the body as does the practice of temperance. It is this temperance that serves as a control to those youthful passions and desires."[5] St. Gregory the Theologian has also noted in his poetry: "No satiety has brought forth prudent behavior; for it is in the nature of fire to consume matter. And a filled stomach expels refined thoughts; it is the tendency of opposites to oppose each other." Job, too, assuming that one could fall into sin through eating, offered sacrifice to God for his sons who were feasting among themselves. "And when the days of the feast had run their course, Job would send and sanctify them, and he would rise early in the morning and offer burnt offerings according to the number of them all; for Job said: 'It may be that my sons have sinned, and cursed God in their hearts' " (Jb 1:5–8). In interpreting this passage Olympiodoros wrote: "We learn from this that we ought to avoid such feasts which can bring on sinfulness. We must also purify ourselves after they have been concluded, even if these are conducted for the sake of concord and brotherly love as in the case of the sons of Job." Surely then, if the sons of Job were not at a feast but in prayer or some other spiritual activity, the devil would not have dared to destroy the house and them, as Origen interpreted the passage: "The devil was looking for an opportunity to destroy them. Had he found them reading, he would not have touched the house, having no reason to put them to death. Had he found them in prayer, he would not have had any power to do anything against them. But when he found an opportune time, he was powerful. What was the opportune time? It was the time of feasting and drinking." Do you see then, dear reader, how many evils are brought forth by luxurious foods and feasting in general?

Hierarchs, Priests, and Every Christian Ought Not to Break the Fast of Each Wednesday and Friday

Let me add here that after abstaining from rich foods and sumptuous feasts, you must also keep the prescribed fast of each Wednesday and Friday throughout the year, except of course for those times when no fast is required by the practice of the church calendar. Even if others may break this fast by including wine and oil in their diet on Wednesday and Friday, you ought not to imitate them, whoever they might be, for the holy canons require this rule to be kept. The Sixty-ninth Apostolic Canon considers the fasting rules of each Wednesday and Friday to be the very same as that of Great Lent. "Any bishop, priest, deacon, subdeacon, reader, or chanter who does not fast during Great Lent and each Wednesday and Friday is to be deposed, except if he is prevented from doing so because of a bodily illness. If the person is a layman who does not fast, he is to be rejected." The same kind of austerity is expressed by the Fifth Canon of Peter of Alexandria: "I agree with St. James who called the well fed sheep for slaughter: 'You have lived on the earth in luxury and in pleasure; you have fattened your hearts in a day of slaughter' " (Jas 5:5).[6] St. Gregory the Theologian had no kind compliments for feasting when he considered it to be nothing but manure. St. Isaac the Syrian too considered the wasting of food as only appropriate to swine. This is why a wise man, seeing that inscription on the tomb of Sardanapal the glutton which read: "I have as much as I have eaten and have drunk and have enjoyed," concluded: "This inscription is indeed appropriate for a pig!"[7]

God Will Put Gluttons to the Test

I praise the most high God many times who has never neglected to put the gluttons who are always feasting to the test. Sometimes he permits the sons of Job to be crushed to death in the house of their cohorts; sometimes he destroys through Sampson the palace where the gentiles were eating and reveling. God disrupted the feast of Balthasar by that fearful hand which was writing on the wall, and he brought great sorrow to the hearts of the revelers who were feasting with the tetrarch Herod on account of the beheading of the Forerunner. Do you see, dear brother, how hateful a thing this gluttonous feasting and drinking is in the sight of God? This is why the Prophet Amos condemned such unrighteous feasting. "Woe to those who lie upon beds of ivory, and stretch themselves upon their couches, and eat lambs from the flock, and calves from the midst of the stall; who sing idle songs to the sound of the harp . . . who drink wine in bowls, and anoint themselves with the finest oils, but are not grieved over the ruin of Joseph!" (Am 6:4–6). Whatever I have said so far about sumptuous foods, I also say about

111

aromatic wines. St. Gregory the Theologian has noted, "Let us not honor the wines that have the scent of flowers."[8] It should also be noted that the quantity of wine be limited to two or three glasses, especially for the young. The elder Sisoes was once asked if it is too much for someone to drink three glasses of wine. He answered that if there were no Satan, then it would not be too much. The Spartan Leotychides, too, was asked why the Spartans did not drink wine. He answered that the Spartans refrained from drinking wine so that others would not receive instruction from their consequent bad behavior. And he was right because wine clouds the mind and does not permit it to know the truth and the correct and benevolent advice. Now, when much wine is consumed, then the mind is totally clouded, like the extra oil that snuffs out the lamp. Thus another sober person is required to offer advice and guidance to him who is drunk.

What One Must Do to Avoid Overeating and Other Sins of the Tongue

When eating and drinking, always remember the Psalm: "What profit is there in my blood, if I go down to the Pit?" (Ps 30:9). St. Basil has advised that we recall this verse in order to help us avoid overeating and overdrinking, as he has interpreted it in the following manner:

> What is the need for robustness of flesh and an abundance of blood if their future is to be delivered over to the common corruption of the body? For this reason I constrain and deprive my body, otherwise my blood becomes so robust and overzealous that it makes my flesh to sin. Do not therefore flatter your body with sleep and baths and soft beds, but always recall the saying: "What profit is there for my blood if I go down to the Pit?" Why do you care for the lesser thing that will later become corrupt? Why do you bother to make yourself fat? Do you not know that the fatter you make your body so much heavier will be the soul's prison?

In this sense of the mouth are also included all those sins which are enacted by the tongue: condemnation, slander,[9] mocking, insults, unreasonable excommunications, curses, reprimands, obscene talk, and all the other idle and vain words. From all of these we must guard ourselves as much as possible, for as you know, we must give an account for every vain and idle word, according to the Sacred Scriptures (Mt 12:36). "Let your speech always be gracious, seasoned with salt" (Col 4:6), as St. Paul has directed, so that those who hear the grace of your words and appreciate the sound of your voice will say what the Bride (Church) was saying to her Groom: "His cheeks are like beds of spices, yielding fragrance. His lips are lilies, distilling liquid myrrh" (Sg 5:13). For you know that the sweet tongue exceeds the sweetness of flutes and harps: "The flute and the harp make pleasant melody, but a pleasant voice is better than both" (Sir 40:21). This is why that wise Socrates himself advised the young people to possess three things: simplicity of heart, silence of mouth, and modesty in their appearance. To the elders he advised that they possess three different qualities of character: seriousness in their appearance, pleasantness in their speech and prudence in their heart.

Hierarchs and Priests are not to Curse but rather to Bless

Above all seek, for the love of Christ, not to curse or depose anyone at random without careful thought and consideration. This kind of behavior is typical of barbarians and uneducated people. Moreover it is forbidden by the sacred canons and altogether inappropriate to the character of the hierarch. It is after all appropriate for the hierarch to bless his flock and not to curse it. For if God did not want that ancient people Israel to receive a curse but rather a blessing, as it is written: "Balaam saw that it pleased the Lord to bless Israel" (Nm 24:1), how much more now does He not want curses but blessings to come upon the New Israel, the chosen people of God that have been redeemed by the blood of Christ? St. Peter wrote to the believers: "Do not return evil for evil or reviling for reviling, but on the contrary bless, for to this you have been called, that you may obtain a blessing" (1 Pt 3:9). [10] If St. Paul himself beseeched all Christians to "bless and do not curse" (Rm 12:1), how much more does he direct his counsel to the holy hierarchs and priests who are the source of blessings?

There are many examples exhorting us to bless. Many are the sayings which show the evil of condemnation, of insults, of slander and one could write a whole book by just listing them all. The Apostle James, having said many things against the abuses of the tongue, also added: "Thus the tongue becomes among our members the cause

113

which stains the whole body, sets on fire the whole cycle of life and is itself burned up by hell" (Jas 3:6; trans. by author). This is why the saintly Pamvo remarked that in forty-nine years he was unable to put into practice the saying: "I will guard my ways, that I may not sin with my tongue" (Ps 39:1). Having achieved this, though, he used to say in his final days: "As often as I have spoken, so many times have I not repented." The elder Sisoes for thirty years only prayed this one prayer: "Lord Jesus Christ protect me from the corpses of my tongue." Also the elder Agathon kept a stone in his mouth for three years in order to learn to keep silence. Thus the wise Sirach said: "Many have fallen by the edge of the sword, but not so many as have fallen because of the tongue" (Sir 28:18). "Blessed is he who has not made a slip with his tongue" (Sir 25:8). St. Basil too said that "the most common and multifaceted sin is the one enacted by the tongue." He also said in conclusion that "it is loose talk which brings about the myriad evils of the tongue, as security of the tongue provides for so many virtues."[11]

Some Thoughts on Laughter

Laughter, too, falls into this sense of taste and not to another, and must be avoided, especially violent laughter that is so uncontrolled and loud that it often produces tears. Such excited laughter causes the gums and the teeth to show in those who laugh loudly just as they do with horses when they neigh. St. Basil has strict rules against loud laughter. "To be overcome by uncontrolled and meaningless laughter is a sign of intemperance and the lack of modesty in our behavior; it is also a sign that the foolishness of the soul is not controlled by precise reason."[12] St. Basil also said: "Loud laughter and violent reactions of the body are not proper to one who is contrite of heart, mature, and self-controlled." This is why this form of laughter is discouraged in the Bible as something especially harmful to the stability of the soul: "I said of laughter, 'It is mad' " (Eccl 2:2).

Solomon was right in pointing out that the laughter of the foolish is similar to the sound of thorn bushes being burned. "For as the crackling of thorns under a pot, so is the laughter of the fools" (Eccl 7:6). St. Gregory the Theologian in his Iambic Poetry wrote: "All laughter deserves the laughter (contempt) of wise people, especially the sinful laughter; but disorderly laughter brings about tears." St. Basil has set a boundary to acceptable laughter: "The mirth of the soul may be revealed to the point of a happy smile which is not improper, as long as it only reveals what is written in Scripture: 'A glad heart makes a cheerful countenance' " (Prv 15:13). Also the wise Sirach wrote: "A foolish man raises his voice in laughter, but a prudent man will smile in silence" (Sir 19:30; 20:5–6).

Moreover, when we take into account that our responsible and sinful life is carried on in a valley of sorrows, then even our laughter must be turned to mourning and our smile and joy to grief, as St. James the Brother of the Lord has said: "Let your laughter be turned to mourning and your joy to dejection" (Jas 4:9).[13] St. Isidore the Pelousiotes wrote to the presbyter Dorotheos:

> If the priest is called and is the model for the flock and the light for the church, then it is imperative that this be impressed upon his way of life as a seal is impressed upon wax. If he really wants to be a light to his people he must hate coarse jesting and the show of laughter, so that he may not teach many to misbehave. After all, he is a priest, an angel of the Lord God Almighty. An angel can not be versed in laughter when his purpose is to serve with the fear of God.[14]

The Lord Himself Did Not Laugh but Cried Four Times

There is one thing that I often ponder about laughter and I am puzzled. I see how the philosophers consider laughter as the counterpart of reason and say that every man is reasonable therefore he must also be laughing. And vice versa: Every laughing person must also be reasonable, because the ability to laugh is, as they say, an essential attribute of the faculty of reason. But, beyond this, I see that our Lord, though he received all the natural attributes of human nature, did not appear to have ever used this attribute, as St. Basil noted: "It appears that the Lord submitted to the necessary passions of the flesh and to those that bear the mark of virtue, such as physical weariness and compassion for the suffering. He never once demonstrated laughter, as far as the evangelical history is concerned."[15]

What conclusions can we draw from this? We conclude that it is not the ability to laugh but rather the ability to cry that is natural to man. For this reason our Lord not only did not laugh himself, but he also spoke against laughter. "Woe to you that laugh now, for you shall

115

mourn and weep" (Lk 6:25). Christ himself did cry on four occasions in his life: (a) He cried over his friend Lazarus (Jn 11:35); (b) he cried at the time of his passion. According to the Apostle, "In the days of his flesh, Jesus offered up prayers and supplications, with loud cries and tears, to him who was able to save him from death" (Heb 5:7). Also, the prayer and agony in Gethsemane before his betrayal is well attested in the Gospels. (c) On another occasion Jesus drew near and saw the city of Jerusalem and "wept over it," mourning the sad fact that she "did not know the time of her visitation" (Lk 19:41, 44). (d) Jesus cried a fourth time when he sat with his disciples at the last supper for the loss of Judas. "He was troubled in spirit, and testified, 'truly, truly, I say to you, one of you will betray me' " (Jn 13:21). According to St. John Chrysostom, this troubling of spirit is to be understood as an expression of his sadness accompanied with tears. So the Lord himself not only shed tears indeed, but he also blessed with his words the capacity to weep. "Blessed are you that weep now, for you shall laugh" (Lk 6:21). When therefore the theologians reason and say that Christ in his human nature is a rational being, they do not add that he is also a laughing being. This has not been revealed in the Scriptures, and we therefore prefer to imitate the example of our Lord and avoid laughing as much as possible as something that may bring eternal mourning. Let us therefore embrace a contrite spirit of weeping that is the cause of blessed and eternal joy and laughter.[16]

But again we have said enough about the fourth sense of taste and the mouth.

Notes

1. Homily 5, On The Lord's Prayer.
2. Quoted in the *Gerontikon*.
3. Why does luxurious eating and drinking degrade one to irrational passions of the flesh, to ungodliness and unbelief? Because the smells and smokes which they produce not only obstruct, as clouds, and exile the supernatural enlightenment of the Holy Spirit, they also obscure the natural discretion of the mind, and cause man to rush headlong toward irrational animal desires. St. Basil has confirmed this by saying, "The illuminations of the Holy Spirit are obstructed from reaching us by the 'clouds' of rich foods" (Homily 1 on Fasting). Also, St. Cyril of Alexandria said: "Every worldly luxury presents itself as something to be partaken

readily, but whoever partakes of it is greatly clouded and inebriated by it" (*Octateuchos*, vol. 2). What do you say to this, those of you who foolishly claim: "What evil is there in eating and drinking? Foods and drinks are not sinful. God does not condemn man for food and drink and other similar things." Note, however, from the above how very wrong and foolish you are to be saying such things. From this you can see what degree and grade you are and what truth you have been taught. For all the evil things are born from luxurious eating and gluttony. Cease then to project thoughtlessly such justifications. I know that you can only be saying them in order to console your conscience, which is in effect condemning you for doing evil. Such thoughts and practices however close the door of repentance and do not permit you to repent. Begin then to examine yourselves more carefully and to criticize yourselves. This self-reproof is in itself a part of repentance and salvation, as St. Timothy of Alexandria wrote (Canon 17), but it can also cause us to refrain from sumptuous eating and to learn true repentance through works of virtue.

4. Homily on Pentecost.
5. Broad Rules 15.
6. I read once an amusing story about two men who met each other. One loved to eat a lot and was fat and robust, the other exercised self-control and was very thin and ascetic looking. The fat man greeted, "Welcome, spirit without a body!" And the thin man responded, "Welcome, body without a spirit!" Is it not true that this is the only gain of such well-fed persons: a heavy body that is difficult to maneuver and often troubled by ailments? While the body of the ascetic person is thin, healthy, and resilient. Moreover, it has been shown that gluttons die much sooner than those who exercise self-control in their eating habits. Hippocrates said: "The fat people die much sooner than thin people do. . . . The mother of health is not to be oversatisfied with food, and the ability to bear pains."
7. Remember that the ascetic fathers on the Holy Mountain, who sit to eat on the ninth hour on days of fasting, experience greater sweetness and joy in tasting their simple meal and drinking their simple water than the gluttons who devour sumptuous pheasants and other rich foods and drinks. And as the wise Solomon said: "He who is sated loathes honey, but to one who is hungry everything bitter is sweet" (Prv 27:7). St. Basil too made the same point:

"If you wish to make your meals desirable, accept the change that is brought about by the period of fasting. Something that is enjoyed to satiety through continuous use is easily rejected. The things rarely acquired are the things most especially enjoyed" (Homily 1 on Fasting).

. . . It can be said about all those who love to eat in excess all sorts of rich foods that they do not simply eat to live, as in the normal and reasonable case, but rather they live in order to eat, which is characteristic of irrational beings and beasts. The mind of Christians will surely be much more miserable than these if, after the grace of the Gospel and the hope of eternal life, it becomes like that of pagans of old who had no other concern but to enjoy sumptuous and endless feasts. And, again, the Christian becomes a miserable person if he abandons his proper nourishment, which is the study and practice of spiritual things, to preoccupy himself with unworthy bodily foods and the worship of the stomach, which will be done away with.

8. Homily on the Nativity.

9. The reasoning of certain moral philosophers is very correct concerning the nature of slander. They say honor is greater than life. Since slander destroys the honor of a person, while murder kills life, then slander is greater than murder. And indeed it is a greater evil to kill someone with the tongue rather than with the sword, to wound with words rather than with arrows. A murderer kills only those who are alive and his own life is in danger, but the slanderer can also kill in relative security even those who are already dead.

10. When our Lord Jesus Christ was about to be ascended to heaven he raised his arms—arms almighty that created the world, arms most sweet and kind that provide all good things, arms that fashioned us in the beginning and refashioned us later. When Christ raised these arms he blessed all of his disciples and through them all of those who believed in him and bear his name. This is to say that with the motion of the hands he also blessed them with his mouth, so that the hands together with the tongue, in deed and in word he blessed them, not only once but always. He is always blessing those who believe in him. This is what St. Luke wanted to convey when he wrote in his Gospel: "Lifting up his hands he blessed them. While he blessed them, he parted from them, and was carried up into heaven" (Lk 24:51).

. . . I believe that even now, sitting at the right hand of God the

Father, sweetest Jesus Christ has his arms outstretched to bless us for he is the source of blessings. Why all these things and for whom? Thus an example is given to the holy hierarchs, who on earth preserve the type of Jesus, so that they may always bless their flock and always bless it with deeds and words, with hands and mouth.

But why do I say that he should pray and bless simply his flock? He must also bless and pray for his greatest enemies and not curse them, according to the Lord's commandment: "Love your enemies, bless those who curse you, do good to those who hate you and pray for those who despitefully use you and persecute you" (Mt 5:44, traditional text).

. . . I have written these comments for those who may have errored personally before a hierarch. But as for those who openly sin and scandalize the people and who after many exhortations persist in their evil ways unrepented, the appropriate penance provided by the canons must be applied. This penance does not mean the excommunication from the Holy Trinity and other similar curses as has become the current practice and which do not at all differ from the anathema, but rather involves at first the separation of the sinner from the sacramental life of the Church and beyond that his separation from the community of the faithful.

11. Commentary on Matthew, ch. 12.
12. Broad Rules 17.
13. St. John Chrysostom wrote in his homilies: "The present time is one of mourning and sorrow, of constraints and servitude, of sweat and tears, and you laugh!" (Homily 15 on Hebrews). Again he wrote elsewhere: "The present time is not for warm expressions of mirth and joy, but rather for mourning and sorrow and grief, and you spend your time in urban ribaldry!" (Homily 17 on Ephesians).
14. Epistle no. 319.
15. Broad Rules 17.
16. . . . Time has introduced into the world two types of people: Democritos and Heracleitos. One pondered upon the foolishness of men and had a great capacity for laughter. The other meditated upon the sufferings of mankind and had an aversion to laughter, preferring to cry and mourn. Even if both of these men exceeded the bounds of moderation, it is Democritos, who was always laughing, that is criticized by the moral philosophers as intemperate and facetious, while Heracleitos who was mourning is considered more temperate and more prudent.

119

CHAPTER SEVEN

Guarding the Sense of Touch

The Sense of Touch and Its Activities

We have reached in our discussion the fifth sense, which is the sense of touch. Even though the activity of this sense is generally considered to be concentrated in the hands, it actually encompasses the entire surface of the body so that every feeling and every part and every organ of the body both external and internal becomes an instrument of this sense of touch. Guard yourself then with great attention from such tender touches that arouse strong feelings, feelings that are mostly in the body and most vulnerable to sin. St. Gregory of Nyssa, in interpreting a passage in the Song of Songs, commented that the sense of touch is the subservient sense, the one most likely created by nature for the blind. It is most difficult for one to be free from the power of this sense, once it has been activated. This is why one must be careful to guard it with all his power.

Even though the power of the other senses seems to be active, it nevertheless seems to be far from the enactment of sin. But the sense of touch is the closest to this enactment and certainly the very beginning and the initial action of the deed.

One Should Not Even Touch His Own Body if It Is Not Necessary

Be careful not to bring your hands and your feet close to other bodies, especially of the young. Be especially careful not to stretch your hands to touch anything, unless it is necessary, nor upon members of your body, or even to scratch yourself, as St. Isaac the Syrian and other holy Fathers have taught. Even from such minor activities, the sense of touch becomes accustomed, or to put it more correctly, the devil seeks to arouse us toward sin and at the same time to raise up into our mind improper images of desire that pollute the beauty of prudent thoughts. This is why St. John Climacus wrote: "It so happens that we are polluted bodily through the sense of touch."[1] Even when you go out for the natural needs of your body respect your guardian angel, as St. Isaac has reminded us.[2] Elsewhere this same father has written: "Virgin is not one who has merely preserved one's body from sexual intercourse, but one who is modest unto oneself even when alone."[3]

The pagan Pythagoras taught that even if there were no other spectator of human evils in heaven or earth, man should have a sense of modesty and shame for himself. When someone does evil, he dishonors and degrades himself. The ancient Athenians had a temple dedicated to the goddess of modesty that would act in the place of God upon the true conscience. Now, if these pagans taught this and had such shame for themselves, when alone, how much more should we Christians be ashamed of ourselves when we are alone in a closed room, or in an isolated lonely place or even in the darkness of night? For it is only right that the modesty and reverence we feel when in a holy temple be also felt for ourselves, since we are a temple of God and the grace of the Holy Spirit. "For we are the temple of the living God" (2 Cor 6:16). Again St. Paul wrote: "Do you not know that your body is a temple of the Holy Spirit within you, which you have from God?" (1 Cor 6:19). St. John Chrysostom has taught us also that our bodies are even more honorable and more revered than a temple. We are a living and rational temple, while a building-temple is lifeless and irrational. Moreover, Christ died for us and not for temples.[4] Therefore it follows that more shame and modesty should be kept for ourselves and for our bodies than for the temple. For this reason, then, anyone who would dare to degrade the holy temple of his body by committing some sinful deed will in truth be more sinful than those who would desecrate the most famous temple.

Again, our pagan forefathers sought to teach men to avoid shameful deeds by asking them to imagine the presence of some important and revered person. If the imaginary presence of mortal men can avert one from doing evil when found alone, how much more can the true and abiding presence of the true and omnipresent and immortal God, who not only sees the external deeds of men but also knows the inner thoughts and feelings of the heart?

Most foolish then are those who are by themselves alone in an isolated or dark place and who have no self-respect and shame, nor remember the presence of God. They may say: "I am now in this darkness, who can see me?" God condemns such persons as being foolish. "Can a man hide himself in secret places so that I cannot see him? . . . Do I not fill heaven and earth?" (Jer 23:24). "A man who breaks his marriage vows says to himself, 'Who sees me? Darkness surrounds me, and the walls hide me, and no one sees me. Why should I fear? The Most High will not take notice of my sins.' His fear is confined to the eyes of men, and he does not realize that the eyes of the Lord are ten thousand times brighter than the sun" (Sir 23:18–19).

A Hierarch Ought Not to Stretch Out His Hand to Receive Gifts out of Greediness, Nor to Strike Anyone or to Ordain Those Who Are Unworthy

Be careful not to stretch out your hands to do evil. For as David said, "The righteous ought not to put forth their hands to do wrong" (Ps 125:3), that is, to receive bribes, to be greedy, to be unrighteous, to be graspy. Moreover, it also means not to seek shameful profits, not to carry out shameful beatings, and not to ordain unworthy candidates to the priesthood. God himself forbids the taking of bribes. It is written in Holy Scripture: "And you shall take no bribe, for a bribe blinds the officials, and subverts the cause of those who are in the right" (Ex 23:8). St. Basil too has written: "He who has not first placed true righteousness in his soul, but is corrupted by money or by consider-ations of friendship,⁵ he who defends enmity or beseeches power can-not direct and obtain justice."⁶

Do not stretch out your hands in greediness, in wrongdoing, in stealing, for the Apostle has written: "Do you not know that the unrigh-teous will not inherit the kingdom of God? Do not be deceived; neither the immoral, nor idolaters, nor adulterers, nor sexual perverts, nor thieves, nor the greedy, nor drunkards, nor revilers, nor robbers will inherit the kingdom of God" (1 Cor 6:9). Do not therefore stretch out your hands to acquire unlawful gain or to strike anyone. For according to the Apostle, "a bishop must be above reproach . . . temperate, sensible, dignified, no drunkard, not violent but gentle, nor quarrel-some, and no lover of money" (1 Tm 3:2). Any hierarch or priest who strikes with his hand or with a rod anyone is deposed, according to the Twenty-seventh Apostolic Canon. "A bishop, priest or deacon who strikes the faithful who may have sinned or the unbelievers who may have done wrong, and who does this for the purpose of disciplining them through fear, must be deposed. The Lord has never taught us to do this. On the contrary, he was struck but did not strike back. He was abused but did not abuse others. He was beaten but did not threaten others." The same discipline of deposition is required by the Ninth Canon of the Protodeutera Synod.

Do not be hasty to place your hands for ordination upon unworthy candidates. The Apostle again has instructed Timothy about this matter: "Do not be hasty in the laying on of hands, nor participate in another man's sins" (1 Tm 5:22). The bishops who have ordained unworthy candidates must render an account to God for all the sins that have been committed and may be committed by those whom they have so ordained. St. Chrysostom has also emphasized this point. "Do not tell me that the presbyter has sinned, or that the deacon has sinned. The responsibility of all these is placed upon the heads of those who have ordained such unworthy candidates."[7] Who then, as the Prophet David has asked, can inherit the mountain and the kingdom of God? He who keeps his hands pure from all of these. "Who shall ascend to the hill of the Lord? And who shall stand in his holy place? He who has clean hands and a pure heart" (Ps 24:3–4).

The Use of Luxurious Clothing and What Its Use Implies

The use of soft and fine clothing is another matter that we can relate to the sense of touch. Now, if I may be permitted to be more blunt, I want to emphasize especially to hierarchs and priests that they not fall into the error of fantastic apparel which unfortunately many experience because of their bad habits from childhood and the bad examples of others. St. John Chrysostom, first of all, reminded us that the very custom of covering the body with clothing is a perpetual reminder of our exile from Paradise and our punishment, which we received after our disobedience. We who were previously in Paradise, covered by the divine grace and having no need of clothing, find ourselves now in need of covering and clothing for our bodies. The forefathers were naked before the disobedience but not ashamed; after the disobedience they sewed fig leaves together and coverings for their bodies (Gn 3:7). Therefore, what is the reason for this reminder of our sin and punishment to be done with bright and expensive clothing? "The use of clothing has become a perpetual reminder for us of our exile from the good things of Paradise and a lesson of our punishment which the human race received as a consequence of the original sin of disobedience. There are those who are so affected in their vain imaginations that they say to us that they no longer know the clothing that is made by the wool of the sheep and that they now wear only clothes made of silk. . . . Tell me now, for whom do you so clothe your body? Why are you glad over your particular set of clothing? Why don't you heed St. Paul who wrote: 'If we have food and clothing, with these we shall be content.' " (1 Tim 6:8)

The Usefulness of Clothing. The Early Bishops Did Not Wear Expensive Clothing

According to St. Basil the usefulness of clothing is to protect our bodies from the cold in the winter and from the heat in the summer. "What is the difference for one who is sensible to have long robes with a flowing train or to wear foolish and unnecessary clothing that do nothing to keep you warm in winter and to protect you from the heat in the summer?"[9] For the clothes to be made of silk and other expensive materials is a vanity that derives from unreal fantasies and misleading desires of the heart. In other words, such vanity is a shadow, smoke, dust thrown into the air, and bubbles that are blown around and broken. Solomon at first experienced the use of expensive clothing but later condemned them. I agree with him when he wrote that they are a vanity of vanities and a deliberate choice of one's spirit. But what is this choice of one's spirit? St. Gregory the Theologian considered it to be "a desire of the soul that is irrational and a temptation of man deriving perhaps from the ancient fall."[10] Is it characteristic of a prudent person to follow such vanity? Should he ever allow himself to seek the shadows of dreams? No, please do not accept to do this. Perhaps you will argue the pressures of your youth is forcing you to do this. But what is youth? Solomon again has told us that "youth and the dawn of life are vanity" (Eccl 11:10). Therefore one vanity loves another vanity, but never prudence and right reason. Perhaps you will say that it is the office of being a bishop that prompts you to wear expensive clothes. Well! Take a look at those ancient bishops. See the poor garments of St. Basil and St. Gregory, the cape of St. Athanasios and the cape of Bishop Serapion. Moreover, those blessed men traveled great distances on foot and alone. They did not use animals and

124

horses of great value[11] that were richly saddled, and without the accompaniment of many persons leading and following the procession. One can see from this vain fantasy that having expensive clothes is not a substantive element but rather a destructive one for the office of a bishop.

The Present Things Are Vain and Temporal

Leave such vanity, brother. Remember that according to the Apostle: "The form of this world is passing away, and those who deal with the world [live] as though they had no dealings with it" (1 Cor 7:31). Remember also, "We look not to the things that are seen but to the things that are unseen; for the things that are seen are transient, but the things that are unseen are eternal" (2 Cor 4:18). For death comes and death is unknown. Judgment follows death and this judgment is quick. After judgment comes hell, an endless hell. When death comes, youth passes away, so does vanity. Every luxury of clothing and all the pleasant things of this life come to an end with the end of the life of each person. Where are your predecessors and those before them? Having the same vain imaginations, have they not played out the short scene of life and the empty sentiments? Are they not now also deceived by the shortness of life and are already earth and dust in a forgotten place, according to David? What do you think? Will you not in a short while follow them? Will you not follow the same way of life and will you not reach the same goal of the grave?

According to the psalmist David and St. Basil who interpreted him, this life is likened to a journey on account of the tendency to reach the goal of each created being. Listen to what he said: "Those who on board a ship are sleeping are nevertheless led to the harbor automatically by the power of the prevailing wind. Even though they may not be aware of it, their journey is continued toward its goal. So is it with us in passing the time of our life. In a certain unique movement that is continuous and ceaseless we are pressed on the unknown course of our life that is appropriate to each of us. You may be sleeping and yet the time passes on. You may be awake and intellectually active and yet your life is spent, even if it escapes our perception. We are all indeed on a journey, each of us running toward our appropriate goal. This is why we are all on the way. In the case of those who travel, once the first step is taken the next one will follow and the one after that in

125

succession. Consider the affairs of life if they are not similar. Today you have cultivated the earth, tomorrow another person will do it. And after him still another will continue. Therefore isn't our life a journey on which we partake differently from time to time and on which we all succeed each other?"[12]

In the book of Job, Zapar the Naamathite, wanting to indicate the shortness of human life, said: "Though his height mount up to the heavens, and his head reach to the clouds, he will perish for ever. . . . Those who have seen him will say, 'Where is he?' He will fly away like a dream, and not be found; he will be chased away like a vision of the night" (Jb 20:7f.). These examples and even the mere meanness, the vicissitudes and the disorder in human affairs and good things, all of these I hope will convince you to turn down such a vain quest and irrational desire.

What are gold and silver and all those precious stones (as one moralist noted) but bright products of the earth? When these are kept locked up in treasuries they also hold therein the heart of him who has so locked them up and they thus prevail over their owner. What are those famous compliments and honors but smoky emissions which come out of the mouths of the public and are diffused in the air and which are often mixed with the criticisms of envy? What are those supreme, those hierarchal, those patriarchal offices and those great kingdoms, but great servitudes in which those who rise to them find also at the same time their fall? And those who seek after extreme honors find extreme catastrophes. What sort of thing is pleasure but a change that is irreconcilable with self-control? What is good health that we so desire, but a mild and well-tempered condition of the four liquids in our bodies that are always combated by the other four opposing qualities of the elements? What is life but a flow of successive moments in which one is born when the other dies, so that man begins to die just as soon as he begins to live? Finally, what is this body of ours that we so care for but transformed clay and an extolled hospital that contains more diseases than members and nerves? And, speaking in general, what are all the external and useful and so-called fortunate good things but vain and rather more useless than useful, more harmful than helpful? Are they not founded simply on opinions? And what are all the bodily, the physical, and the pleasurable, the so-called good things, but the common properties of the plants and the irrational animals? By the way, these irrational animals are in a sense more well off than we, by realizing less than we do that they can be deprived of these good things, which are after all always united with opposing suffering.

With all this in mind, St. Gregory spoke well when he said: "Do not marvel at anything that does not remain, and do not overlook anything that does. Do not moreover try to grasp at something that simply escapes us when held."[13] A certain wise man also said: "If you are a mortal, O great man, you will concern yourself with mortal things." Another one said: "The shadow of glory is glory itself. No one who sees a loaf of bread in a painting will ever reach to take the drawing, even if he is a thousand times overcome by hunger. Now, if you want to receive glory, evade glory, for if you seek after glory you will fall away from it."[14] St. Isaac said: "He who runs after honor causes it to flee from before him. But he who avoids it, will be sought out by honor that becomes a herald to all of his humility."[15] Now, meditating on these things prudently, dear brother, say to yourself the words of the wise Joseph Vryennios:

> Soul, be a stranger to all these things; soul, you have been redeemed by the precious blood of the immaculate and spotless Lamb—Christ; soul, for you the good shepherd has offered his own soul; soul, raise up your eye to your Creator, be sober, see your redeemer, know and love the Savior; acquire a blameless conscience. . . . Why do you stand before those things that do not exist? Why do you fret over the things that are corruptible? Why do you find joy with vain things? Why do you trouble yourself with what passes away? Why are you attracted by imaginations? Why do you delight in things that you will abandon as if you will not? And of whose vision will you be deprived in eternity? How long will you be deceived by the eyes? by the attraction of pleasures? by random preoccupations? by evil thoughts? by thoroughly vain glories—all of which cause you to be separated from the vision of the most sublime and desired spiritual reality?

I find myself out of breath in struggling in every way, dear brother, to find supportive arguments and proofs to show you how empty and vain a thing it is to preoccupy yourself with fine clothing. For I love your salvation as I love my own. And in order to make my words more understandable, I bring the example of the reflux of water of Euripus where the tide changes so often that the ancients chose to refer metaphorically to the frequent changes in human affairs with the term *euripus*. What else is this troubled life but a strait of troubled waters that flow to and fro? A place where good and bad, happiness and misery, are always flowing and mutually replacing each other; sometimes sending man to the depths of goodness and happiness and sometimes leaving him on the dry shore and in misfortune. Therefore learn even from this name of Euripus and put an end from here on to the desire and the fantasy of these fleeting vanities.

Luxurious Clothing Is the Cause of Many Evils and All Clergy Must Avoid It

Up to now I have assumed that luxurious clothing is a simple vanity. I am afraid however that it is more than that. It also nourishes vainglory; it is the mother of pride; it is the way to prostitution and it is the panderer of virtually all the passions. I said that it is the nourishment and the mother of vainglory and pride because the soul naturally has the tendency to be fashioned internally according to the body. Now, if the body, as it should, wears humble clothes the soul will also be humbled. If the body wears vainglorious and prideful clothes, the soul too will be vainglorious and prideful, as St. John Climacus has written: "The soul becomes similar to its external appearance and pursuits; it is impressed by what it does and fashioned according to such deeds."[16] I also noted that luxurious clothes lead to prostitution. St. Basil has said: "A person who beautifies himself and is so called is like being promiscuous and a schemer against other marriages."[17] St. Paul disallowed luxurious clothing in women, who are by nature beings who love beauty and who love to dress themselves up: "Women should adorn themselves modestly and sensibly in seemly apparel, not with braided hair or gold or pearls or costly attire" (1 Tm 2:9). St. Peter too did not permit women "the outward adorning with braiding of hair, decoration of gold, and wearing of fine clothing" (1 Pt 3:3).

If women are not permitted such luxurious apparel, how much more then are we to assume that this is not permitted either among men and especially among hierarchs, who are to keep modesty and propriety in all things. This is why the Sixth Ecumenical Council decreed, through its Twenty-seventh Canon, that the hierarchs and all the clergy be dressed modestly and not use secular and luxurious clothing. The canon says in part that "no one among the clergy should dress with inappropriate clothes while in the city or while traveling on the road. They should wear the apparel that has already been determined for the clergy, that is, modest and simple. Anyone who disregards this rule will be deposed for one week." Similarly, the Seventh Ecumenical Council with its Sixteenth Canon decreed the following: "Every foolish beautification of the body is foreign to the priestly order. Those bishops and priests who dress themselves with luxurious apparel must be reprimanded and corrected. If they persist in their wrongdoing, they must be given a penance."

From early times every priestly man was dressed with modest and moderate apparel. Everything that has no practical use but is merely cosmetic only adds to our condemnation, as St. Basil noted.[18] They did not wear clothing made out of silk, nor did they add colorful decorations on the edge of their clothing. They heeded the sacred word saying, those who wear the soft and fine apparel are in the palaces of kings (cf. Mt 11:8; Lk 7:25). St Basil once asked, "Have you ever seen a man of high principles wearing a flowery garment made of silk? Despise such things."[19] St. John Chrysostom also noted, "When you see a man wearing silken apparel, laugh him to scorn!"[20] St. Isidore Pelousiotes also, explaining the seamless garment of the Lord, noted: "Who can overlook the simplicity of that garment which the poor Galeleans used to wear? In fact they had a special skill in weaving such garments. Imitate the simple garments of Christ. For if the roughness in apparel here on earth is foolishness, wearing the garment of light in heaven is certainly not."[21] The prophets of God too used modest humble and poor garments. Listen to what Clement of Alexandria said of them: "Prophet Elijah wore a garment made of sheepskins which he tied around his waist with a belt of animal hairs. The Prophet Isaiah went about virtually naked and with bare feet. Oftentimes he would wear sack cloth as a symbol of humility and mourning. Jeremiah too only wore a simple linen garment. As the strong members of the body are seen clearly when uncovered, so also is the beauty of virtue demonstrated magnificently when it is not entangled with a great deal of idle talk." The Synod at Gangra in its Twelfth Canon pronounced anathema upon those criticized for wearing velvet and silk garments. Finally, the same Synod in its Twenty-first Canon decreed: "We accept and praise the simple and modest garments, but we avoid those which are soft and luxuriously ornamental."

GUARDING THE SENSE OF TOUCH

Luxurious Garments Are Scandalous to Both Men and Women

Let me leave aside the sense of folly and looseness that is created on the body, especially on a body of a young person, by the luxury of clothing. I leave aside also the uselessness of such clothing, as St. Gregory the Theologian noted.[22] I keep silent about the greed for money that is incited in those who desire to acquire such clothing. I also sidestep the vanity and pride and all the other passions that act as so many poisonous fruit of this death-bearing tree. And I consider only the common scandal that it is for both men and women. It is indeed a great scandal for men to see their bishop dressed in such luxury, and wherever they are they comment that the bishop is altogether given over to a desire for fine garments and an air of haughty pride. It is even a greater scandal for the women. For as they themselves often scandalize the men who look upon them and excite in them certain passions, in the very same way the men who are decorated in fine clothing, especially bishops and priests, scandalize the women and kindle the coals of passion in their souls.

Even if we assume that it is permitted for you to be so dressed, even if you guard yourself and are a prudent person in dressing yourself well, should you not take into account the scandal of those misfortunate souls? Should you not consider the evil desires and the spiritual harm that may be caused in their souls? Who will give an account for this? Certainly no one else except you, for in seeking to serve your foolish desires, it is you who have allowed all these evils to come into being. And this because you have not chosen to imitate the holy hierarchs of old, who dressed humbly and spent their days in great humility. I had the opportunity to know St. Macarios of Corinth, who in his diocese and in his later life always wore humble black clothing. How serious is the punishment for creating a scandal is noted by the Lord himself: "But whoever causes one of these little ones who believe in me to sin, it would be better for him to have a great millstone fastened round his neck and to be drowned in the depth of the sea" (Mt 18:6). Listen to this story and be informed: When St. Anthony was about to die, he ordered his disciples to give one of his garments to St. Athanasios and the other to Bishop Serapion. These two churchmen received the garments with all of their heart and used to wear them on the dominical feasts. These simple and coarse monastic garments did more to dignify them in a most reverent way than any royal garments ever could in all their luxurious splendor!

Having learned about the luxury of garments and the many evils which come from them, strive to avoid such luxury as harmful to the soul.

Soft Beds Should Be Avoided for They Are the Cause of Many Evils

In this sense of touch we must also include the soft and comfortable beds and everything that has to do with our comfort. Inasmuch as these may contribute to our spiritual harm, they must be avoided by all, but especially by the young. Such comforts weaken the body; they submerge it into constant sleep; they warm it beyond measure, and therefore kindle the heat of passion. This is why the prophet Amos wrote: "Woe to those who lie upon beds of ivory, and stretch themselves upon their couches" (Am 6:4). Once a young monk asked an elder [monk] how to guard himself against the carnal passions. The elder replied that he should avoid overeating, avoid slander and all those activities which excite carnal passions. The monk however was unable to find the cure for his passion even after observing carefully all the admonitions of the elder. He would return to the elder again and again for advice until he became a burden to the elder. Finally, the patient elder got up and followed the brother to his cell. Upon seeing the soft bed where he slept, the elder exclaimed: "Here, here, is the cause of your struggle with carnal desire, dear brother!"[23]

Heracleides has also noted in the *Lausaikon* about Iouvinos, the famous bishop of Askalon, that on a very hot day near the Pelousion mountain he washed with a little water his hands and feet and laid out a camel skin to rest a little in the shade. This was done in the presence of his most holy mother, who directly began to reproach him. "Oh son," she said, "you are most daring to flatter your body with such care and at such a young age. The more you fuss over it the more it becomes agitated like a serpent against you, seeking to harm you. I am already sixty years old, and I have not yet washed my face and feet in such a way, except for my hands. Even though I suffered certain illnesses and the doctors advised me to take advantage of therapeutic baths and other cures for the body, I have never entrusted in my body nor have I allowed myself to flatter it in any way, knowing full well the enmity that exists between it and the soul. For this reason, my son, I have even refused to recline in a soft bed to sleep."

Behold what an ascetic reaction is prompted by the simple laying out of a camel skin to rest upon it. Behold how a little washing prompted such austere criticism by a mother to her son. Do you see, dear brother, what great exactness and care is needed and especially by the young? Once the Patriarch of Alexandria, St. John the Merciful, seeing that he had need of it, accepted a precious bed covering offered to him by a certain ruler. Throughout that night the blessed hierarch struggled with his thoughts and was most critical of himself for having accepted such a precious covering when so many poor brothers did not even possess a straw mat to lie on. He finally threw it away from his bed and in the morning had it sold in the marketplace, distributing the money to the poor. Notice well how what is for the comfort of the body, or (what amounts to the same thing) what is unnecessary and more than what we need, was used then by the hierarchs of that time.

In the Psalms the Prophet David has made a distinction between "bed" and "couch." The bed is commonly used for sleeping, while the couch is in the area prepared for sitting. Now, if your sitting room is furnished with soft chairs and couches, this, I believe, is not harmful since it is also thus prepared for the comfort of guests.

The Clergy Must Not Play Games of Chance Nor Take Baths

In this general sense of touch must be included the playing of cards and dice and all other such games that one plays with his hands. I beseech you as strongly as I possibly can to avoid these completely. Such games are improper and altogether alien to your high character and profession and they are the cause of much scandal among Christians. They may even become the cause for deposing someone from the hierarchy. The Forty-second Apostolic Canon decreed the following: "Any bishop or priest or deacon who spends his time playing the dice and drinking must either be defrocked or deposed." Going even further, the Forty-third Apostolic Canon provided that a lay person who is involved in such games of chance is excommunicated. Why do I simply say that you must not play such games? You must not even look upon those who do. The law of Photios decreed the following:

Any bishop or clergyman who plays the dice or other such games of chance, or who simply keeps company with those who do and sits beside them when they play, must be deposed from doing any of his sacred duties and must not receive any of the provisions given by his diocese for a certain period of time until he repents. If he should persist in his evil even beyond the given time for repentance, he must be entirely banished from the ranks of the clergy and may become a secular officer of some kind for the province where he had been a clergyman.[24]

According to Armenopoulos, the One hundred and twenty-third Law of Justinian requires that the clergy who become drunkards and those who play the dice must be confined to a monastery. I say nothing of all the harm that comes to those who play cards and other such games, about which St. John Chrysostom wrote the following: "The vice of dice brings blasphemy, anger, harm, abuse and a myriad more evils greater than these."[25] Aristotle himself, even though a pagan, numbered the gamblers among the thieves and robbers: "A dice player, a thief and a robber are among those who are not free, for they acquire their gain shamefully and illegally."[26]

You have already heard above from the holy nun and mother of Iouvinos how harmful even simple bathing can be, especially to the young. In the act of bathing the sense of touch is certainly sorely tested and tempted. As we read in the sayings of the Fathers there were many ascetic fathers who hesitated even at the crossing of rivers, not only because they were ashamed to bathe their bodies but also because they did not even want to uncover their legs. These holy men were often in a flash transported across the river by an angel of God. St. Diadochos, bishop of Photiki, has written that the avoidance of baths is a manly achievement. "It is a manly and prudent thing to avoid baths. This way our bodies are not effeminated by that pleasurable flow of water over them, nor do we come to a remembrance of that shameful nakedness of Adam, so that we too seek to cover the shame with the [fig] leaves of a second excuse. Those who desire to keep their bodies spiritually pure are especially required to be united with the beauty of prudence and chastity."[27] Of course, it is understood and acceptable that occasionally one must bathe out of necessity for the sake of health and the requirements of an illness.

Notes

1. The Ladder, step 15.
2. Homily 26.
3. Homily 56.

4. Homily 14, On Ephesians; Homily 20, On 2 Corinthians.
5. Cleon the king of Athens was highly praised when he was made king against his will and then proceeded to call all his most dear friends and with sighing and sorrow took his leave from them, fearing that he might be forced to transgress the law because of their friendship. As a prudent man he had realized that friendship and authority cannot sit together at the same time upon the same cathedra. He who would exercise justice must put friendship aside. The story is also told of Routelios, the dear friend of Skouros. When Skouros requested an unjust favor from his friend Routelios and did not receive it, he was disturbed and retorted: "And what need have I of your friendship if I cannot get one small favor from you?" To this reproach Routelios replied: "And what need have I of your friendship if I am to do for you unjust deeds?" And their friendship came to an end. Above all the praise goes to Pericles the Athenian, who was being beseeched by a friend to take a false oath in order to support him. Pericles responded with the famous saying: "Friend up to the sanctuary," that is to say, "I want to be your friend but only until we come up to the holy sanctuary" (where it was customary to place the hand when taking a public oath). It is necessary here to grieve bitterly! For if these persons who were far from the grace of the Gospel were able to rise to such heights of virtue with only the natural law, you who are an Orthodox Christian, a leader, a bishop, a ruler, what do you think? Can you disobey the law of God? Do you think that you will be saved? You are deluding yourself!
6. Homily on Proverbs.
7. Homily 3, On Acts.
8. Homily 18, On Genesis.
9. Address to the Young Men.
10. Funeral Oration to Caesarios.
11. The Lord himself through his own example taught us to travel in a humble manner. He himself used the humble donkey to enter Jerusalem and not a stallion. However, when the road is difficult or long it is permissible for bishops and Christians in general to travel with horses and mules, but these should not be animals of great value nor richly saddled and adorned.
12. Commentary on Psalm 1.
13. Homily on the Lord's Day.
14. Quoted in the Life of Cyril Phileotos.

15. Homily 5.
16. Homily 25, On Humility.
17. Address to the Young Men.
18. The Short Monastic Rule, 49.
19. Homily on the Hexaemeron.
20. Homily 11, On I Timothy.
21. Epistle 74 to Caton the Monk.
22. Homily on the Birth of Christ.
23. From the *Gerontikon*.
24. The first Book of the Codex, Statute 34, Title 9, ch. 27.
25. Homily on the Statutes.
26. Nichomachean Ethics, Book 4.
27. Diadochos of Photike, ch. 52.

CHAPTER EIGHT

Guarding All the Senses
in General

What the Senses Are in General and What They Resemble

With the help of God, I have to the extent of my ability commented briefly on each of the senses and indicated the harm that they can bring to the soul when they are abused. You need all of your strength to control these senses from passionate desires and to protect yourself from any evil form that they may bring upon you. These senses after all, are, as we have noted, those very doors and windows through which either life or death may enter. Life enters when they are governed well and do not partake of their usual passions. Death enters when they partake of "corpses" as do the birds of prey; when they taste the dust of the earth as do the serpents; when they eat rotted food as do the flies. Or to put it in another way, when they partake of those sinful and death-bearing passions, which are harmful to the soul. This is why the prophet Jeremiah alluded to these senses when he said: "For death has come up into our windows, it has entered our palaces" (Jer 9:21). St. Gregory of Nyssa, interpreting this reference, explained that "the windows" through which death enters "our palace" are indeed the senses.[1] Make every effort then to purify your soul from the impurities which the senses bring within from the outside. These senses may be likened to mountain torrents, which as soon as they swell up with the force of abundant water from the winter rains drag downhill with them everything that happens to be in their way—rocks, logs, mud, and other debris.[2] The senses too, when allowed free reign by the controlling mind, are driven out with great force toward the physical things of life and thus draw with themselves every indecent vision, every shameful word, every evil sound, and generally every dirt and impurity of the passions. Afterward, when they return they bring back all these things into the troubled soul, causing it to be darkened, to be full of so many shameful images and so many conflicting sounds that, generally speaking, it is overwhelmed by the passions that make it into a den of thieves and a harbor of impurities. It was perhaps at a time when the prophet David was troubled by such torrents of the senses that he shouted to God in spiritual anguish: "The cords of death encompassed me,/the torrents of perdition assailed me" (Ps 18:4).

Why One Must Struggle to Control One's Senses

According to St. Gregory the Theologian we must struggle to block our senses and to control them, for they are the easy ways toward evil and entrances of sin. Let us not give in to the easy ways of evil and to the easy entrances of sin. I say to you then, put all your strength forward to protect your senses. I also say to you to be attentive, to struggle, and I insist on this, by using various synonymous words. I wish to prove to you that the devil is always standing before us, observing and studying the condition of our senses. Just as soon as we open even one sense to him, he enters into our soul directly and brings death to us, as St. Isaac has noted: "The enemy is standing and observing day and night directly against our eyes to detect which entrance of our senses will be opened to him to enter. Once he enters through one of our senses because of our lack of vigilance, then this devious shameless dog attacks us further with his own arrows."[3] We must also struggle to protect our senses because it is not only through curious eyes that we fall into the sin of desire and commit fornication and adultery of the heart, as the Lord noted. There is also the fornication and the adultery of the sense of hearing, the sense of smell, the sense of taste, the sense of touch, and of all the senses together. Therefore, St. Gregory the Theologian has written in his heroic counsel to the virgin: "Virgin, be truly a virgin in the ears, in the eyes and in the tongue! Every sense that wanders with ease sins." St. Gregory of Nyssa also said: "The Lord has spoken, I believe, about all the senses, so that following His words we can include that the one who hears lustfully, the one who touches and the one who uses every inner power in us to serve pleasure has actually committed the sin in his heart."[4]

GUARDING ALL THE SENSES IN GENERAL

Those Who Live in the World Must Protect Their Senses More than Those Ascetics in the Desert

You who are in the world, dear friend, must guard yourself even more than those who are in the desert. St. Basil wrote to someone living in the world the following advice: "Do not relax your efforts because you are in the world. In fact you are in need of greater efforts and more vigilance to achieve salvation. After all you have chosen to live in the midst of all the pitfalls and in the very stronghold of the sinful powers. You have before you constantly the instigations of sins and day and night all of your senses are being attacked by their evil desires."[5] If we are overcome by the desire for food or drink, we do not experience such a strong attack. Being in a desolate place where one does not see or hear anything out of place or experience the other causes of sin, we are thus surrounded by a protective wall that helps to win our battles without wars, as St. Isaac said: "When one does not receive a sense perception, then he can have a victory without a struggle."[6] In other words, the monks who have removed themselves from the world are fighting behind trenches, but you are fighting an arm-to-arm combat against the enemies. The attacks are coming from all directions. And the causes of sin are all around you. While they stand afar off from the precipice, you are at its very edge. That great luminary of spiritual discretion, St. Poimen, once said: "Those who live far away from the world are like those who are far from a precipice and, whenever they are misled by the devil, before they reach the edge, they call upon God who comes to save them. Those who live in the world, however, are like those who are near the precipice and when the devil draws them toward it, they have no time to call upon God and be saved but fall directly into the abyss."[7] Therefore, because you are so close to this abyss, you are in immediate danger just as soon as you neglect or open one of your senses. God forbid! This is the reason why you want to use all your energy to protect your senses from coming into contact with sin. As it is impossible for a house not to be darkened by smoke entering from the outside, it is similarly impossible for a man not to be harmed when he is not careful to guard his senses, but rather opens them without restraint, allowing all manner of passionate images to enter the soul. The wise St. Syngletike said, "Even when we do not want it, the thieves will enter through the senses. For how is it possible for a house not be darkened by the smoke entering from outside through the doors and windows that have been left opened?"

How Can We Interpret the Aristotelian Axiom—"Nothing Is in the Mind That Has Not Previously Entered the Senses."

The famous axiom of the philosopher Aristotle which says that "nothing is in the mind that has not previously entered the sense" is indeed legendary. Many have written many opinions in favor and against the truth or falsehood of this axiom both in the past and now. In this case the proverb is apropos that says: ρητάτ᾽ ἄρρητά τε, φατάτ᾽ ἄφατά τε."[8] In view of this divided opinion, I shall say briefly that the axiom is false, if it refers to the virtues. Since the mind has been created by God as naturally good, it has received innately its appropriate goodness from God. "And God saw everything that he had made, and behold, it was very good" (Gn 2:31). "For everything created by God is good" (1 Tm 4:4), as the Apostle wrote. Granted that at infancy and early childhood there is no other impression in man except perhaps the very impression of having no other good idea in mind that has entered through the senses and that the mind is simple, without forms and shapes and like an unwritten sheet of paper (a "tabula rasa"). Still, we must say that this simplicity which the mind has in itself is indeed one good thing, the original and the most appropriate to its nature. God created the mind to be pure and simple, as Scripture and the Fathers affirm.

The mind was thus created pure and simple without predetermined shapes so that its image may have similitude to its Creator who is invisible. "So God created man in his own image, in the image of God he created him" (Gn 1:27). This way the mind can be united with the divine Archetype. Thus the whole struggle of secular and worldly philosophers is to fashion their minds with different ideas and imaginary knowledge of natural and human things. This is after all the whole power of secular philosophy. On the contrary, the whole struggle and effort and goal of virtuous and spiritual persons is how to erase from their minds every shape and image and thought that has been impressed upon it and to make it (again) simple and pure and unimpressed by anything external, so that through such simplicity it may be united with God and restored to its original condition. This is the return about which the Lord spoke: "Truly, I say to you, unless you turn and become like children, you will never enter the Kingdom of heaven" (Mt 18:3). Therefore the wise St. Neilos said: "Blessed is the mind that acquires in the time of prayer a complete absence of images."[9] St. Basil too said: "As God does not dwell in temples created by hands, similarly he can not be contained by intellectual creations and expressions." St. Diadochos also said: "The blessed light of God shines in the heart when the heart has been released from all and has become free of all. In the deprivation of all thoughts, that divine light is revealed to the pure mind."[10]

Now if we are to talk about the evil things that are in the mind, then I must say that Aristotle's axiom is most true. Evil is, after all, unnatural and a foreign element that has entered the nature of the mind, that was created good. Evil has no other way to enter the mind except through the senses from the outside. A ready proof and a trustful witness of this saying is Adam himself, that simple man who was the first to be created by the hand of God. Evil and the idea of sin entered into the mind of Adam not from inner thoughts, but from external influences through the senses, when the devil deceitfully advised Eve to eat of the forbidden fruit. This is confirmed by St. Macarios, who said about Adam the following: "Adam was created pure by God to serve him. . . . However, the devil approached him and spoke to him and it was from without through the hearing that he was first received. It was after this that the devil entered his heart and pervaded his entire being."[11]

In What Way Can One Guard the Senses from the Passions?

What should we conclude from this? That every idea of evil and every form of passion enters the heart through the mediation and service of the senses. And if the senses are not guarded, then the evil passions are also not guarded. How can they be guarded and closed to such passions? Listen. The windows of the Temple of Solomon were covered with fine nets to prevent the entry of impure insects (cf. Ez 41:6). This may serve as a reminder that he who does not want any impure passions of the senses to enter into his soul must drape his senses with [spiritual] nets. What are these nets? It is the memory of death, for one; our account before Christ on the day of judgment; the memory of eternal suffering. Through these, man can put away the evil passions and sins, when they come before his eyes and his other senses. St. Neilos has confirmed that this is so: "Those who desire to keep their mind as a clean and pure temple, where the doors and windows are covered with fine nets to prevent the entry of any impure insects, must similarly cover their senses by meditating on the sobering realities of the future judgment which prevent the entry of any impure images to creep in."[12]

St. Isidore Pelousiotes also has taught us how to guard the senses from evil passions. He said that the mind of man must stand firm like a king and emperor with awesome thoughts which are armed like soldiers to guard the entries of the senses and to prevent the enemies from entering. For, if they do not enter, the war and the victory will be easy. But if, on the contrary, they do enter then the war becomes difficult and the victory uncertain.[13] This is why you too, brother, can through these means guard and close the windows of your senses, so that all the evil passions that are commonly referred to as bodily and external can be readily overcome. But are we to overcome only these bodily and external passions? No, we must also overcome the inner passions of desire that are commonly called inner and spiritual. These, too, will gradually be weakened and overcome as the passions of the senses cease to enter and rule. This is why St. Poimen used to say: "When a serpent is shut within a vessel and does not receive any food, it will gradually die. So also with the inner passions of our heart, if they are isolated and do not receive the evil nourishment they need from the outside through the senses of the body, they in time are weakened and eventually die."[14] Again the passions can be likened to certain tiny creatures found in the mud at the bottom of a lake. As long as they do not have anything to eat they are content to lie there in peace. But as soon as food is put into the water, you can see them immediately moving and rising up from the depth to get the food. In the same manner the passions remain peacefully within the heart as long as they do not receive from the outside through the senses any nourishment and pleasure. But as soon as such a pleasure enters, especially through the eyes, these passions move directly toward the desirable nourishment.

The Devil Dies When He Does Not Receive the Pleasure of the Senses

Since the devil has as nourishment the passions and pleasures of the senses, he too will die as he is deprived of this nourishment. "The strong lion perishes for lack of prey" (Jb 4:11). St. Neilos has noted that the devil is often referred to as an "ant-lion," just as the passions are. This means that at first these passions appear as something very small, but later become great and strong like lions. Do you see, dear brother, what great enemies you have to defeat? Do you see that by cutting off the passions of the senses, you are also going to put Satan to death? But alas this cutting off and this victory cannot be won without a war. It is like the external wars, no one can win a victory without first waging a war against the enemy. It is certain that you have to experience a great struggle in each of your senses both from the point of view of habit and of the enemy. For the bad habit desires to draw each sense toward its pleasurable object when it is present. On the other hand, the enemy desires to wage a great battle in the memory and imagination of the mind in order to achieve its consent to enjoy that pleasure, so that, in doing so, the devil can also enjoy the same pleasure. But you must stand courageously and never consent to the will of the enemy. Say to yourself that iambic proverb of St. Gregory the Theologian: "No one can excel by beginning from cowardice; it is the victories that bring praise."

An ancient people recognized their children to be their genuine offspring only after placing before them a viper and observing them catch it courageously. You too, dear brother, must make the enemy realize that you are a true child of Christ who is your heavenly Father, and who has overcome the passions and the devil—through the courage you demonstrate in fighting against the evil passions of your senses. And if the enemy stands to fight you, be not afraid to tell him what that brave Spartan said to Xerxes: "Oh king, you managed to sail the sea and to cut a channel across the peninsula of Athos, but you will not pass the side of one armed Spartan." For this reason then show the enemy that you are not a slave of your senses, but lord and king. Show that you are not only flesh and blood, but a rational mind, appointed by God to be leader and sole ruler over the irrational passions of the body. Say to yourself that wise proverb about evil habits: "The best learning for man is to unlearn evil." Now, if I have learned, wrongly, to give to my senses their sensual objects, and this wrong learning has brought about a bad habit, and this bad habit a still further bad condition, why can I not now learn to do the opposite? Let, therefore, the good learning become a good habit and the good habit a good and permanent condition. If, in doing this, I am to experience difficulties and bitterness at first, let me experience them. Afterward I will be able to experience both ease and joy. The first efforts to learn and practice the virtues and establish the habit of virtuous living are often very bitter and most difficult for the senses. The activity that follows after these initial efforts to acquire the habit of virtuous living is very easy, ineffably sweet, and enjoyable.

Briefly we can say that angels are invisibly present, holding crowns in their hands. Christ himself is the one who will crown you every time you are victorious in the battle against the evil passions of the senses and you do not succumb to them. St. Basil said: "Suffering brings glory, and tribulation brings crowns." But you have been beaten once or twice (I hope not!). Be not completely overcome. Stand firm and courageous, calling upon God for help. If you do so, the grace of God will come directly to your help and will not leave you to be completely overcome by the enemy. Do you want to be sure of this? Follow me and let us travel to Sodom. Have you come? Behold the five kings of Sodom mentioned in Holy Scripture (Gn 14), who were then under the hegemony of the Assyrian king Chedorlaomer and who were paying tribute to him and to the other kings with him for ten years. In the thirteenth year they rebelled and did not want to pay the tribute to the Assyrian king, who then declared war on them. It appeared soon afterward that the five kings were subdued and captured by the Assyrians. What happened next? When Abram heard about this, he ran to their aid; he fought, he won, and he liberated them for the sake of his nephew Lot.

What Is the Symbolic Meaning of the War at Sodom for the Senses?

The war at Sodom can be seen as an allegory on the five senses. The five kings are the five senses who up to the twelfth year of childhood enjoy the bodily pleasures and, in a sense, pay tribute to the Assyrian devil and to his three associate kings, who are the three initial and universal passions of forgetfulness, ignorance, and laziness. As soon as the mind begins to have discretion between good and evil and to understand the harm one suffers, then the five senses are checked by the mind and they no longer want to pay tribute to the enemy. That is, they do not want to give free reign to the passionate pleasure. This is why the enemy renews his attack, seeking to incite the senses to their usual pleasures, and overcomes them. Jesus, a descendent of Abraham, when called upon to help, hears and responds. He strengthens the mind through his Grace and liberates the senses from being completely overrun by the enemy. Here is how St. Neilos explained this story:

GUARDING ALL THE SENSES IN GENERAL

From this story we learn about ourselves and the war that is going on with our senses and sensible things. Each one of us from our birth to our twelfth year of age, not yet having the ability of rational discretion, allow the senses to be impressed indiscriminately by everything sensible. . . . During this time there is no intellectual power, because of the infancy, that would seek to guard any of the senses. When our intellect is made stronger and begins to understand how we are harmed, we seek to rebel and avoid such slavery. If one finds himself becoming stronger intellectually and spiritually, he will be confirmed in this realization and will remain free in all things, having escaped all bitter tyrants. But if one finds himself wanting in judgment, he will again betray his senses to captivity, being overcome by the power of the material things.[15]

It Is a Great Victory to Overcome Ourselves

Do not think for a moment that this victory is small and insignificant. In fact it is a greater victory to overcome one of your passions and a pleasure of your senses than to overcome one hundred of your enemies. It is a more glorious trophy of victory to shed willingly a few drops of perspiration and one drop of blood, for the love of God, in order to overcome one of your evil wills and to spite the devil, than to shed rivers of blood to subdue entire armies. Again it is a greater triumph to subdue your senses and your entire body to your hegemonious mind than to subdue large kingdoms. Once, when King Alexander was praised for having conquered the whole ecumene, he responded with the prudent remark: "All of my victories will prove to be vain, if I do not succeed to conquer myself." Many who have subdued their enemies, cities, and countries have later been subdued miserably by their own improper passions and have shamefully become slaves of their own passions. A certain Father was very correct when he said that "the first victory is the victory of self." St. Isidore Pelousiotes also said: The true victor is not he who subdues the foreign barbarians, but he who wages spiritual warfare against the evil passions. Many who have conquered barbarians have in turn been shamefully subdued by their own passions."[16]

GUARDING ALL THE SENSES IN GENERAL

It Is Most Important to Be Victorious in Spiritual Warfare

If you stand courageously to fight the unseen warfare against your senses and the enemy and in fighting you win, know that the angels will assist you and will crown you victor. St. Isidore has informed you of this. "Angels will assist you after the battle and will crown you with victory."[17] If you should lose heart and fall in this battle and appear to be defeated, God forbid, you will not only be the object of malignant joy to the enemy, not only will you cause sadness and shame to Christ for being deprived of heavenly crowns, but even according to human standards, you will become an insignificant person. . . . The ancient Greeks had a law that required a soldier to be without name and fame as long as his weapons did not bear the sign of a victor and his spear the blood stain of his enemies. But he who would lose his weapons was the most dejected of men. Therefore the Spartans exiled their own poet Archilohos because he simply wrote in his poems a verse which said: "It is better to be deprived of weapon than life."

Notes

1. Homily 5, On Our Father.
2. St. Basil, Homily on Virginity.
3. Homily 26.
4. On Virginity, ch. 21.
5. Homily on the Renunciation of Life.
6. Homily 44.
7. Quoted in the *Gerontikon*.
8. "Inexpressible things are expressed and ineffable things are spoken."
9. On Prayer, ch. 117.
10. Quoted in Kallistos Xanthopoulos, ch. 65.
11. Homily 11, ch. 5.
12. Ascetic Homilies quoted in the Philokalia.
13. Letter 107 to Eutonios the Deacon.
14. Quoted in the *Gerontikon*.
15. Philokalia.
16. Letter 1177 to Germanos.
17. Letter 75 to John the Hermit.

CHAPTER NINE

Guarding the Imagination

What the Imagination Is and That It Produces the Same Passion as the Senses

Because I have already commented to you about the five external senses of the body, it is proper now to also comment briefly on the internal sense of the soul, that is, the imagination. Imagination is more refined than sense perception, but more coarse than the mind and for this reason it stands between the mind and the senses, according to St. Gregory Palamas.[1] The imagination is the map of the ruling mind, about which we spoke in the beginning, and upon which everything is recorded; it is the broad board on which things are painted; it is the wax on which things are imprinted. What things? All the things that we see with our eyes; all the things we hear with our ears; all the things we smell with our noses; all the things we taste through our mouths; and all the things we touch through the general sense of touch. According to the wise Vryennios who borrowed the saying from St. Maximos, "The body's world are the external objects, and the mind's are the thoughts."[2] Aristotle called the imagination a common sense, because it alone contains all those images, all those sensations and dispositions which have entered from the outside through our five senses. He called it sense because the same passion and movement caused by all the external senses upon the soul is also caused by the imagination alone. In order to prove this [fact] many examples are brought forward by the metaphysicians, the physicians, the physicists and ethicists. I like to present my proof with this example only: Someone eats a lemon. Someone else stands by and sees him, and in seeing him he thinks that he too is tasting the sharp taste of the lemon so much so that the taste buds are affected in his own mouth. Now, what is experienced by the observer can be experienced also by someone who is not observing the phenomenon of eating a lemon, but who is affected with a strong impression through the imagination. He who imagines strongly the sensation received by the one eating a lemon imagines himself to be eating a lemon also and gradually has almost the same reaction in his mouth. There is obviously a very close interplay between the external senses and those of the imagination which are affected by both one's physical and spiritual capacities.

This is the reason why, dear friend, knowing this you must guard your external senses from passionate objects, as we said before. At the same time, however, you must also guard the internal sense, that is the imagination, and not permit it to envision and remember passionate and shameful visions seen by the eyes, or the improper words heard by the ears, or the fragrances smelled by the nose, or the rich and delicious foods tasted by the mouth, or the soft things touched by the hands. No, for what is the value of guarding the external senses and then not guarding the imagination, which possesses all the passionate impressions of the senses and causes through them the same passion and agitation to the soul? Joseph Vryennios has borrowed a quotation from St. Maximos to express this close relationship between the senses and the imagination: "As the body is capable of fornication with the body of a woman, the mind can also fornicate with the thought of the woman, through the imagination of that same body. A man imagines in his mind the form of his own body to be united with the form of the woman's body. The same is true with the other sins as well. Those things which the body does actively in the physical world, the mind also does in the world of thoughts."[3] But why do I say that you must guard the imagination as you do the external senses? Actually, we must take greater care in guarding our imagination than our senses.

How Does the Imagination Differ from the Senses?

The external senses are active only when external stimuli are present. The imagination however can open its "book" and reveal its sights and sounds, and so forth, even when the perceptible things are absent and man is alone enclosed within the walls of his home or in a far and isolated place. The imagination is a sort of very fine sense of touch, especially when a certain passion is invoked strongly. In fact it is often the imagination itself which prompts the external senses to enjoy some imagined passion and thus exercises a sort of influence over them. The imagination being itself a more refined sense than the external senses, as we said before, is consequently more rapid in movement, being able in a flash to impress and fashion passionate images of sin, and at the same time to attract the heart to consent. This is why greater care is needed to guard the imagination. St. Maximos said: "To sin in thought is so much easier than to sin in deed, as to wage war indeed is so much more difficult than to do so in thought."[4] St. Basil also spoke about this when interpreting the passage in Job 2:5: "For Job said, 'It may be that my sons have sinned, and cursed God in their hearts.' " "The just Job was reasonable in considering the possibility and praying for hidden sin, since men have a tendency to readily fall into the sins of the mind. The activities of the body require both time and opportunity and toil as well as other persons to cooperate. The activities of the mind, however, are enacted in an instant, without toil, without burden and every time for them is appropriate to act."[5] The imagination has a certain natural attribute and all the impressions it receives from the senses it wants to make them all visible so that it can see, as St. Gregory Palamas has noted.[6]

For example, you hear, "Martha, Sophia." These are two simple sounds which have struck your eardrums and you have heard them. The imagination is not content to hear them as simple sounds, so it proceeds to fashion even the images of Martha and Sophia, thereby creating greater agitation and passionate pleasure in the soul. By the same token when you hear "kingdom of heaven" or "hell" or anything else that you have not actually seen before, you undergo a certain effort through the imagination to give them some visual form or image. Generally speaking, as we said in the chapter on sight above, the sense of sight sees things substantially; the imagination similarly makes visible what is imagined and in a sense represents them substantially. This is why imagination instigates a more serious war and a greater agitation. These then are the two natural consequences which follow one after the other: Namely, the effort one makes to imagine an object that is absent is the same effort one makes when it is present physically. Conversely, the less one tries to imagine a thing, the less one tries when it is physically present. Oftentimes the senses receive sense perceptions of things and simply leave them without curiosity. Later when one returns home, the imagination then remembers and describes with curiosity whatever the senses saw or heard or spoke in passing, and thus creates a greater war and agitation to the soul. The imagination, as soon as it receives and records the image of a beautiful person, can only with great difficulty wipe out that image, as we have noted in the chapter on sight. "The things we have suffered are the things we carry around with us through their passionate imaginations," as St. Maximos wrote.[7] What is very strange is that we often imagine that person to be dead, while other times we touch with our hands the lifeless skull and the bones and yet our foolish and unreasonable imagination does not want to remember it as dead. It holds on to that first image that was impressed on the mind when that person was alive and does not cease to trouble us with it. And this can happen when we are awake or when we are sleeping. Also, the imagination not only records things, that is, receives images of things seen, but also recalls those images that have been forgotten, fashions other images on its own which it substitutes for others by adding or subtracting or changing. Thus it can change insignificant images insignificantly, both when we are awake and when we are asleep through our dreams, in which dreams, I suggest, you never believe. It is written: "For dreams have deceived many, and those who put their hope in them have failed" (Sir 34:7).

From this we conclude that passionate imagination has greater power and authority over man than the senses themselves. Once someone is overcome by a passionate imagination he becomes altogether subservient to that imagination. Thus he may not be able to see even though he has the sense of sight; he may not hear even though he can hear; neither can he smell or touch. Having all his sense organs open, he appears to have them closed and totally inactive.

The Devil Is Greatly Related to the Imagination and for This Reason Uses It as an Organ of Deception

The devil has a very close relationship and familiarity with the imagination, and of all the powers of the soul he has this one as the most appropriate organ to deceive man and to activate his passions and evils. He indeed is very familiar with the nature of the imagination. For he, being created by God originally as a pure and simple mind without form and image, as the other divine angels, later came to love the forms and the imagination. Imagining that he could set his throne above the heavens and become like God, he fell from being an angel of light and became a devil of darkness. St. Dionysios spoke about this devil: "What is the evil in the devils? Irrational anger; unreasonable desire;

149

and reckless imagination."[8] St. Gregory Sinaite also wrote: "The devils were originally minds who fell from that immateriality and refinement and each of them received a certain material thickness."[9] The devil uses the imagination as his organ. He deceived Adam through the imagination and raised up to his mind the fantasy of being equal with God. Before the disobedience Adam did not have the imaginative attribute, as St. Maximos noted:

> In the beginning, passion and pain were not created together with the body; nor forgetfulness and ignorance together with the soul; nor the ever changing impressions in the shape of events with the mind. All these things were brought about in man by his disobedience. He who would remove passion and suffering from the body achieves practical virtue; he who would remove forgetfulness and ignorance from the soul has properly attained the natural vision; and he who would release the mind of the many impressions, has acquired the mystery of theology. For the mind of Adam at first was not impressed by the imagination, which stands between the mind and the thoughts, setting up a wall around the mind and not allowing it to enter into the most simple and imageless reasons of created beings. The passionate physical perceptions of the visible things are scales that cover over the clairvoyance of the soul and prevent its passage over to the authentic word of truth.[10]

Adam, however, was able at first to be attached to the thoughts of the mind and to enter into them without the intermediary of the imagination.

The Lord Did Not Have Imaginations

The new Adam, our Lord, did not have imaginations, according to the theologians. One of them, Georgios Koresios, wrote in his theological treatise on the Incarnation: "The Lord deserved merit not for his blessed vision and knowledge and the love that flowed from it, but for the knowledge that was poured upon him from God, and which was always active in Christ voluntarily and never interrupted by sleep or any other cause, as it happens in the mind of other men. The mind of

Christ was completely independent of the imaginations which become a wall blocking our penetration into the immaterial realities of the spirit." Not only Adam but most persons who have ever fallen into sin and deceptions, into irrational superstitions and heresies and evil and corrupt doctrines, have all been deceived through the imagination. This is the reason why the holy Fathers call the devil a pantomime and an ancient painter, as we have seen especially in St. Chrysostom.[11] St. Maximos has noted that the devils deceive men not only when awake but also when they are sleeping, by inciting them with the passions of the body through the imagination. This imagination is considered by the Fathers to be a bridge of the devils. St. Kallistos has written: "Imagination is like a multiform and many-head monster similar to the mythical Daedalos and Hydra, which the devil utilizes as a sort of bridge, as the saints have previously noted. These murderous villains communicate and unite themselves with the soul, making it into a hive of parasites, a place of passionate and fruitless thoughts."[12] St. Gregory the Theologian said that imagination is the cause of both the consent and the act of sin. Do you see now, dear friend, how many evil things imagination brings about? I beseech you therefore, to guard your imagination as much as you possibly can so that no images harmful to the soul are impressed upon it, as they seek to enter through the senses. And if they have already entered, seek not to compromise with them or to give your consent in your heart, but run directly to God through prayer of the heart, which we are going to discuss in the following chapter. St. Syngletike has noted: "It is important not to give your consent to the imaginations. For it is written that if the spirit of the devil arises in you, do not leave the place of your heart, for such a consent is tantamount to worldly fornication" (cf. Eccl 10:4).[13]

How Should Imagination Be Used and That We Will Be Judged by the Images Imprinted Upon It

I have referred to images harmful to the soul because there are other images which are permissible, as St. Kallistos noted. Such images include the contrition, the grief, and the humility of the heart; the meditations upon death, the future judgment, and the eternal punishments; the study and meditation upon creation and the Incarnation of the Lord; the phenomena of creation, the miracles, and the mysteries of the Lord's Incarnation—the birth, the baptism, the crucifixion, the

151

burial, the resurrection, and so forth, as we said before. Finally, it is permissible, when fighting against certain inappropriate and evil imaginations presented by the enemy, to use other appropriate and virtuous imaginations. Do not pay any attention to the shameful and fearful images of the foolish and irrational imagination and do not be frightened by them. Ignore them and consider them unworthy of your attention. They are empty playthings without any true substance. He who is used to ignoring the imaginations can also ignore the real things themselves that are depicted in the imaginations, as St. Maximos has noted: "He who conquers over the passionate fantasies will also be able to prevail over the realities they represent."[14] Let me conclude this chapter and summarize what I have been saying. Know that if you impress upon the board and chart of your imagination beautiful and appropriate images, you will be praised on the day of judgment, when what each person imagines secretly will be revealed. But if you allow inappropriate and evil images to be recorded and to dwell in your imagination, you will then be condemned, as St. Basil has noted.[15]

Notes

1. Physical Chapters, ch. 27.
2. Third Century, ch. 53.
3. Third Century on Love, ch. 53.
4. First Century on Love, ch. 63.
5. Homily on Guard Thyself.
6. Physical Chapters, ch. 6.
7. First Century on Love, ch. 63.
8. Divine Names, ch. 4.
9. St. Gregory the Sinaite, ch. 123.
10. Second Century of Theology, ch. 75.
11. Homily on Prayer.
12. Philokalia, ch. 64.
13. Quoted in the Biography of St. Syngletike.
14. The Centuries on Love, ch. 63.
15. Homily on Virginity.

CHAPTER TEN

Guarding the Mind
and the Heart

*One Must Guard His Heart from Evil Thoughts More Than His
Senses from Harmful Objects*

Have you learned how to guard your external senses? Have you
learned to guard also the internal and common sense of the imagination? Learn now also how to guard your heart from evil passions and
thoughts. The heart is the mystical and hidden chamber of the mind
or, in other words, the soul, as we said in the beginning. For, as St.
Syngletike said, a ship can sink for two reasons: externally by the
waves of the sea, or internally by the failure of the pumps. Thus the
soul, too, can be harmed from without through physical things and
from within through evil thoughts and desires that rise up in the heart.
This is the reason we must guard our senses from hedonistic and
harmful objects, as well as our heart from evil thoughts and passions. It
is therefore necessary to be vigilant and to guard both, for both of these
may become our downfall. However, one must be more vigilant to
guard his heart from evil thoughts and passions than to guard his
senses from external harmful influences. For if we neglect our evil
thoughts, they will become our downfall and perdition, much like the
ship that suddenly finds itself sinking at a time of calm seas when the
sailors are sleeping, because they neglected to man the pumps. We
must therefore keep in mind that as the center of a wagon wheel has a
certain number of spokes going out to the circumference of the circle
and returning to the center where they meet, so also is the heart of man
like a center where all the senses, all the powers of the body, and all the
activities of the soul are united. The heart is a center that has three
aspects: It is a natural, a supernatural, and a para-natural center.

153

GUARDING THE MIND AND THE HEART

The Heart Is a Natural Center, and the Essence of the Soul Is to Be Found in the Heart

The heart is a natural center. Of all the members of the body, it is the heart that is fashioned first. St. Basil said: "In the creation of animals the heart is the first to be founded by nature in accordance with the animal that must be analogous to it."[1] Thus the physicians too are of the common opinion that the heart lies at the center of the chest with a slight inclination toward the left side. Thus we can say that the heart, because of the sense itself and the central place where it is found, holds a key position in relation to the whole body. For this reason it is not only the first to be created of all the members, but it is also the last of the organs to die. The heart is the seat, the root, the beginning, and the source of all the physical energies of the body—generation, nurture, growth, life, sensation, emotion, desire, and the others. Also the heart is the center of all the natural energies of the soul—thought, reason, and will. Therefore the essence of the soul as the inner form of the body may not be contained as if in a vessel, since it is bodiless; and yet the soul, as in an organ or carriage, is found at the very core of the heart and at the very core of the most sincere and most pure spirit that intercedes between the body and the mind. Thus the essence and the power of the mind, that is the soul, is not found in the brain as an organ. Only the energy of the mind is found in the brain, as we said at first, (and never mind the newer physicists and metaphysicists who argue that the essence of the soul is found in the brain). To say this is the same as to say that the soul of growth is not originally in the root of the tree but in the branch and the fruit. The teaching of Sacred Scripture and the holy Fathers is truer than the teaching of men.

One of the newer moral philosophers has expressed excellently this position of the heart: The heart as the first of the organs and root of life is also the organ of desire and the interpreter of passions and emotions, because of its marvelous activities. The ocean has received from nature a moderate and appropriate flow, called high and low tide, providing a rest for the ocean as it flows back and forth, like a baby in a cradle. But if this ocean is blown by the cold north wind or by the warm south wind, it is no longer contained within itself, but comes and goes, sometimes rising high toward heaven and sometimes lowering itself to the abyss. The same divine providence has given to the heart a sort of perpetual and physical motion appropriate to the nature of man that is extended and contracted by innumerable measures to inter-

154

change the breathing and to distribute the vital spirits to the whole body. Now, if the heart is troubled by the winds of passions, then by a paradoxical extension or contraction, changing the analogy of physical movement, it changes the emotions. The changes of the heart are as many as are the passions. It is obvious that the soul is moved first by thought and then the heart by the soul. The first is a physical movement, the second a moral one. It would be a most desirable sight to be able to look through a crystal and to see through the chest the movements of the heart as we see those of a clock. If the understanding accepts some subject as lovable, the heart as a whole extends itself and rushes forward to receive it. But if a subject is hated, the heart again is all contracted, drawn back, and appears to be going away. In utter joy the heart rejoices and jumps. In sadness and grief, the heart is withdrawn and apparently closed. In anger the heart is agitated and pumps the blood quickly. In fear, it is choked, struggling, and trembling. The smallest part of the ship is the rudder, but every small movement of the rudder causes the whole ship to turn on a wide circle left or right. Similarly every small movement of the heart, situated at the center, can cause great movements throughout the periphery of the human body: those sweet smiles and tight embraces which one does in answer to a beloved friend; the expression of abhorrence and turning away from something that is undesirable and abominable; the clapping of hands and the jumping up and down when one is pleased; the expression of sighs and laments when one is grieved; the burning sensation in the face; the turning of the eyes and the biting of the teeth in anger; the cold paleness and the terror of fear—all of these are external results of the internal movements of the heart: small at the center but great at the outer perimeter.

The Heart Is a Supernatural Center

The heart is also a supernatural center. The supernatural grace of God which we have received through holy baptism is found in the heart—its seat and throne. Sacred Scripture is the first witness of this. For the Lord has said: "The kingdom of God is within you" (Lk 17:11). St. Paul said: "God's love has been poured into our hearts through the Holy Spirit which has been given to us" (Rom 5:5). Again he said: "God has sent the Spirit of his Son into our hearts, crying, 'Abba! Father!' " (Gal 4:6). Elsewhere he said: "That according to the riches of his glory he may grant you to be strengthened with might through his Spirit in the inner man, and that Christ may dwell in your hearts through faith" (Eph 3:16). The holy Fathers agree with the Holy Scripture. St. Macarios said: "The heart affects the whole organism, and as soon as grace enters the place of the heart, it rules over all the members and the thoughts, for the mind and all the thoughts of the soul are there."[2] St. Isaac wrote: "If you are pure, behold heaven is within you; and you will see in yourself the angels and their light and their Master with them."[3] Elsewhere St. Isaac wrote: "Seek to enter into your inner chamber and you will see the heavenly chamber, they are one and the same."[4] St. Diadochos also said: "I have learned from Sacred Scripture and from the mind of perception that before holy baptism grace prompts the soul to good externally, while Satan lies hidden in its depths. But at the hour of our rebirth in holy baptism, the devil is banished from our soul while grace enters."[5] St. Gregory Palamas, interpreting a saying of St. Macarios: "It is necessary to look *there* to see if the grace of the Spirit has written any laws," asked, "Where is *there*?" And he answered: "In the leading organ, in the throne of grace where the mind and all the thoughts of the soul are present, in the heart, of course." This is the universal confession of all the Fathers and especially of the *neptic* Fathers.

The Heart Is a Para-natural Center

The heart is also a para-natural, that is, an unnatural center. All the unnatural passions, all the blasphemous, proud, shameful, and evil thoughts and all the evil passions, tendencies, appetites, attempts, and consents that we have come to receive from the things of the world are born in the heart and are to be found there. All of these evils can cover over the divine grace which we received at Holy Baptism, much like the ashes covering the spark of fire, as St. Kallistos has noted. There in the heart are the roots and origins of all the unnatural sins, which we have committed after Holy Baptism, through evil thoughts and deeds and which we even now do and desire to do. There in the heart is also Satan, even though he is not at its core (for divine grace is at the core as St. Diadochos said above). Nevertheless, Satan is at the surface of the heart and simply around the heart, as again St. Diadochos has noted, smoking up the mind through the dampness of the body and the desires and pleasures of the flesh. Thus he is able to project, through the inner reasoning that is naturally spoken in the heart, all the passionate and improper thoughts. This situation is confirmed by Sacred Scripture. The Creator of the hearts has taught us to know: "For out of the heart come evil thoughts, murder, adultery, fornication, theft, false witness, slander. These are what defile a man" (Mt 15:19). Again another passage: "When the unclean spirit has gone out of a man, he passes through waterless places seeking rest, but he finds none. Then he says, 'I will return to my house from which I came.' And when he comes, he finds it empty, swept, and put in order. Then he goes and brings with him seven other spirits more evil than himself, and they enter and dwell there; and the last state of that man becomes worse than the first" (Mt 12:43–45).

Do you hear? "They enter and dwell . . ." Where? In the heart, of course, in the inner man. The tradition of the holy Fathers confirms this word of Scripture. St. Gregory the Theologian wrote in his Homily on Baptism and in his heroic elegies: "You came to me again, O deceiver, as you planned, grazing within the depths of my heart."[6] St. Basil too wrote: "We must first of all consider it a blessing to be pure in thought. The reason is that the root of the activities of the body is the will of the heart. For the sin of adultery begins to burn first in the soul of the hedonist and then the corruption of the body is brought about. Therefore the Lord warned us that the things which defile us come from within."[7] St. John Chrysostom and generally all the Fathers agree in their interpretation of this passage from Scripture. Especially significant is the comment of St. Macarios about guarding the heart: "Enter by controlling your thoughts into your mind that is a captive and a slave of sin; detect there him who is lower than mind and deeper than your thoughts, in the so-called chambers of your soul; see there the cowering serpent that has brought death to your most vital members. The heart is indeed an incomprehensible abyss. Only when you succeed in killing this demon in your heart can you dare to take pride in being pure before God. Otherwise, humble yourself as wanting and sinful and pray to God for your hidden sins."[8]

In What Way Does the Mind Return to the Heart and That This Return Is Not a Deception?

In addition to everything that has been said, let me also say that you must guard your mind, that is, the activity of the mind, and your heart. You know that every essential activity has a natural relation with

157

the essence and power that activates it. Naturally, it returns to it, is united to it, and finds rest in it. For this reason, you too, must do this because you have liberated the activity of your mind and of all the external things of the world by guarding your senses and your imagination, as we have already noted. Now it is necessary to return this activity to your own essence and power, that is, to return your mind to your heart, which is the organ (and the center) of the essence and power of the mind, and thus to review spiritually the whole of the inner man. This return of the mind in the beginner is usually done, as the holy Fathers teach, with the bending of the head so that the chin is touching the chest. This spiritual meditation is referred to by St. Dionysios Areopagites, who mentions three forms: the direct, the spiral, and finally the circular, which alone is certain and without deception. It is referred to as the circular meditation because as the periphery of the circle returns to itself and is united, so also in this circular movement the mind returns to itself and becomes one. St. Dionysios noted: "The movement of the soul is circular; leaving the externals, it enters into itself and unites its spiritual powers in a circular movement that provides a gift of truth."[9] St. Basil also noted: "A mind that is not distracted toward the externals, nor is scattered by the senses to the world, returns to itself and through itself rises to the understanding of God."[10] St. Gregory Palamas has noted that it is possible for deception to enter the direct and spiral meditations, but not into the circular meditation.[11] Direct meditation is the activity of the mind based on external perceptions that raise the mind to a simple intellectual activity. Spiral meditation occurs when the mind is illumined by divine knowledge, not entirely spiritually and apophatically, but rather intellectually and cataphatically, combining direct and some circular meditation. Therefore, those who love to meditate without deception must occupy themselves more with the circular meditation of the mind, which is accomplished by the return of the mind to the heart and the spiritual prayer of the heart. The more this prayer is difficult and painful the more fruitful it becomes because it is free of deception. This is the most important, the most sublime activity of the mind. This sublime meditation, this prayer of the heart, unites the mind with God; it purifies, illumines, and perfects the mind much more than all the algebra, all the physical and metaphysical and all the other sciences of secular philosophy. This prayer of the heart makes man spiritual and a seer of God, but those other intellectual disciplines make him only a natural (ψυχικός) man. "The unspiritual (natural) man does not receive the gifts of the Spirit of God, for they are folly to him" (1 Cor 2:14).

Man is not made worthy of this purity and this illumination and perfection by simply meditating briefly in this circular way from the mind to the heart. One must practice this prayer for a long time; it is only then that it reveals the ineffable mysteries of God, as St. Gregory Palamas wrote.[12] Man must humble himself, retire in silence, and cut himself off from everything that will cause agitation and obstruction to his prayer. But even then he must leave everything to God. If God considers it advantageous to offer spiritual graces, all well and good. But if not, we must continue to do our work, which is this return of the mind to the heart, this vigilance and this most spiritual prayer. We must be careful not to be overcome by a desire for spiritual gifts and allow deception to enter instead of truth. Above all one must keep even in this spiritual activity "a perfect measure" without excess or want.

When the Mind Is in the Heart It Must Be Praying

When your mind is in the heart it should not simply be there. Having discovered reason, that is, the inner reason of the heart through which we can reason intuitively to ourselves, composing, judging, analyzing, and reading whole books mystically, without ever saying a single word with the mouth, then, let the mind not say anything else except the short prayer of the heart: "Lord Jesus Christ Son of God, have mercy on me." But it is not enough to do this only: It is necessary also to overcome the willpower of the soul so that the prayer is said with all of your will and power and love. Let me say it more clearly. Let your inner understanding say only the Jesus Prayer; let your mind pay attention through its spiritual vision and hearing to the words of the prayer only and especially to the meaning of the words, without any forms or shapes and without imagining any other perceptible or intelligible thing internal or external, even if it is good. Because God transcends all beings both visible and invisible, the human mind seeking to be united with him through prayer must go out of all beings that are perceptible or intelligible in order to achieve this divine union. Therefore, as St. Neilos said: "While you are praying do not attempt to give shape to the divine, nor allow any image to be impressed upon your mind, but approach the spiritual spiritually and you shall understand."[13] At the same time have your will join itself through love to the same words of the prayer. Thus the mind, the inner reason, and your will—these three aspects of your soul—will be one and the one three, so that in this way man, who is an image of the Holy Trinity, is united with the prototype, as St. Gregory Palamas, that great teacher of spiritual prayer and vision, has taught us. "When the unity of the mind is made triune, while remaining unified, then it is attached to the divine principle of the triune monad and excludes every entry of deception, transcending thus the flesh, the world and the ruler of this world."[14]

Why One Needs to Control His Breath in Prayer

The mind, the activity of the mind, is used from a very early age to be scattered toward the external physical things of the world. For this reason when you say this sacred prayer do not breathe continually as is natural to our nature, but hold your breath until your inner consciousness has a chance to say the prayer once. Then let your breath out, as the holy Fathers have taught us. By holding your breath even for this short interval the heart is pressed and troubled and feels pain for not receiving natural oxygen. The mind on the other hand is much more readily controlled to return to the heart, both because of the pain and suffering of the heart but also because of the pleasure that is created from this warm and vivid memory of God. When God is remembered a pleasure and a gladness is experienced by the one who remembers, as the psalmist said: "I remembered God and was made glad" (Ps 77:3–LXX). Where there is a sense of pain and suffering there the mind is summoned to return, according to the philosopher Aristotle. By holding the breath, the usually hard and thick heart is somewhat refined and warmed through this slight suffering. Consequently it becomes soft, sensitive, humble, and more capable of contrition and tears. At the same time the mind becomes more refined and its activity is more refined, more clear and more capable of a supernatural illumination from God. When the breathing is interrupted, the heart feels pain. Through this pain the heart expels the poisonously baited hook of pleasure and sin, which had been previously swallowed, and thus you have the therapy of action and reaction, according to the physicians. This is why St. Mark said that "the memory of God is a pain to the heart [that is done] for the sake of piety; everyone who forgets God experiences sweetness but remains unhealed."[15] Again he said, "The mind that prays without distractions grieves the heart; a broken and humble heart God will not despise."[16] This controlling of the breathing also unites all the powers of the soul to return to the mind and through the mind to God, which is the marvelous thing. Thus man offers to God the whole of the visible and invisible creation of which he is the link and the arena of both, according to St. Gregory of Thessaloniki.[17]

I said above that the beginners especially have need of this momentary control of breathing when they pray. Those who are already advanced in this spiritual activity can enter the heart and remain there without the control of breathing but only through the inner consciousness. Nevertheless, even these when they want to return the mind into the heart more earnestly (and especially at a time of war with thoughts and passions) and through this return to pray in a more unified way, they do this by controlling momentarily their breathing (cf. 1 Kgs 18:42—Prophet Elijah praying on Mt. Carmel). Such then in brief is the remarkable prayer of the heart of the holy Fathers, and if you desire to know more about it, read in the Philokalia the Homily of St. Nikephoros, the discourses of St. Gregory Palamas in defense of the Hesychasts, and the hundred chapters of Kallistos and Ignatios Xanthopoulos, as well as the writings of St. Gregory Sinaite. I advise you fervently then to preoccupy yourself with this prayer of the heart as a permanent and ceaseless activity together with the other seven-part service of prayer, which you read daily according to the ancient practice of the Church. In doing so you will be speaking in your heart through your inner consciousness the sweet name of Jesus that is so beloved by the people and by all. You will be contemplating Jesus through your mind. You will be desiring and loving Jesus through your will. You will be returning all the powers of your soul to Jesus and from him will be seeking mercy and contrition and humility. If however you are not always able to find time for this because of your concerns in the world and the many disturbances, you should at least set aside one or two hours especially at night when you can remove yourself to a quiet and dark place for this sacred and spiritual activity. I assure you that you will enjoy many benefits from such prayer and will reap an abundant harvest. Listen now to what are, in brief, the fruits of this prayer of the heart.

GUARDING THE MIND AND THE HEART

The Fruits of Spiritual Prayer

1. These are the fruits of this spiritual work, when the mind becomes accustomed to remaining in the heart and away from the beautiful things of this world, avoiding and hating the physical pleasures of the senses. St. Diadochos said: "He who remains always in his heart avoids all the beautiful things of the world, and living in the spirit he cannot experience the desires of the flesh."[18] Similarly, such a person also avoids the delusion of the imagination that activates evil and shameful thoughts. By lowering quietly his activity, bare and refined, down to the inner consciousness of the heart, he dismantles every heavy idol or image of the imagination, on account of the narrowness of the place of the heart, just as the serpent sheds his old skin when it passes through a narrow passage. In fact when the mind becomes accustomed to remaining in the heart, it not only loves to close the door of its cell and to remain quietly; it not only loves to close the door of its mouth and remain silently; it also uses its authority to close even the door of the inner consciousness so that it does not permit evil spirits and devils to speak through it those evil and sinful thoughts that they do desire to impose upon us. For it is through such evil thoughts that man becomes impure before God, who discerns the hearts and inner life of men. Thus St. John Climacus wrote: "Close the cell-door to the body, the door of the tongue to talking and the inner gate to the (evil) spirits."[19]

2. When the mind enters the heart and sees there spiritually with the eyes of the soul the ugly and shameful form with which it is covered, and the despicable mask it has put on from the improper visions which it has looked upon, and the shameful hearing which it has heard and simply from the baser activity of the senses and the world, then it acquires humility, sorrow, and tears. And as St. Mark noted, how can one not be so humbled after seeing the whole place of his heart so darkened and clouded with a thick and deep darkness brought about by the sins committed by word, deed, and thought?[20] How can the poor man not grieve and be sad, seeing his consciousness so filled with pride and with so many irrational, blasphemous, and satanic thoughts? How can he not shed tears, the miserable one, seeing his soul or will so captivated by so many shameful and evil thoughts and by so many undisciplined passions against the neighbor? And, in a word, how can he not feel contrition and shed tears of blood? Or how

can he not in his misery cry out to Jesus to show mercy upon him and to heal him? Does he not see his heart enslaved and tied down by so many passions? Is it not hardened by a rocklike insensitivity and by so many wounds? Does he not see the whole inner man, not as the temple of God and of grace, but as a den of thieves and a workshop of sin and the devils? Therefore through this humiliation, this sorrow and tears, God shows compassion for him and comforts him from the onslaught of the passions and liberates him from the attacks of devils and devilish thoughts.

3. This return of the mind to the heart and its firm abode there to contemplate and to guard itself in maintaining spiritual prayer becomes a clear mirror, as St. Kallistos said, for the mind to see therein the evil tendencies of his heart, the evil movements of his thoughts, the attacks and robberies and ambushes of the evil spirits. There man can simply see all his faults, even the most insignificant. Thus he can call upon Jesus to help him, to forgive him; he repents, he grieves, he prostrates himself, he adds sorrow to sorrow, humility to humility, and does everything he possibly can to correct himself and to sin no more. This is the reason why St. John Climacus wrote about this type of prayer: "Your prayer will reveal to you your [spiritual] condition, for it is called the mirror of the monks by the theologians."[21]

4. Another fruit is the purity of nature and through this purity of nature the given supernatural activity of divine grace of the Holy Spirit. For as the holy Fathers discovered natural organs, manners, and methods in the use of fasting, of vigils, of sleeping on the ground, of prostrations, of obeisances, of self-control and the rest of the deprivations and hardships imposed upon the body, in order to purify the human nature from the passions which entered it against nature, they also by the same token discovered this natural method of returning the mind to the heart in order to purify somewhat more readily and more quickly the mind and the heart. These, of course, are not only the most important organs of man, but also the most vulnerable to evil and capable of attracting all the other members of the body to sin. Thus through the mind and the heart the human nature as a whole is purified of the evil passions and made capable of receiving the supernatural grace and activity of God. This method of prayer purifies our nature faster, because the very work and the subject matter with which it is preoccupied is the first, catholic, and most comprehensive commandment of all: for man to love God with all of his soul, all of his heart, all

of his power, and all of his mind. Through this commandment especially, (but through the others also) man receives the supernatural
grace of God.

In guarding the heart and keeping it pure, one can also keep all the
divine commandments of Christ. For in truth this is how it is. The
guarding of the mind and the heart and the spiritual prayer of the heart
that is thus made possible has as its subject matter the commandment
to love God. But by virtue of the power of this one commandment all
of the other commandments are also included and fulfilled. This is
why the Lord said: "If you love me, you will keep my commandments"
(Jn 14:15). It is obvious that because the commandment to love God is
the first, the most universal, and the most comprehensive, he who
keeps it well will also keep all the other commandments included in it.
For in the love of God is also included the love of neighbor: "He who
loves God should love his brother, also" (1 Jn 4:21). Again, in the love
of neighbor all the other more particular commandments are included
and recapitulated, as St. Paul wrote: "Owe no one anything, except to
love one another; for he who loves his neighbor has fulfilled the law.
The commandments 'You shall not commit adultery, you shall not kill,
you shall not steal, you shall not covet,' and any other commandments,
are summed up in this sentence, 'You shall love your neighbor as
yourself' " (Rom 13:8–9). Even though there are many commandments, they are all recapitulated in the one word to love the Lord God
with all of your strength and your neighbor as yourself. He who
struggles and keeps this word of God also keeps all the other commandments of God.

5. When the mind of a person becomes accustomed to entering
the heart, to converse with his inner consciousness and to find his will
and to contemplate upon himself and all his activities, it does not
remain without joy and gladness. Thus, as when a person who has
been away from home rejoices to return and to see his wife and his
children, so also the mind rejoices to return to the heart. Leaving all
the other benefits and the supernatural gifts which a person receives
from this spiritual return of the mind to the heart and the prayer of the
heart, I come now directly to the main purpose and say this only:
Dearest friend, through this spiritual prayer of the heart you can guard
your mind and your heart, if not completely pure and dispassionate—
for this is very difficult to achieve in the world—[not to mention that
this is also difficult in the desert and in silence because of the evil and
the laxity of our generation, as St. John Climacus noted] at least you

can guard them to be in the least passionate and as much as possible pure. God has given us such a commandment to guard our heart from the evil passions and the evil thoughts which rise in our mind. "Take heed lest there be a base thought in your heart" (Dt 15:9). Solomon also wrote: "Keep your heart with all vigilance; for from it flow the springs of life" (Prv 4:23).

Why We Must Guard Our Heart

Why does Solomon insist with such great emphasis: "Keep your heart with all vigilance." As we said, the heart is the center of all the senses. (These senses considered externally are five and different, but considered internally in the heart the five become one unified sense, according to St. Diadochos.[22] By the same token, the lines in a circle when seen outside the center appear to be many and separate, but when they are observed at the center they all appear to be one.) The heart is also the center of all the powers of the soul and of the body. It is therefore difficult, rather impossible, for this heart to be cleansed unless all the other senses and powers of the soul (and body) are cleansed. For if one sense only or one power of the soul is polluted, the pollution is sent directly to the heart, just as each spoke in a wheel goes directly to the center. When the heart is polluted, the pollution is transmitted and divided into all the other senses and powers of the soul, as the wise St. Gregory Palamas has noted in his treatise on prayer.

St. Isaac has taught us that, while the mind is easily cleansed, it can also be easily polluted; the heart however as it is cleansed with great difficulty it is also difficult to be polluted: "The purity of the mind is one thing, but another of the heart. The mind is one of the senses of the soul, and if one attempts diligently to study Sacred Scripture or to struggle a little in fasting and vigils, his mind will be cleansed. . . . But since it is easily cleansed it is also easily polluted. The heart contains and holds the inner senses and is the root. If the root is holy so are the branches holy. That is, if the heart is purified, it is obvious that all the senses will also be pure. Once the heart is purified, it is not easily polluted again by small things."[23] For all these reasons then, it is necessary to guard the heart so that it is not polluted by evil thoughts and consents to sin which would attack it either by the external senses or by the inner thoughts and activities of the soul. For as the antlers of deer or other chemical substances when burned can cause snakes to flee from a place, so also must the guarding of the heart banish evil thoughts and passions from it by the fragrant incense of spiritual prayer. St. Syngletike reminded us of this constant vigilance: "It is necessary constantly to clean out the house and to see that nothing harmful to the soul penetrates into the chambers of the soul, by censing these places with the divine incense of prayer. For as poisonous creatures are sent away by certain other strong poisons, so also are evil thoughts banished by prayer and fasting."[24]

Through Spiritual Prayer We Find the Hidden Grace in the Heart

If you guard your heart to be pure, knowing, as we said, that it is the center of the supernatural, the natural, and the unnatural, it is obvious that through this guarding of the heart you will also guard there the good things and virtues of nature. Also you will obviously protect yourself from other unnatural and evil influences. In time and with the help of sweetest Jesus who will be constantly remembered and found in your heart, you will rise up to the level of the supernatural. By rising up through this spiritual work and by removing the dirt and the ashes of evil passions and thoughts and superstitions from your heart, which contains within itself the covered spark of the supernatural grace of God, you will also find this very spark which Christ came to light upon the earth of the heart. And when you do discover this most precious spark in your heart you will experience an ineffable joy and this joy will cause you to shed tears of great sweetness. Afterward, by placing over this spark as kindling the work of the life-giving commandments of the Lord and the various other acquired virtues, and by blowing upon them with fervent willingness and love, you will light up a strange and supernatural fire in your heart. Rather it will be Jesus whom you remember who will light this fire, and who will burn up with His warmth the evil passions and the demons that attack you, banish the insults of evil thoughts, and sweeten the whole inner disposition of your heart—granting you joy, peace, love for God, and love for your neighbor. "A devouring fire is the Lord your God" (Dt 9:3), who destroys matter and evil habits, who enlightens your mind with his light and fills it with the light of knowledge and discretion. Thus through this spiritual work you will establish the whole of your inner self to be a temple and a dwelling place of the Holy Spirit, while your heart especially will be a holy altar, a sacred sanctuary. Your mind, moreover, will be a priest; your will and disposition will be a sacrifice; your prayer of the heart to God will be an offering of spiritual fragrance, as St. Basil used to say. May our most beloved Jesus make us worthy of such graces—first all those who read this book of spiritual counsels and finally the one who is writing it.

This is why again I beseech you not to neglect this beneficial to the soul and salutary work. Abandon constantly going out and the many companionships and the untimely conversations. Remain quietly in your home and preoccupy yourself with this return of your mind to your heart, as St. Isaac has instructed us. "We must insist and persist monastically and with simplicity toward our inner self where there are no impressions of thoughts nor visions of composite things."[25] Visit therefore frequently your inner temple that is holy unto God, as David desired to do by visiting God's temple: "O Lord, I love the habitation of thy house, and the place where thy glory dwells" (Ps 26:8). Banish out of this holy temple every evil passion and thought, as the Lord banished out of the sacred temple of God all the sacrilegious merchants. Such passions and evil thoughts pollute the heart and the temple of God in the heart and deprive us of the grace of God. As Solomon said: "For perverse thoughts separate men from God" (Wis 1:3). And again, "The thoughts of the wicked are an abomination to the Lord" (Prv 15:26). The Lord himself alluded to this when he expelled the merchants from the temple: "My house shall be called a place of prayer; but you make it a den of robbers" (Mt 21:13). No doubt you will have to make a certain amount of effort in the beginning, but afterward when you become used to it and taste of the spiritual sweetness you will receive great comfort.

The Mind Has the Natural Attribute to Find Rest in the Heart

Everybody finds calm and rest at their center. As snails find rest within their crusty shell, as octopus in their chamber, as four-footed land animals in their dens, and as birds in their nests, so also with man, whose mind has the natural attribute to be calm, to find rest and to be in peace when it enters the heart and the inner man. Man too has the body as a region and a dwelling, and the heart as its own center and room for resting. St. Isaac called the heart "the house of understanding."[26] And as the animals when troubled and frightened run to their dens to be protected, so also the mind of man, when troubled by some assault of evil thoughts or some other internal or external circumstance, runs to the heart and shouts, "My Jesus help me! My Jesus save me!" and is thus liberated. St. John Climacus said: "The name of Jesus chastises enemies" and "Let the memory of Jesus be united with your breathing and then you will know the benefit of silence."[27] The Apostle Peter preached: "And there is salvation in no one else [except Jesus], for there is no other name under heaven given among men by which we must be saved" (Acts 4:12). This is why St. Macarios also noted: "For as it is not possible for the eye to see without light and for speech to be made without a tongue, or for hearing to take place without an ear, so also it is not possible without Christ to be saved and to enter the kingdom of heaven."[28]

But even if you acquire no other benefit from this spiritual return of the mind into the heart, you will in the very least acquire a knowledge of your sins and your illness. With this knowledge you can be humble and can repent before God. This is why St. Isaac said: "A man who comes to know the extent of his illness has also attained the perfection of humility."[29] Without this guarding of the mind and of the heart, it is impossible to know when one is mistaken either by words or by thoughts. Also one will often fall into sin, into serious sins, but will not be sensitive to it. Consequently, he does not grieve for such sins and does not repent. A certain Father was right when he said that he who examines carefully his thoughts will also keep the commandments of God. St. Isaac said: "Man's victory and his loss, his treasure and his understanding and everything that has to do with an ascetic are all together in his thoughts and can take place with a small gesture."[30] For as another Father said, "One thought saves and another thought destroys a man." This is why the Preacher said, "One sinner destroys much good" (Eccles 9:17).

The Perpetual Memory of the Name of Jesus Cultivates Our Love for Him

Let me again for a third time beseech you to have Jesus as the sweet contemplation of your heart; let Jesus be the preoccupation of your tongue; let Jesus be the honorable shape and idea in your mind. In brief, let Jesus be your breath and never grow tired of calling upon Jesus. From such a perpetual and most sweet memory of Jesus, those great theological virtues—faith, hope and love—will grow and mature and become great trees in your heart. Know that when a lover is far from his beloved there is no other consolation for him but to constantly remember the name of the beloved person. When Emperor Leo the wise was banished from Constantinople, his mother found some consolation in repeating his name constantly: "My Leo, my Leo, my son." She spoke these words so often that the parrot who heard them learned to repeat them. Thus the soul that loves Jesus but cannot see and enjoy him because he is in heaven and not present cannot be consoled in any other manner except by constant remembrances of his holy name, calling him always with love and tears and pain of heart: "My Jesus, my beloved Jesus!" This is why St. Isaac told us: "When the mind is moved to remember God, the heart is directly moved in love and the eyes produce many tears. It is the habit of love to shed tears when remembering the beloved person."[31]

By remembering Jesus and saying the Jesus Prayer we cultivate in our heart love for Jesus and His commandments. What is more blessed, what is more happy, what is more sweet than to contemplate always the most glorious, the most pleasant, and the most beloved name of Jesus Christ, through whom anything anyone asks of the Father and of him himself one receives without fail? "Whatever you ask the Father in my name, he may give it to you" (Jn 15:16). And again, "Whatever you ask in my name, I will do it, that the Father may be glorified in the Son" (Jn 14:13). What other thought and recollection is more graceful and divine than the thought and recollection of the salutary, divine, and fearful name of Jesus Christ, the Son of God, whose name is above every name and before whom every knee shall bow? St. Paul said: "Therefore God has highly exalted him and bestowed on him the name which is above every name, that at the name of Jesus every knee should bow, in heaven and on earth and under the earth, and every tongue confess that Jesus Christ is Lord, to the glory of God the Father" (Phil 2:9–11).

I have said these things to you out of the abundant love which I have for your salvation. All of these things, like a parrot, I have learned well out of the sacred books of the God-inspired Fathers and have heard through the living voice of certain spiritual fathers who have in part experienced these things. Because of my own laxity and my passions, I have not been able to learn any of these things through my own experience.

169

GUARDING THE MIND AND THE HEART

It Is Very Appropriate to Teach Those Who Are in the World about Spiritual Prayer

Yes, I am aware that some may criticize me for writing to a person living in the world about those things that are appropriate for monks living outside the world. But if these persons are justified or not in criticizing me, I will keep silent and say only that indeed I have done it. I have done this, first, because of my great love for your salvation. For it is characteristic of friends to reveal to each other their secrets. "I have called you friends, for all that I have heard from my Father I have made known to you" (Jn 15:15). God is not a body, and does not delight in worship offerings made to him through the body (even though God's worshipers who have a material body are obliged to worship God with bodily worship); God is spirit and mind and of all the spirits and minds he is the first. Therefore God delights more in the worship offered to him through the mind and the spirit because they are more akin to his nature. "Every creature loves its like" (Sir 13:15). The Son of God taught us this truth when he said: "The true worshipers will worship the Father in spirit and truth, for such the Father seeks to worship him. God is spirit, and those who worship him must worship in spirit and truth" (Jn 4:23–24). Such spiritual and true worship is especially carried out through the spiritual prayer of the heart.

St. Paul too has given a direction to all the Christians without exception to "pray without ceasing" (1 Thes 5:17). According to St. Basil and St. John Chrysostom this constant prayer is best achieved through the prayer of the heart that can be activated anytime, anywhere, and during all forms of activity. Again St. Paul has directed Timothy to remember Jesus Christ: "Remember Jesus Christ, risen from the dead" (2 Tm 2:2). St. Gregory the Theologian said: "It is more important to remember God than to breathe."[32] Another Father has said that God requires of us to remember him always because he always provides for us everything—our existence and our breath.

St. Gregory Sinaite did not teach the art of spiritual prayer only to the monks of the Holy Mountain, but beginning from the mountain he travelled and taught all the people all the way into Blachia. St. Gregory Palamas too in many of his homilies encouraged all the Christians to pray spiritually in the heart. He even devoted an entire treatise which he sent to John and Theodore, the philosophers who were in the world, and in which he revealed to them all the mysteries of this sacred prayer and purification. St. Diadochos said that the devil does not like to see people learn and believe, for he is in the heart and from there he attacks them. However, he just loves to make them think that he attacks them from the outside. Therefore most persons, and oftentimes highly educated persons, do not realize that these thoughts come to them from within—from the heart—and not from the head or some other place, as they think. Thus by not learning the truth they are unable to attack him through the contemplation of Jesus Christ in the heart. This then is the reason why I have explained to you the deceptive ways of the devil, so that you may know and fight against him through prayer of the heart.[33]

Notes

1. Commentary on Psalm 1.
2. Homily 15.
3. Homily 44.
4. Homily 30.
5. St. Diadochos, ch. 76.
6. Ἤλυθες αὖθις ἔμοιγε δολόπλοκε, ὡς ἐνοήθης. Βένθος ἐμῆς καρδίης, ἔνδοθι βοσκόμενος.
7. Commentary on Psalm 1.
8. On Guarding the Heart, ch. 1.
9. Divine Names, ch. 4.
10. Epistle 1.
11. In one of his letters to Barlaam.
12. On Prayer, ch. 2.
13. St. Neilos, ch. 67.
14. On Prayer, ch. 2.
15. On Those Who Think They Are Justified by Works, ch. 1.
16. Ibid.
17. Quoted in the Life of Peter.
18. St. Diadochos, ch. 57.
19. The Ladder of Divine Ascent, Homily 27.
20. On Those Who Think They Are Justified by Works, ch. 1.
21. The Ladder of Divine Ascent, Homily 28.
22. St. Diadochos, ch. 24.
23. St. Isaac, ch. 83.
24. Biography of St. Syngletike.
25. St. Isaac, Epistle 4.

26. St. Isaac, Homily 69.
27. St. John Climacus, The Ladder, Homily 27.
28. St. Macarios, Homily 3, ch. 4.
29. St. Isaac, Homily 73.
30. St. Isaac, Homily 54.
31. St. Isaac, Homily 85.
32. Against Eunomios.
33. See more about this subject in the introduction and at the end of the Philokalia.

CHAPTER ELEVEN

The Spiritual and Proper Delights of the Mind

The Six Areas of Spiritual Delight

Have you guarded your external senses so that they do not partake of the physical delights? Have you guarded the external sense of imagination so that it does not receive impressions of evil passions? Have you also guarded your mind and your heart from passions and evil thoughts? Listen now to what are the spiritual and proper delights of the mind, about which we said a few things at the beginning. I suppose there are six main sources or areas from which the proper delights are born and derived. These may be ennumerated as follows:

1. Doing the divine commandments and fulfilling the will of God.
2. Acquiring the God-enacted virtues.
3. Reading and understanding the word of God in Sacred Scriptures.
4. Contemplating the reason and beauty of creation.
5. Knowing the reason for the incarnate economy of the Son of God.
6. Contemplating upon the attributes and perfections of God.

Each of these topics will be discussed briefly, for if one were to attempt a thorough discussion one would have to write many books.

PROPER DELIGHTS OF THE MIND

1. An Area of Spiritual Delight Is the Doing of the Divine Commandments and Fulfilling the Will of God

Dear friend, obey the commandments of God which are contained in the decalogue and in the holy Gospel. Do them all with simplicity without exceptions. The Lord commanded that we observe all that he has commanded. We must not observe some and neglect others. "Go therefore and make disciples of all nations . . . teaching them to observe all that I have commanded you" (Mt 28:19–20). If all the commandments of Christ were not necessary for our salvation, we would not have been commanded to observe them, as St. Basil has noted. You must not only observe all the commandments of God; you must also be careful to do them not for the sake of receiving human praise or glory or anything else worldly, but only for the sake of obeying, pleasing, and loving God who has given us these commandments. Otherwise, you run the risk of losing the true reward of your labor and effort. For the Lord said that those who do the commandments to be seen and praised by men "have received their reward" (Mt 6:2).

It is important to note here that according to St. Mark the Ascetic and all the Fathers in general, there are two types of divine commandments: the catholic or comprehensive and the particular. For example, to love God and neighbor, to give up all your possessions, to subdue all thoughts to an obedience of Christ, to guard the mind and the heart in purity, etc.—all these are catholic and comprehensive commandments. Particular commandments include charity to those who are deprived, the avoidance of the negative commandments: not to lie, not to steal, not to covet, not to commit adultery, and all the other particular commandments contained in the Gospel and in the Apostles. Both the comprehensive and the particular commandments must be observed and kept by both soul and body, spiritually through the heart, and practically through actual deeds.

As much as possible, seek to do the will of God, which "is good and acceptable and perfect" (Rom 12:2). The "good" will of God is to simply do that which is good either by deed or by word or thought. God's "acceptable" will is to do the good for no other reason than for God only. The "perfect" will of God is to do the good with all of your heart and power and love. In this regard, St. Theophylactos said, "First of all, look to see the will of God as good; when you realize this, look to see it as 'acceptable'; many things that are good are not always acceptable either because of the time or because of the person. . . . But when the will of God is both good and acceptable, seek to have it be perfect, complete, and observed fully as it is required and not only partially."

According to St. John Damascene and all the theologians, the will of God can be considered to be of two kinds: the preceding and the subsequent. God who is good desires the good; God who is just may permit some sorrows to come for our benefit. This is why it is necessary for you too, dear friend, to bear graciously all the sorrows which come to you, either from men, or from devils, or from corrupt nature. Choose that remarkable maxim which St. John Chrysostom used to say: "Glory be to God for all things."[1] Remember, also, what the cunning Odysseus said to his heart: "Bear this suffering also, my heart, because you have suffered worse things before." In fact, it is better to sing in every circumstance the sacred refrain of David: "Be strong and let your heart take courage; yet, wait upon the Lord" (Ps 27:14). In doing the commandments of the Lord and in fulfilling his holy will, your mind can enjoy great delight! Oh, what great joy your heart will receive! "Nothing is better than the fear of the Lord, and nothing sweeter than to heed the commandments of the Lord" (Sir 23:27). For if as a servant, you observe out of fear the commandments, you rejoice and are blessed because you comfort your master by doing his will. "Blessed is the man who fears the Lord, who greatly delights in his commandments" (Ps 112:1). If you work as a laborer in the vineyard of divine commandments, you rejoice because you hope to receive your wages in full from the lord of the vineyard who has hired you. "Call the laborers and pay them their wages . . ." (Mt 20:8). Now, if you observe the commandments as a son out of love only for the Father, you rejoice and are glad because you have pleased and glorified your heavenly Father through your obedience. "A son honors his father, and a servant, his master. If then I am a father, where is my honor?" (Mal 1:6).

He who observes all the commandments of the Lord acquires a blameless conscience. Not only is he unembarrassed and unashamed, but [he] also acquires a boldness before God, as the beloved disciple noted: "Beloved, if our hearts do not condemn us, we have confidence before God; and we receive from him whatever we ask, because we keep his commandments and do what pleases him" (1 Jn 3:21–22). By the same token, he who fulfills the will of God by doing willingly what is good or by forbearing the unwanted sorrows, graciously acquires a blameless conscience. "We rejoice in our sufferings, knowing that suffering produces endurance, and endurance produces character, and character produces hope, and hope does not disappoint us, because God's love has been poured into our hearts through the Holy Spirit which has been given to us" (Rom 5:3–5). When one has his conscience blameless before God, it is truly a delight of delights and a joy of joys. Not only does one who observes the commandments receive a blameless conscience, but he who willingly and with love fulfills them as a sacred privilege also acquires a similitude and a union with God, who has given us these life-giving commandments. This is confirmed by the bird of heaven, St. Dionysios: "Similitude to God and union with him is accomplished only by loving and fulfilling reverently the most revered commandments of God."[2] Think how much delight, how much joy, and how much happiness is derived from becoming like God and being united with God!

On the contrary, he who disobeys even one commandment of the Lord is condemned in his conscience because he becomes guilty of all the others, according to St. James: "For whoever keeps the whole law but fails in one point has become guilty of all of it" (Jas 2:10). Why guilty of all of the law? Because, as St. Basil said, "The commandments all have the same purpose according to their true and interrelated reason, so that by breaking one, you by necessity break the others."[3] Therefore, to have a guilty and shamed conscience that condemns us is in truth the suffering of sufferings, and sorrow of all the sorrows. St. Gregory of Nyssa also said, "Nothing burdens the soul and draws it down as the consciousness of sin."[4] St. John Chrysostom also said that the person who is troubled by his conscience is like a person who constantly has winter in his soul and waves breaking upon it one after the other. Sleep to such a person is not sweet but filled with fear and terror. There is no pleasure in his eating nor in his conversation with friends, and these cannot change and relieve this person from such a struggle.[5] Again, St. John said that "he who lives in evil is punished in hell prematurely, being pierced by the conscience."[6]

2. An Area of Spiritual Delight Is the Acquirement of All the Virtues

In acquiring the divine virtues the mind experiences an ineffable joy because it is made worthy to possess an inexhaustible treasure. This treasure (in heaven) is more valuable than any number of sapphires or diamonds, more valuable than gold or silver and more valuable than all the precious vessels of earthly kings. Seek therefore, dear friend, to acquire in your soul this treasure of virtues which cannot be corrupted, nor stolen nor lost as any material wealth, but remains in your soul always and is immortal. St. Basil said, "All other possessions do not really belong to the one who has them or to the one who has acquired them for they are exchanged back and forth like a game of dice. Only virtue among our possessions cannot be taken away, but remains with us when we live and when we die."[7] Seek therefore to win the virtues. Not only some of them and not others, but all of them. It is not enough to have one or two virtues, but all of them, as St. Chrysostom has noted: "As we have five senses and they are all necessary, so also we need to have all the virtues. If someone is prudent but uncharitable, or charitable but greedy, or if he avoids taking what belongs to others but does not give of his own, then everything is without purpose and vain. One virtue does not entitle us to stand with boldness before Christ; we need them all in all of their variety and magnitude."[8] St. Mark has also commented on this: "No one single virtue alone can open our physical door unless all of them follow as interrelated.[9] If you acquire all of the virtues your soul will rejoice and your mind will be delighted with this spiritual gain. You will be imitating God and you will possess the virtues and will seek to rise up to the likeness of God.

The virtues bring delight and joy not because we have the habit of virtue, but when we actually practice them actively. In other words, the merciful person does not rejoice and find delight only when he has the habit of charity in his heart, but rather when he activates this disposition and actually practices charity. An artist or a craftsman does not experience delight when he does not practice his skill or his art, but rather when he actually practices it. This is why one must first practice the virtues until he acquires their habit, which is often called "a second nature." After the habit is acquired the virtues are then practiced for their delight, for the first acts of virtue have no joy, when they are done with strain and difficulties until the habit is established. These first acts of virtue may be likened to the planting of a tree. The habit of virtues may be likened to the tree that has taken root and has blossomed. The acts of virtue that follow after the habit is established are likened to the tree bearing fruit.

There are three reasons why I suggest that you acquire all of the virtues. (A) All the virtues are interrelated one with another like a golden interlocking necklace. Therefore if one virtue is untied from the series and removed because of neglect, all the other virtues will by necessity be untied at the same time and become weakened. Let me show you how one of the Fathers described the interrelatedness of the virtues. Faith bears fear of perdition; fear of perdition bears abstinence from passion; this abstinence bears patience in tribulation; patience bears hope in God; hope in God bears indifference to worldly matters; this disregard for worldly things bears love for God, which is the highest of all the virtues. (B) The second reason is that the virtues are close to the evils and related to them. Each virtue is in fact in opposition to two evils, as the two extremes of excess or of deficiency standing on either side of each virtue. When one virtue is absent the nearby evil comes to fill the gap, or rather, the two evils on opposite sides of the missing virtue come in its place. (C) When the mind is preoccupied with all of the virtues, it does not have time to be preoccupied with evil, but becomes in a sense blind to it. On the contrary, he who is preoccupied with evil has no time to consider the virtues and is in a sense blind to them. Evagrios put it wisely: "Both the virtues and the evils blind the mind; the virtues blind us from seeing the evils and the evils from seeing the virtues."[10]

Virtue Is Timeless and Makes Men Wise and Praiseworthy

Every virtue has its beginning from God, but in terms of time, it is eternal as God is. St. Maximos has noted: "All good things and virtue itself are obviously works of God. All virtuous things have a beginning; there was a time when they were not. But virtue itself has no such beginning in time, for there was no time when it was not."[11] The mind rejoices and the heart is happy when we acquire the virtues. Besides this, every virtue and especially the fear of God produces knowledge, prudence, and wisdom, making those who have this fear of God virtuous, prudent, knowledgeable, and wise. Moreover, it makes those who have it praiseworthy, happy, and zealous. This is why a certain wise man said: "The majesty of virtue is that it magnifies the person who magnifies virtue. Even among opponents and enemies, virtue makes persons to be virtuous and praiseworthy." As evil brings about every kind of ignorance, conversely virtue and, before it, the fear of God bears every wisdom and prudence. This is why one of the Fathers said: "The source, the mother, and the root of prudence is virtue; while every evil has its beginnings in thoughtless foolishness. The virtuous man who also fears God is more prudent than everyone else."

PROPER DELIGHTS OF THE MIND

The Benefits of the Fear of God

This is why David said, "The fear of the Lord is the beginning of wisdom" (Ps 111:10). And Solomon said, "The fear of the Lord is instruction in wisdom" (Prv 15:33). Sirach said, "How great is he who has gained wisdom! But there is no one superior to him who fears the Lord. The fear of the Lord surpasses everything" (Sir 25:10–11). Notice that David said that the fear of the Lord is "the beginning of wisdom," and Solomon said it is "instruction in wisdom" or wisdom itself, while Sirach said that it "surpasses everything." Each of these men praised the fear of God in greater degrees. See also the golden line of virtues which comes from the fear of God, and which St. Gregory the Theologian praised so marvelously: "He who truly has the fear of God in his heart, he it is who keeps the commandments of God: he it is who is purified, who is illumined, and he it is who has reached the love of God, which is the highest of all the virtues."[12] Do you see to what height of virtue the fear of God raises man? This is why St. Isaac used to say that "the fear of God is the beginning of virtue."[13]

The Benefits of Meekness

Seek therefore, dear friend, to have always in your secret heart the fear of the Lord. Seek also to have meekness as an inseparable companion when you teach and when you do charitable work, and generally in all of your works, maintain a willing and patient goodness. This meekness and goodness is a title and a virtue of our Lord, Jesus Christ. "Learn from me—I am gentle and lowly in heart"(Mt 11:29). St. Paul instructed Timothy to "aim at gentleness" (1 Tm 6:11), and to "correct his opponents with gentleness" (2 Tm 2:25). Sirach also instructed: "My son, perform your tasks in meekness" (Sir 3:17). You will acquire this meekness and gentleness if you are not conceited, especially if you happen to be a bishop or some other high official. On the contrary, humble yourself, and be as one of the persons you govern, as Sirach has instructed: "If they make you master of the feast, do not exalt yourself; be among them as one of them" (Sir 32:1). Now, if all of the Christians in general are obligated to have formulated in themselves the virtue of their Teacher Christ, as St. Peter has instructed us (1 Pt 2:9), how much more are you obliged to have these virtues formulated within and without as a disciple and imitator of Christ? This meekness, as we have said, is a title and a virtue of Jesus Christ, the holy

179

Apostles and the Fathers of the Church. Thus, you will always want to acquire this virtue and demonstrate it in all your works. Especially, however, you will want to have this virtue of meekness at the time when you are the celebrant of holy mysteries. At this sacred time, I beseech you fervently, not to imitate in words, in forms, and in movements, the disorders, the anger, and the impatient confusion of the others. No! All these things are most out of place and create a great scandal for the Christians who see and hear such things. Stand therefore before the holy altar with much fear and reverence. Be complete, calm, peaceful, and untroubled in body and spirit, in words and movements, as you are standing there before the Prince of Peace himself and King of all. Offer the Holy Eucharist—the peaceful and bloodless sacrifice—for yourself and for the people. But if you ever see yourself confused and immersed in passions, I advise you to withdraw peacefully and avoid an immediate reaction.

The Value of Acting without Malice

To act without malice is to invite into our soul the very appearance and indwelling of God himself, as St. John Climacus said.[14] Also, great joy is created in the soul by the prevalance of innocence. Indeed, look at the young children who are simple and free of malice; they are always most happy simply on account of their gracious simplicity and guilelessness. Later, when they grow up and come to know evil, joy leaves them because they are no longer without malice.

Who can depict the pleasure you can enjoy when you have love for your neighbor? This is especially evident when you show him also the results and fruit of true love, which are compassion, charity, sympathy, forgiveness of his wrongs, patience with his shortcomings, and simply every beneficent work and grace which you would want to show him in word or deed, spiritually or bodily. I believe that he who shows mercy and beneficence experiences greater joy than the one who receives the benefit or the mercy. The reason for this is simply the fact that one imitates God by doing good. As St. Gregory the Theologian said, "Love is clean money, worthy of God, and its work is to be given." He also said, "Man becomes similar to God in nothing else as much as in doing good."

Another reason for this greater joy lies in the fact that man draws other people to himself by his love and encourages them to be subject to him willingly and not by force. The wise Themestios once said:

Nothing is more conducive to good will than to be beneficent. For it is best of all to draw someone out because of your good will than to hold him (captive) by fear. In the former, one is lord with willing subjects and in the latter with unwilling ones.

This is why a certain moralist has said that good works for the people are the elements which constitute the love of the people, the food which nourishes this love to grow and be perfected, and the golden chain which binds the heart of the beneficiaries with the love of the benefactor. This is why we have that common proverb: "Man is God to man." Through his good works a man appears as God to his fellow man. The beloved disciple said, "He who does good is of God" (3 Jn 2). What words can depict the joy you will be able to safe keep in your soul if you love prudence, virginity, purity, and long-suffering? If you love repentance, moreover, you will be able to make up for any oversights in the other virtues and thus receive the mercy of God for the mistakes you make all day in deeds or words or thoughts. You will thus be able to examine your conscience each evening and to say that familiar proverb, "How have I transgressed? What have I accomplished? What was not done that is necessary for me?" David too instructed us to examine ourselves: "Feel compunction upon your beds for what you say in your hearts" (Ps 4:4). Simply then your joy will be ineffable if you love the other chorus, the golden species of virtues, especially the spiritual prayer of the heart, about which we have spoken above, and the continuous memory of the most sweet name of Jesus who is the giver of joy, of grace and light.

A Bishop and Every Leader Must Be Humble and Ready to Benefit Not Revenge Enemies

If you struggle to acquire the virtue of humility and forbearance, you will not simply have joy, but a source of joy in your heart. You will acquire this source of joy through humility, if you do not take pride in your office as hierarch, as we said before, and if you do not consider yourself to be a governor, but rather one of the governed. Moreover, you must not consider yourself a hierarch of the people, but as counselor of the people, appointed by God to serve them and to advise them what is the right way and to convince them of this rather than to order them, as St. Basil wrote: Because each one of us is not capable by himself to find what is necessary, God has provided us with counselors [that is, the hierarchy], not with rulers. The attribute of a

181

king is to give orders to those he rules; the attribute of a counsellor is to convince those he counsels. Thus, each of you must consider yourself, not as a ruler, but as a counselor given by God to the people. "The leader must not exalt himself in his office so that he may not lose the blessedness of humility."

Again, you can gain this source of joy through forbearance by not returning evil for evil, nor by revenging those who have grieved you, or have treated you unjustly, or have mistreated you in any way. It is a great condemnation in a bishop or other leader to be seeking revenge. For, how will he be able to teach others not to return evil for evil received, when he himself does the opposite and revenges his enemies? The prophet Isaiah, in his time, condemned the rulers of Jerusalem for seeking revenge. . . . But why do I say that you must not seek revenge on your enemies? We have a commandment of God to love them and to do good to them. "Love your enemies and pray for those who persecute you" (Mt 5:44). If you do good to them, you are bound to receive many blessings from God, as did David when he did not kill Saul in the cave (1 Sm 24:10f). St. John Chrysostom interpreted this passage and said that we will receive greater rewards from God when we do many good things for our enemies and receive from them the opposite. If we cultivate these virtues and acquire all of them, mentioned above, our joy and gladness will be boundless and inexpressible.

What Are the Praises of Virtue

St. Gregory of Nyssa said that "nothing gives wings and flight to the soul as much as justice and virtue."[15] St. Isidore was right in praising virtue: "Virtue is useful and necessary; virtue is beneficial, good, proper, advantageous, and profitable. Virtue is necessary, for there is nothing more essential than to live correctly; it is advantageous for it leads to blessedness; it is good and right, for it beautifies those who possess it."[16] Again he wrote, "We define true philosophy to be the one which does not overlook anything in those who have come to piety and virtue."[17] St. John Chrysostom was right when he wrote, "If we want to enjoy [spiritual] delight, we must before all others avoid evil and seek after virtue; there is no other way to partake of this delight even if we rise to the royal throne."[18] This is why St. Paul used to say "the fruit of the Spirit is love, joy, peace, patience, kindness, goodness, faithfulness, gentleness, self-control" (Gal 5:22). St. John also wrote: "The pleasure of evil is short lived, but its suffering is eternal; on the other hand, the pain of virtue is short lived, but its advantage and blessedness is eternal."[19] In agreement with St. John, his disciple, St. Mark also wrote: "As every evil ends in the prohibited pleasure, so also does every virtue lead to a spiritual comfort. The former endures and increases evil, while the latter similarly increases virtue."[20]

The Virtues Must Be Acquired in Order

St. Basil has written in his letter to Chilon that we must seek to acquire the virtues in order, that is, one by one, and not all of them together. St. John Chrysostom also has taught this principle. We must distribute to ourselves the various virtues as the farmers their plantings. During this month, we will control abuse, hybris-slander, and the wrath of the unrighteous. During another month, we will train ourselves to avoid malice. During still another month, we will work on another virtue. When we acquire the habit of each virtue, then we proceed to another one. The virtues must be acquired one by one in order, and not all of them together, so that they do not become burdensome and difficult, but easy and light, as St. Isaac said.[21] The virtues must be acquired one by one, for the sake of being helpful and harmless. St. Isaac said, "Each virtue is the mother of the next one. But if you leave the mother who gives birth to each virtue and you seek after the daughters before you acquire their mother, those virtues will prove to be vipers in your soul. And if you do not put them away from yourself, you will surely die."[22] For example, if someone seeks to reach the love of God, the highest virtue, before he has already acquired the fear of God, which is a lower virtue, capable of bearing the love for God, he will be greatly harmed. By the same token, one must not seek the vision before the practice, or the divine *charismata* before observing the divine commandments. This is why St. Gregory the Theologian said: "We do not begin from spiritual vision to reach fear of God, but are rather supported and purified and in a sense, refined by fear in order to rise to greater heights."[23]

The Spiritual House of the Soul Built by the Virtues

Since, as we have said, the virtues must be acquired in order, we have such an order from St. Peter the Damascene. When placed together in an orderly fashion, these virtues constitute the spiritual house of the soul. I think you will enjoy a pleasant vision if we attempt to construct this house here. Just as the physical house in order to be built needs (1) firm ground, (2) a foundation, (3) stones, (4) mortar, (5) walls, (6) roof, and (7) a builder, also the spiritual house needs these very same elements. Now, instead of firm ground for the construction of the spiritual house, one needs to have perfect patience in every temptation that may come our way, either from men, demons, or from corrupt nature, as St. Basil said. Instead of a foundation, we need steadfast and undoubting faith. By this I mean not only the faith with which we believe in the Holy Trinity, the Incarnation of the Son of God, but the inner faith by which we believe that everything that God has said is true, both the promises of good things and the warnings of sufferings, as St. Symeon the New Theologian said. Instead of stones, this spiritual house needs the many virtues about which we spoke above. Instead of mortar, we need humility. As the mortar binds the various stones together, so also humility binds and holds together in harmony all the virtues. Instead of four walls, the spiritual house needs the four cardinal virtues. That is, prudence which determines what must be done and what avoided. Chastity is needed to control the desires of the soul and the body. Courage is needed to harden the heart only against the devil and sin. Finally, Justice is needed to offer each part of the soul what properly belongs to it, as St. Maximos said; "If you want to be just, give to each part of you what rightly belongs to it, that is, to the body and to the soul. Give to the intellectual aspect of the soul readings, spiritual contemplation and prayer. To the emotional aspect of the soul give spiritual love to combat hatred. For the desirous aspect of the soul provide prudence and self-control. For the body, provide food, clothing, and shelter, but only the essentials." The roof of this spiritual house is the perfect love for God and neighbor, the end and the head of all the virtues. The builder, finally, is discretion and wisdom, as it is written: "By wisdom, a house is built, and by understanding, it is established" (Prv 24:3). Rather, we should say that the builder is our Lord Jesus Christ without whom we cannot do anything (Jn 15:15). For as it is written, "Unless the Lord builds the house, those who build it labor in vain" (Ps 127:1). St. Theodore the Studite has written in the Anavathmoi hymns: "If the Lord does not build the house of virtues, we labor in vain." For all these reasons then, dear friend, use the spiritual prayer of the heart to beseech with fervent tears and with your whole heart and soul the architect and builder of this house, the most good Christ and most sweet Jesus, to build this spiritual house within your heart. Then invite him to come in to dwell there and to make you rich with his blessing of grace and to illumine you with the light of his divine knowledge.

The Various Types of Practical and Theoretical Virtue

It is necessary to note here that according to St. John Damascene some virtues are considered bodily virtues and some spiritual. Bodily virtues are, for example, self-control, fasting, hunger, thirst, vigilance, standing, kneeling, physical labor, and every other hardship of the body. These are more properly called "tools" of virtue and not virtues as such. They do, however, bring man to the true virtue and to humility and dispassion when they are practiced not hypocritically and for the love of man, but in true knowledge and for the love of God alone. Among the spiritual virtues are the aforementioned four cardinal virtues of prudence, chastity, courage, and justice, which bring about the other spiritual virtues, such as faith, hope, love, prayer, humility, meekness, long-suffering, serenity, divine knowledge, joy, simplicity, imperturbability, unselfishness, and so many more which are truly called and indeed are virtues. When therefore someone is unable to practice the bodily virtues because of illness or old age or any other circumstance or need, he can be excused by God, who knows the reasons. But if we do not practice the spiritual virtues we have no apology and no forgiveness, for these virtues are not under any constraints and everyone can practice them regardless of what illness or physical need they may suffer. These spiritual virtues are enacted by the mind and the heart alone. For example, if someone is unable to fast because of an illness, he can still pray spiritually and thank God with his lips for his illness. This is why St. John the Karpathian, allegorizing the evangelical saying "When they persecute you in one town, flee to the next" (Mt 10:23), taught that when we are troubled by illness to leave the "town" of fasting we must go on to the next town of virtue, that is, to prayer and thanksgiving. If you cannot work the bodily virtues then at least grieve in your heart that you cannot keep them and this sorrow will take their place, as St. Isaac said: "A heart that is filled with sorrow because of an illness that renders one unable to do external deeds takes the place of all the bodily virtues. The deeds of the body, however, without the understanding mind are like a dead body."[24]

Ask the Lord also to make you worthy not only of the two types of practical virtue, which are the social one, namely modesty, and the cathartic one, namely dispassion, but also of the two types of theoretical virtue, that is, the spiritual and the *divine*, according to the wise Psellos. He has written about virtues that it is one and the same to say that one is deified or that one is made a dwelling place for Christ and his Father and the Holy Spirit, as promised: "If a man loves me, he will keep my word and my Father will love him and will come to him and make our home with him" (Jn 14:23). This is the goal of both practical and theoretical virtue and the true happiness and blessedness of man, which is experienced in part in this life as a sort of foretaste or engagement of the future. The wise Vlemides has written about virtue: "One is blessed who has immortalized himself through practical virtue; he who also is made worthy of complete catharsis through theoretical virtue attached to a spiritual way of life and who is completely united to God by grace becomes indeed most blessed."

By being yourself deified first by grace, you can in turn as a hierarch provide blessings to those Christians under your care through the grace of the Holy Spirit. In this way, you may be called a God-father, bearing spiritual sons and daughters. According to the philosopher Psellos, those who have the divine virtue are called God-fathers.

Be careful also to have a doorkeeper of this spiritual house of yours, not some "woman," that is, a low feeling or a weak thought, as did (Iebosthe) who was killed because of this. Your doorkeeper must be a manly and careful reason, as St. Neilos has allegorically noted. This doorkeeper is the vigilant guard of the mind and the heart, that we spoke about before. If an enemy enters or some evil or passion into the house, the king is angered and departs, which I hope does not happen.

3. Ultimate Truth and Sweetness Is to Be Found in Reading and Understanding Holy Scripture

A source of spiritual delight is the word of God contained in Holy Scripture because there is to be found ultimate truth that enlightens the mind, which, being mind, has truth as its object. Moreover, there is ultimate sweetness and grace in the words of Scripture, which draw like a great magnet the hearts of the readers to agree with them and to be convinced. This is only natural. After all, the words of Scripture are the words of God and of the Holy Spirit. This is to say that they are the words of truth itself and grace itself. "Thus says the Lord," "The word of the Lord came," and "The Spirit of the Lord spoke to me" are all too familiar phrases throughout Scripture. St. John Chrysostom said, "The reading of Holy Scripture is the opening of heaven, and the mouths of the prophets are the mouth of God." I say nothing of the height of theology, the depth of divine economy, the breadth of beneficence, and the width of knowledge and wisdom which are contained in Scripture, each of which constitutes a source of delight for the mind and the heart. The whole of Scripture—old and new—contains the above, but more especially the New Testament. St. Basil said: "The voice of the Gospels is much more magnificent than the other teachings of the Holy Spirit. In the other teachings God spoke to us through his servants the prophets, but in the Gospels he spoke to us personally through his Son and our Lord."[25]

We find in the New Testament many simple words which in truth possess such remarkable grace that they attract the hearts of the hearers. It is written that "all spoke well of him, and wondered at the gracious words which proceeded out of his mouth" (Lk 4:22). "The people sought him and came to him to hear him" (Lk 4:42). David, foreseeing that the Lord will speak in this manner in the New Testament, wrote: "You are the fairest of the sons of men; grace is poured upon your lips" (Ps 45:2). St. Basil, when interpreting this verse, wrote:

> The prophet wanted to emphasize the abundant grace in the words of the Lord, for we have seen how richly God has poured out his grace upon the words of Christ. This is why in a short period of time the Gospel has reached virtually the whole ecumene. This happened because the grace of God was poured abundantly upon the preachers of the Gospel who are called the lips of Christ by Scripture. Thus, in simple and insignificant words the Gospel contains great power to draw us to salvation, and every soul is held fast by established doctrines and confirmed by grace with an immovable faith in Christ.

In Holy Scripture we see humble words, simple words, but within they possess such great depths of the knowledge of God that the passing wisdom of this world cannot even stand beside it. St. Paul wrote about this wisdom of God: "Among the mature we do impart wisdom, although it is not a wisdom of this age or of the rulers of this age, who are doomed to pass away. But we impart a secret and hidden wisdom of God" (1 Cor 2:6–7). St. Gregory the Theologian also wrote about this divine wisdom: "I praise and value this wisdom; this is the wisdom I accept. This wisdom has glorified simple and uncultivated people. Such insignificant people have been exalted and preferred because they have overcome the wisdom of this world that is temporal through the word of divine wisdom that is eternal."[26]

It is important to note here that those who study the Sacred Scriptures must be convinced and must believe from within that all the words of the Lord contained in the Scriptures are credible, in agreement with each other, certain and true as it is written: "The sum of thy word is truth" (Ps 119:160) and "The ordinances of the Lord are true, and righteous altogether" (Ps 19:9), and "The works of his hands are faithful and just; all his precepts are trustworthy, they are established for ever and ever" (Ps 111:7–8). One must believe the message of Sacred Scripture with simplicity, as small children trust their parents and pupils their teachers.

If we find in Scripture a word or thought that may appear to us obscure or contrary to other words or thoughts of Scripture or to right reason, then we must read the entire passage before and after that saying, in order to find the true meaning. Moreover we must compare it with other clearer passages found elsewhere in Scripture and thus discover the meaning of the unclear passages. Even if after such effort the meaning is not found, it is better to blame oneself rather than to claim conceitedly that something in Scripture is not correct.

Two Reasons Why a Bishop Must Read the Holy Scripture

Read the Holy Scripture, dear friend, read the Scriptures and be immersed in them; receive their sweetness, nourishment, and delight, which is not empty and transient. St. John Chrysostom said: "Insatiable is the sweetness of spiritual thoughts. Just as the earth that is not watered cannot bring forth wheat even though it may hold within itself thousands of seeds, so also the soul cannot show forth any spiritual fruit unless it is first enlightened by the Holy Scriptures. Again, as wine when drunk helps to put an end to our sorrow and brings gladness to the heart, so also the spiritual wine brings joy to the soul."[27] You must read especially the New Testament as St. Basil instructed us in his letter to Chilon, just for your own benefit and secondly for the benefit of the people under your care. ". . . Read the Scriptures for your own sake, for you will find there the remedy for everyone of your ailments."[27]

From the meadow of Holy Scripture you can select, like a bee, the flowers of all the virtues. From Abraham we select the virtue of faith and the virtue of hospitality and assistance to strangers; from Job we receive the virtue of courage and patience; from Joseph we receive prudence; from Moses and David, meekness and the absence of malice; from the Evangelists we receive our faith in Christ; from St. John we receive theology; from St. Peter the confession; from St. Paul the fervent zeal, and so forth. In general, we receive from Scripture and learn all the traditions and teachings of all the virtuous deeds and promises and warnings all of which help to make mature and perfect the person who believes in Christ, as St. Paul wrote: "All scripture is inspired by God and profitable for teaching, for reproof, for correction, and for training in righteousness, that the man of God may be complete, equipped for every good word" (2 Tm 3:16).

The New Testament Completes the Old and the Lord's Testament Completes the New

If you love to delight, to move, and to attract your heart with the sweetness and the attraction of the love of Jesus, read continuously the Testament of the Lord as contained in the Gospel of St. John. The new Scripture is greater than the old; the four Gospels are greater than the new Scripture as a whole; the fourth Gospel is greater than the other three; and the Lord's Testament (ch. 13–17) is greater than the Gospel of St. John as a whole. In the Lord's Testament the Lord himself spoke in a very special and most sweet and loving manner, not as a lord and teacher to his servants and disciples, but rather as a most compassionate and loving father to his beloved sons. He emptied himself and poured upon his holy Apostles, and through them upon all of us, that depth of his heartfelt love. He revealed the most sublime, the most salutary, the most hidden mysteries of his heart. Think about this: In this section, the Lord does not refer to his Apostles as sons, but rather in a more tender, more authentic and familiar manner. He calls them *teknia*—"little children," something he never called them before: "Little children, yet a little while I am with you" (Jn 13:33). Oh, what great and tender love you have for us, dearest Jesus, most compassionate and lover of mankind. I knew a man who had the habit of reading

189

each day, besides the Scriptures in general, a section from this sacred testament of the Lord.

The Practical Reading of Holy Scripture and the Fathers Brings Delight to the Soul

If you love to enjoy true and complete delight from the Scriptures, seek to read them not merely with simple understanding, but with deeds and practical realities. Moreover, seek to read them not merely for the mere love of learning but also for the sake of ascetic endeavors and discipline, as St. Mark wrote: "Read the words of Holy Scripture with an eye to practical applications and not merely to be puffed up by any fine thought that you may receive from it."[28] Another Father said: "This is why the lover of knowledge must also be a lover of discipline and practical application. For knowledge alone does not give light to the lamp." You will receive this light if you contemplate on the content of Scripture and realize that it was written to correct you and not the others, as again St. Mark said: "The humble person who has a spiritual life reads the Holy Scripture and understands everything to refer to him and not to others."[29] For this is true wisdom, fear of God, and avoidance of evil: "Behold, the fear of the Lord, that is wisdom; and to depart from evil is understanding" (Jb 28:28). St. Gregory the Theologian also wrote: "The first wisdom is a praiseworthy life purified by God."[30]

Having read Holy Scripture very carefully, you should also read the holy Fathers who interpret the Scriptures. You will receive no less delight from reading the Fathers than you do from the Scriptures. The Fathers develop the hidden meanings in Scripture and with their own writings help us to understand what we did not before. Because of that philosophic axiom that all men by nature seek knowledge, we must say that great delight follows naturally when we learn about hidden and unknown matters. This is why there will be ineffable joy and gladness that will come to your soul from the interpretations and the words of the holy Fathers. You too will be shouting, as did David, those enthusiastic words in the Psalms.

Be careful not to read the books of heretics. Avoid the books of atheists like fire. Do not even accept to take them into your hands. I suggest that you do not even read those apologetic books against the atheists, for they can be harmful to the weak, if not also to the strong in faith.

PROPER DELIGHTS OF THE MIND

The Bishops Should Read Holy Scripture and the Sacred Canons in Order to Teach Their Flock

You should read Holy Scripture and the holy Fathers for the benefit of your rational flock. For as the shepherd grazes and nourishes his sheep in the green pastures and fields, so also a bishop is required to feed his rational sheep in the pasture of Holy Scripture, teaching them always the word of God, or at least on every holiday and Sunday. The Sixth Ecumenical Council had ordered through its nineteenth canon the following:

It is required of the leaders of the Church on each day and especially on Sundays to instruct the clergy and the people in the words of piety out of Holy Scripture, relating to them the thoughts and judgments of truth. They are not to neglect the established canons or the tradition of the God-bearing Fathers. And if a certain passage of Scripture is even placed in question, it should never be interpreted differently from the teachers and Fathers of the Church in their writings. At the same time the people become familiar with what is important and what is not, so that they can reform their lives for the better.

Moreover, you must seek to study the sacred canons, those of the Apostles and those of the councils and the Fathers. These should be your common knowledge because they serve as a rudder in your hand to steer the course of ecclesiastical affairs in your diocese. See what the second canon of the Seventh Council had to say:

We decree that everyone who is to be raised to the authority of a bishop in every way be familiar with the Book of Psalms; he must also be examined by the Metropolitan bishop to see if the candidate has studied diligently and is thoroughly familiar with the sacred canons, the Holy Gospel, and the book of apostolic writings and all of Holy Scripture. Finally, he should also be examined to see if he lives by the Divine Commandments and if he actually teaches the people under his supervision.

PROPER DELIGHTS OF THE MIND

All Christians are Required to Read Holy Scripture and Especially the Bishops

All the Christians who are literate are required to read the Holy Scripture. St. John Chrysostom even wrote that it is not possible for someone to be saved unless he continuously enjoys the spiritual reading of Holy Scripture. Elsewhere St. Chrysostom criticized the lay Christians for neglecting to read the Sacred Scriptures. He overturned the objection often put forth by the laity who say that they are not monks but have families—wives, children, and homes—to be concerned about. He urged the laity to read the Scriptures even more than the monks, precisely because they are in the world and in the midst of greater temptations and they need the fortification of the Scriptures to struggle against evil each day. St. John Climacus also encouraged us to read the Sacred Scripture. It does not only enlighten and put our mind together, it contains the very words of the Holy Spirit that guide anyone who passes through. St. Ephraim noted that the words of Holy Scripture are like a trumpet in time of war that arouses the brave strugglers against the enemy. The Scriptures arouse our desire to struggle for virtue and to be courageous against the passions. For this reason, dear brother, keep a certain spiritual sobriety and seek to read the Holy Scriptures so that they may teach you how to flee from the snares of the enemy and attain eternal life. Therefore, everyone needs to read for himself or to hear the Holy Scripture, for they are most beneficial to our spiritual life. Of course, those who are ordained—the priests and the bishops—have a more essential duty to read the Scriptures. St. Paul instructed Timothy: "Attend to the public reading of Scripture, to preaching, to teaching" (1 Tm 4:13). St. Ignatius gave the same instruction to Heron the deacon in Antioch: "Attend to the public reading, so that you are not the only one who knows the laws, but that you may explain them to others."[31] St. Ambrose considered the Scriptures to be a liturgical book that should always be in the hands of the priests of God. Rufinus the historian has reported that St. Basil and St. Gregory spent thirteen years in the desert studying the Holy Scriptures. Why do I continue to say so many words? To speak of a bishop or hierarch is to speak about a man who is most studious and full of every sacred knowledge of the Holy Scriptures and in whom every hierarchy is enacted and made known, as St. Dionysios the Areopagite noted.[32]

Why the Gospel Book Is Placed upon the Head of a Bishop When He Is Being Ordained

This is the reason why the Gospel Book is placed upon the head of a bishop when he is being ordained. Not only so that they realize that, even though they have become the leaders of others, they are themselves under the authority of the laws of the Gospel. St. John Chrysostom has noted that a bishop who is the head of the people of God is himself under another authority (for it is unbearable to have uncontrolled authority). By having the token of authority over his head, it is indicated that he is led by this law. It is ordered that the head be not bare, but covered in order to teach the head of the people that he too has authority over him. This is why during the ordinations in church of hierarchs the Book of the Gospels is placed upon the head of the ordained to teach him that the Gospel is his true tiara. Thus, he comes to know that even though he is head of all, he nevertheless upholds and is under all of these laws, being controlled and guided by them as he speaks and as he enacts other laws. One of the ancient Fathers, St. Ignatius, who was a bishop of Antioch and who suffered martyrdom, instructed a certain priest: "Let nothing be done without your approval, and you yourself must never do anything without the approval of God."

Not only for this reason then is the Gospel Book placed upon the head of bishops being ordained; it is also done to indicate that the bishops must have precise knowledge and understanding of the Holy Gospels and of all the rest of Holy Scriptures. Do you want to be convinced of this? Listen to St. Dionysios the Areopagite: "The hierarch has the Word of God placed eminently upon his head. . . . As the divine hierarch who partakes completely in every hierarchical power and in all the hierarchical sacred words and deeds he is not only himself enlightened by the true and divinely ordained knowledge, but also transmits to others through sacred rites all that is most appropriate to the office of the hierarch."[33] St. Isidore Pelousiotes also said: "The priest of God because he approaches God must like the many-eyed cherubim be all eyes so that he will not overlook anything, but will see all things. If you should not know something, learn it directly."[34]

PROPER DELIGHTS OF THE MIND

The Love of Holy Scriptures Produces Much Knowledge and Understanding

It is well known that the love and the reading of Holy Scriptures has the ability to produce in you much knowledge and understanding and to relieve you from the ignorance that brings about many stumblings. St. John Chrysostom has indicated that ignorance of Holy Scripture brings about many serious stumblings: the widespread disgrace of heresies, the neglected lives, the unprofitable sufferings. For as one who is deprived of light cannot walk straight, so also he who is deprived of the divine ray of Scripture walks in deep darkness and continuously sins.[35] Therefore, the wise Isocrates said: "If you love to learn you will learn much; what you have learned keep by constant study, and whatever you have not yet learned, seek to do so through the sciences. Thus, what others have discovered with difficulty, you will learn readily." Another wise man said: "The award of victory is given to those who run the race; those who are diligent and industrious receive the primacy of prudence. Ignorance, as a harsh illness, is followed by many sins, while education, as a pleasant region, will produce all good things." Indeed, "there is no substitute for a cultivated soul" (Sir 21:17). "A multitude of wise men is the salvation of the world, and a sensible king is the stability of his people" (Wis 6:24). It is indisputable that the love of learning and the constant reading produces well-educated people even among those who are otherwise unlearned. I have known men who were not only ignorant of the Greek language, but even of the simple vernacular and actually foreigners, who because of their constant listening (reading) in silence learned so much and became so wise that they excelled even the philosophers. Their questions are answered with difficulty even by the great teachers.

Angels Too Desire to Learn

St. Dionysios, that seer of the angelic attributes, tells us that all those other worldly angels and the whole heavenly hierarchy of bodiless minds do not neglect to acquire the knowledge possible to them regarding divine realities. They are moved by a fervent desire to learn always the higher and more sublime mysteries and to be more fully illumined by the light of God. Now, if these bodiless angels, the least of which is wiser than all the wise teachers among men, desire to learn, how much more, incomparably more, must we who are united to matter and to a body not neglect to study the divine knowledge but must seek to learn it from the Sacred Scriptures? Especially when we consider that men are by nature inextricably united to the attribute of not knowing. Moreover, the bishops who hold the highest office upon the earthly ecclesiastical order need this knowledge above all because they are called to perfect not only themselves, but also to enlighten and to teach others in a manner similar to that of the angels. Therefore, take note of St. Basil's admonition: "Let the listening of worldly stories be a bitter taste to you, but a honeycomb of sweetness the teachings of holy men." Therefore, avoid the many conversations of men as unprofitable and vain. For all these many reasons then be diligent in reading and meditating upon the Holy Scripture so that you may receive that blessing which says: "Blessed is the man . . . whose delight is in the law of the Lord and on his law he meditates day and night" (Ps 1:1). Even when someone comes to you for a simple visit, even then let there be readings from Scripture to avoid vain talk. This way he too will receive benefit and be comforted if he truly loves learning. If, on the contrary, the person does not love to learn, but prefers vain talk, he will know your purpose and will not return to bother you.

4. Contemplating the Reasons and the Beauty of God's Creation Is a Source of Spiritual Delight

There is great joy and delight in the mind that contemplates the reasons of creation, that is, the eternal purposes of God in creating and providing for his creatures, both the visible and the invisible. With one glance the mind can look over the visible and invisible creation— angels, heavens, stars, elements, plants, animals, and human beings— and can contemplate that God created all these from nothing and brought them into being with one single word of his: "For he commanded and they were created" (Ps 148:5). By contemplating this, the mind also marvels and wonders how God created everything with the exercise of one single will of his. "Whatever the Lord pleases he does, in heaven and on earth, in the seas and all deeps" (Ps 135:6). For God has indeed created everything by his own will and foreknowledge: "For thou hast done these things and those that went before and those that followed; thou hast designed the things that are now, and those that are to come. Yea, the things thou didst intend came to pass, and the things thou didst will presented themselves and said, 'Lo we are here'; for all thy ways are prepared in advance, and thy judgment is with foreknowledge" (Jdt 9:5–6). St. Gregory the Theologian noted that whatever God considered in his mind to create, he accomplished it by saying the word and he perfected it through the Spirit. The admirable and courageous Solomone, the mother of the seven Maccabee brothers, when she was encouraging her last son to face martyrdom like the other six, said to him: "My son . . . I beseech you to look at the heavens and the earth and see everything that is in them, and recognize that God did not make them out of things that existed. Thus, also, mankind comes into being" (2 Mc 7:28). When the mind contemplates these things, it marvels and is filled with wonder and rejoices with inexpressible gladness for having such a God and Lord who has created with such ease, such beautiful and wise and great and marvelous creatures. So we are moved to say with David: "I praise thee, for thou art fearful and wonderful. Wonderful are thy works!" (Ps 139:4).

The mind, seeing the creation of nature which the theologians define as being created out of nothing, both essence and power and energy, rejoices and glorifies God, calling him Creator. Seeing the unity and cohesion of creation which is the preservation of their essences and powers, the mind calls God unifier. Seeing the mutual interrelatedness and support of nature, which preserves and coordinates its essential activities, the mind calls God active and co-active. From both of these activities of God to provide for his creation, we are moved to call him the provider of all, and to say, "In him we live and move and have our being" (Acts 17:28). Moreover, we can more appropriately say, "For from him and through him and to him are all things" (Rom 11:35). The phrase "from him" denotes the creation; the phrase "through him" denotes the cohesion; and the phrase "to him" denotes the purpose or destiny of creation, which is to say the beginning, the middle, and the end of creation. St. Basil, who has interpreted this passage, said: "*From him* comes the cause of existence to all those things which are. *Through him* comes the constitution and preservation to all, and thus, *to him* all things return looking with ineffable desire and love toward the creator and provider of life."[36]

PROPER DELIGHTS OF THE MIND

The Miracles in Nature Become God's Names in Matter

To put it more simply, let us again consider how the mind rejoices when it observes the wisdom and the artistry in creation. When one rejoices he glorifies; he who glorifies God because of this wisdom and artistry calls him a wise artist. Similarly, God is called powerful because of the power he demonstrates in creation. And from his goodness, he is called good, and so on and so forth. According to St. Gregory of Nyssa, the visible miracles in nature are the matter for the divine names of God. "The miracles seen in everything provide the matter for the theological names by which we call God wise, powerful, good, holy, blessed, as well as external judge and savior and other such names. All of these names indicate some quality of God's myrrh which we may say has been gathered from all of nature and kept there as in a perfume bottle."[37] St. Dionysios considered this kind of theology to be cataphatic, that is, positive theology, which contemplates the spiritual reasons in creation and thus moves from the lower to the higher, or from the caused to the cause.[38]

When the mind rises through the creatures to the Creator and discerns that the reasons in the creatures have similitude with their Creator, the positive or cataphatic theology is used to name God positively—wise, good, creator, light, sun, air, fire and all of the beings as their Cause. But when the mind rises in the Spirit and supernaturally to the Creator and envisions the spiritual reality that God is unlike all the creatures and incomparably beyond them, then the mind uses the apophatic and transcendent theology to name God apophatically and transcendently as more-than-wise, more-than-good. Thus God is not a sun, nor light, nor fire, nor air, nor anything else from among the created beings.

By meditating upon the created beings as mirrors, we contemplate the creator and we praise him and call him by name. St. Maximos said that "God being the cause of all [according to the cataphatic theology] can be called and is in a divine sense all these names, but [according to the apophatic theology] he is none of these transcendently." In agreement with this, St. Dionysios also said: "God is praised by all the created beings according to their analogy for he is their cause. But again, there is the most divine knowledge of God which is known through unknowing according to the union [with God] that is transcendent and beyond intellectual understanding."[39] There is a paradoxical dimension whereby we can say that God is both *in* everything and *everything* and yet is essentially in nothing and nothing (of created nature); and by the same token, God is known to all by all things, and yet he remains essentially unknown, for he is not truly known by anything nor by anyone.

The Harmony in Nature Makes the World More Praiseworthy and Reveals God's Majesty

After all, when the mind sees the relation and reference, the order and harmony which is in all of nature and by which each creature is related to another and to all the creatures; and again all creatures are related to the one and to all of them together; when we see the ends of the former to be related to the beginnings of the latter there is, thus, one whole and unified world as St. Gregory the Theologian said.[40] This marvelous harmony and order in creation which is called the sympathy and the "sympnoia"—the mutual "co-breathing" of nature— brings much joy and satisfaction to the mind. With much joy and enthusiasm, we want to shout with David: "O Lord, how manifold are thy works! In wisdom thou hast made them all!" (Ps 104:24). And again, "O Lord, our Lord, how majestic is thy name in all the earth! Thy glory [and majesty] has been raised above the heavens" (Ps 8:1). This then, is the great majesty of God, the glory which is in his creatures which he has preordained and which he directs, as St. Gregory the Theologian explained.[41] According to this same theologian, the "back-side" of God which Moses was permitted to see is this majesty, that is, the "reasons" of creation. "And what comes after him are also his attributes, just as the shadows and images of the sun reflected in waters can reveal the sun to weak eyes, since they are unable to behold the sheer light which overpowers the sense."[42]

And is it not, dear friend, in truth, a glorious majesty of God to meditate upon the size of the whole earth and to see that it is so very small, so that when compared with the whole heaven, it is only a speck, and when compared with the creative energy of God, it is nothing. God created the whole earth with such ease as if it were nothing, as the prophet Isaiah said. And yet, this speck, this nothing—that is, the earth—is so wide that it contains so many great kingdoms and so many multitudes of nations and people. This earth is so large that its circumference is, according to contemporary calculations, 25,200 miles, or—to put in a more correct and truer way—the earth is so immense that from the beginning of creation (for over 7,000 years now) men have sought and explored it by land and by sea and have not yet succeeded in discovering all of it, but daily they discover new places inhabited and uninhabited. And in the future, they will perhaps discover more such places, for there will always be, to the end of time, some places in creation that will remain unknown.

Is it not a majesty of God to see the most bright sun apparently the size of a disc one foot in diameter and to have this foot be so great in size that it has actually a circumference of about 867,468 miles, according to certain contemporaries? And what about the sizes of planets, stars, and other nonplanet stars that appear as mere oil lamps, are they not larger than earth, according to the astronomers? Is it not then the majesty of God to have all of this visible and invisible world a single drop in the infinite ocean of God's creative wisdom and power? Moreover, this drop, I mean the whole world, is inexhaustible by the collective knowledge of all the aeons from the time of creation. All the wise men of all these centuries have not been able to understand fully and precisely a small fragment of this creation. Truly, then, this creation is an ocean that drowns every mind! This is one miracle that leaves every tongue speechless. And for this reason it should be honored more by silence than by words!

Worthy of every miracle that reveals God to be most glorious and majestic, more than the whole creation of the world itself, is this: Having created with such perfection and wisdom this great wondrous world, God did not choose, after the creation, to inscribe upon the heavens, or upon the earth, or upon some other part of his creation, that he is its creator, as do certain artists of this world. . . . God did not do this. Why? In order to show that this great world, when compared with his infinity, is really a small creation and he did not want to condescend to identify his name with it. But what he himself did not do, the whole world proclaims with a myriad silent voices through the divine wisdom and power that it reflects for those rational beings who observe it. Thus, David could say, "The heavens are telling the glory of God; and the firmament proclaims his handiwork" (Ps 19:1).

Now if God revealed to Moses only after thousands of years that he "created the heavens and the earth" (Gn 1:1), he did this not for his own majesty. No! He did it first to raise mankind from baseness and to lift them up to greatness; from the baseness of polytheism to the majesty of monotheism. Secondly, he did it not to magnify his own name through the majesty of the world, but rather to magnify the world through the majesty of his name.

What Is the Invisible World

Let me say here something about the invisible world according to the contemporary scientists. It is the place and dimension which contains the very tiny living organisms that are completely invisible to our eyes, but which are seen through the microscope in such a way as to see one thousand of them standing on the point of a needle. A contemporary physicist noted that each species of these organisms is a small world in itself that has existed in the whole for over seven thousand years already. Each one of these microscopic organisms has a living body with external and internal members that need to be fed, to live, and to reproduce other organisms like itself. The mind stands in wonder as it learns of these things and it rejoices and glorifies the Creator, who is more marvelous in his slightest rather than his greatest creations. An artist is marveled more by prudent people when he creates works of art on a small scale rather than on a large scale. Pyrgotelis was marveled more for sculpturing Alexander the Great on a small pearl than Pheidias for sculpturing him on a large piece of marble. By the same token, a contemporary watchmaker aroused more admiration for making a tiny watch within the stone of a ring than all the others who make large watches.

How the Mind Glorifies God with All of the Creatures

The mind of man is not alone in glorifying and magnifying the Creator and loving Father of the whole of creation, who, out of his abundant goodness, has produced so many thousands upon thousands, myriads upon myriads, millions upon millions of creatures—spiritual, physical, animate, inanimate, rational, irrational, adorned with such a variety of essences, powers, organs, energies, and perfections. The mind of man is filled by a sort of fulness, so to speak, of joy and gladness and is not pleased to glorify God alone, but as the appointed leader of all the visible creation, man is able to gather unto himself all the creatures that are subject to him and to formulate an all-harmonious choir. Thus, man glorifies God first and then moves the rest of the creatures through a fine personification to glorify him also, and to praise their Creator. Now, man calls upon all of these creatures together with the three Children: "Let all the works of the Lord glorify the Lord; praise and magnify him throughout the ages." And with David we say, "Let everything that breathes praise the Lord!" (Ps 150:6). Man is desirous to see these creatures acquire minds too and tongues and words to proclaim to all the almighty power and the transcendent goodness and wisdom of God, which he has poured out upon them. The divine Creator has not only created them out of nothing and given them existence, but also continuously provides for them everything needed for their preservation and well-being.

How the Mind Rejoices When It Considers Its Own Value

The mind especially rejoices—oh, how it rejoices!—when it glorifies its own architect, its omniscient Creator, God! When the mind returns to contemplate itself and paradoxically becomes its own—the seer and the one seen, the thinker and the one thought about—it realizes that among all the creatures of the whole world, only the mind has been lavished with so many gifts and has been glorified and honored above the angels and above all the creatures of the visible world. The mind has been honored more than the angels because the angels, not being united to a body, are consequently without a spirit that is life-giving to the body, according to St. Gregory Palamas. The mind, however, being united to a body, has consequently also a spirit that is life-giving to its own body. The mind, moreover, has been honored above all the visible and physical creatures because only the mind has been created in the image and likeness of its own Creator; the mind is the head and king of all this expansive sphere of earthly creations. It is also receptive of everlasting blessedness, since it has the natural attribute—if only it would observe the commandments of its Creator— to be united with its prototype and to become willingly by grace what its Creator is by nature. That is to say, the mind has the capacity to be deified and to become divine. As the meditative mind of the prophet David pondered upon these things, he had this to say about the magnificent value of man: "You have crowned him with glory and honor; you have given him dominion over the works of your hands; you have put all things under his feet, all sheep and oxen, and also the beasts of the field, the birds of the air, and the fish of the sea" (Ps 8:5–8).

PROPER DELIGHTS OF THE MIND

The Vision of Creation Is Guided by Sacred Scripture

Dwell with keenness upon these reasons-purposes of creation, dear friend, if you really love to bring joy to your mind and sweetness to your heart by studying them and meditating upon them. As for the other invisible world, that is, the spiritual world of the nine orders of angels, learn the reasons from St. Dionysios, that friend of angels and bird of heaven—(as St. John Chrysostom called him), and from his commentators. The reasons of the physical world you must learn from the holy Fathers, the commentators of the six-day creation, especially St. Basil the Great, who clearly distinguished the nature of created beings. It should be noted that sometimes when one ponders over the rational reasons in nature, he may find some that seem to him to be in opposition to right reason or inappropriate or useless. But one must not for this reason slander or doubt the creation and providence of God, as not having these things properly created and cared for. On the contrary, one must believe that all creatures are good and useful and beneficial, as Scripture confirms: "And God saw everything that he had made, and behold, it was very good" (Gn 1:31). But when one does not understand this, as St. Isaac explained, one may assume a contradiction between nature and Sacred Scripture. God forbid! In fact there is a great symphony and unity between these two, so that nature is an explanation of Scripture and Scripture of nature. For both have the same cause, God, who created nature and who spoke the Scriptures. As God is true in his deeds, he is also true in his words and vice versa. Anyone who would oppose this falls into an obvious contradiction, because he assumes that in one and the same thing someone can be both right and wrong. In expressing this further St. Isaac concluded, "Even those reasons which are not understood by knowledge are nevertheless accepted by us through faith." The same point is made by St. Gregory the Theologian when he said that there comes a time when we are no longer led by reason but by faith, for there are some things which the mind understands and some things which it does not understand.

By forgetting this simple principle, foolish philosophers of our own time have fallen away from the pious faith. In this intellectual conceit they boast of understanding all the reasons in nature and hesitate to admit that there are many things in nature that are beyond their comprehension. In fact, according to the Wisdom of Sirach, "most of his works are concealed" (16:21), and "Many things greater than these lie hidden, for we have seen but few of his works" (43:32). Solomon too, who pondered well on the reasons in creation, said: "I saw all the work of God, that man cannot find out the work that is done under the sun. However much man may toil in seeking, he will not find it out; even though a wise man claims to know, he cannot find it out" (Eccl 8:17). Not wanting to admit this, the wise men of this time either slander the divine providence as not wise but evil or they fall away completely to atheism. Therefore they must admit their every thought to the obedience of Christ in that their reasoning may be purified and they may thus rise to every height according to the knowledge of God, as St. Paul has noted.

We must also add here, as necessary, that those who are spiritually immature and passionate and have not yet attained perfection and dispassion should guard themselves from being preoccupied with the reasons in nature and especially with small animals and man. When the mind is still passionate it cannot see the immaterial and spiritual reasons hidden in the shapes and beauty of physical nature and the passionate and irrational imagination takes precedence to formulate these reasons passionately according to its own standards. Thus instead of selecting from this physical experience knowledge and reasons that are spiritual, such persons select only mere shapes and passions and passionate idols. And instead of rising through nature to the spiritual and incorruptible nature of the Creator so as to marvel at this and to love God and be immersed in him, they remain on the physical level of admiring and being filled by the corruptible beauty of nature only, so as to virtually worship the creation and not the Creator—a condition which many naturalists of the past and of today are suffering. St. Maximos has given clear instruction on this matter: "Before reaching a high degree of control in your habits, it is better to avoid physical theoria so that in seeking spiritual reasons in the visible creation you may not mistakenly gather only passions. For in the imperfect it is much easier for the visible shapes of things seen to be perceived than for the hidden reasons in the shape of events to be received by the soul."[43] Even during the time when the temptations are in revolt, we must avoid physical theoria and must withdraw our mind into our heart (as we noted in the chapter on guarding the heart). This is to say that we must withdraw within ourselves and through our self to run to God with prayer and with the calling upon his name, so that we may thus defeat our enemy who attacks us.

5. As a Source of Spiritual Delight the Incarnate Economy of the Son of God Surpasses the Creation of All the Creatures

What imagination and wonder the mind receives from the incarnate economy of the Lord! What delight and joy it experiences from this inspiration and wonder! Is it ever possible for the mind to ponder how he who is already eternal is begotten of one who is also eternal in a way that transcends both cause and reason? How can the only-begotten and beloved and consubstantial Son, the one in the bosom of the Father; how can the pre-eternal Logos by whom all things were made; how can the true God of true God condescend in these last days to become a man, to appear upon the earth and to associate himself with mankind, and not to have the mind in profound meditation all-enthralled and all-joyful? Especially if the mind realizes that all of this has happened for its own love and for the love of the whole of mankind? "For God so loved the world that he gave his only Son, that whoever believes in him should not perish but have eternal life" (Jn 3:16).

Blessed Augustine said: "God out of love comes to mankind and becomes man. The invisible God through love became like his servants; and for the sake of love he is wounded for our sins. . . . God out of love sent his Son to redeem the slaves, and he sent the Holy Spirit to adopt the slaves. The Son was given as the price of our redemption, and the Holy Spirit was given as the privilege of our love, while God the Father offers himself as an inheritance of our adoption. God became man for the sake of man so that he may be both Creator and Redeemer; God was first born of man so that man may be born of God; God appeared in the likeness of man so that man may love God with greater likeness to him. For these reasons then God received a body and a soul in order that the body and soul of man may be blessed: the soul with his divinity and the body with his humanity."[44]

Is it possible, then, to meditate upon this incarnate economy of God the Logos and his condescension as surpassing the creation of all the angels, of all mankind, all plant and animal life, of all the elements and simply of the whole visible and invisible world and not to be beside oneself from delight and joy? That this is the truth is also confirmed by St. Basil. "There is a tremendous power of proof in God becoming man, much more than the power in the creation of heaven and earth and in the formation of the sea and the air and the greatest of the elements. No creature above the earth or below the earth can represent the power of

God the Logos as does his incarnate economy and his acceptance of the humble and weak circumstances of humanity."[45]

The brother of St. Basil, St. Gregory of Nyssa, explained the reason why the Incarnation surpasses the creation of all the creatures: The creation of the world is a natural creation, the Incarnation is a supernatural one. It should be noted that this condescension of God did not in any way lessen or weaken God, but rather added glory and greater height to him, as St. Gregory of Thessaloniki noted in his homily on the Incarnation of Christ. Because God is by nature supreme and above all, he has no need to rise to a greater height or glory. There was no place from which he could be glorified and exalted other than from here below, that is, from condescending and humbling himself to the level of his creatures. For the glory of the one standing high is his condescension to the humble. This way he wanted to show to his creatures, who have fallen out of a desire for a position of height and glory, an excellent way to be exalted and glorified in truth through humiliation. Therefore the Incarnation of God the Logos, the childhood years, the washing of the disciples' feet, the terrible crucifixion and death, the burial, the descent into Hades and all the humble things Jesus Christ did and suffered upon earth are all so much more glorious and exalted than are heaven itself and all the supernatural powers in heaven. How can the exalted be seen in the humble without descending from its height? How can divinity be united with humanity so that Christ becomes man but remains God? St. Gregory the Theologian sought to explain this in his homily on the birth of Christ: "What wealth of goodness! What a mystery this is for me! I received the image of God and did not preserve it; he partakes of my nature in order to both restore the image and to make the flesh immortal. The second communion is much more paradoxical than the first, for then God offered the greater but now he partakes of the lesser. This latter is more divine than the former; for those who have an understanding mind, true humility is exaltation." For these reasons, then, St. Gregory considered the Incarnation of God the Logos as greater than the first creation of man. It is appropriate to note the words of St. Isaac: "This grace is greater: the one which we received after having sinned in order to be resurrected—than the one we received when we were not and by which we were brought into being."[46] Macarios of Philadelphia also noted that "to become flesh and to suffer for us upon the Cross is a much greater deed for God than to create the whole world and to bring all things out of non-being into being. Creation indicates God's ineffable power and love for mankind, but His Incarnation indicates much more."[47]

The Four Attributes of God (in the Mystery of the Incarnation)

Is it then possible for the mind to meditate upon this mystery of the Incarnation—to see an ultimate goodness, an ultimate wisdom, an ultimate righteousness, and an ultimate power of God, as the Fathers say, and not be filled with inexpressible gladness? The goodness of God was revealed because he did not neglect his own creation, broken by the devil, but with compassion recreated man. The wisdom of God is revealed here in the manner and the means that he thought to use to bring about the recreation and the healing of mankind. The righteousness of God is revealed in that he did not impose tyrannically the salvation of man, who willingly is held captive by sin and the devil. The power of God is revealed in the fact that it was not weakened in bringing to completion such recreation and salvation of mankind. What am I saying? How can the mind not be joyous when it ponders that this mystery is the end toward which all the creatures were from the beginning destined and created in time—both visible and invisible, while the mystery itself was neither destined nor created in time for any other particular end? St. Maximos, in his sixtieth response to questions, has theologized on this mystery: "This is the great and hidden mystery; this is the blessed destiny for which all things were formed; this is the foreordained divine purpose in the origin of beings, and for which all things were made, but which itself was not made for any other." This is to be understood in the sense of the preceding will of God and not in the sense of the subsequent will of God. God created the essences of the beings with this end in mind. This is mainly the end purpose of providence and of those things provided for, inasmuch as there is in God a recapitulation of all that he created. This is the mystery that describes all the ages and which reveals the great will of God that preexisted infinitely all the ages. In proclaiming the will of God, he who is in essence the Logos of God became man and thus revealed the innermost depth of the paternal goodness, and in himself the very purpose for which created beings wisely received their origin.

PROPER DELIGHTS OF THE MIND

The Angels Learned the Manifold Wisdom of God from the Incarnation

How can the mind not rejoice and be glad with an inexpressible and glorious joy when it considers that in this mystery of the divine Incarnation even the angels themselves learned the manifold wisdom of God through the Church, which they did not know before? This is what St. Paul said: "That through the Church the manifold wisdom of God might now be made known to the principalities and powers in the heavenly places" (Eph 3:10). Interpreting this passage, St. Gregory of Nyssa wrote the following:

> Truly through the Church is the manifold wisdom of God made known to the heavenly angelic powers. This wisdom has through opposites brought about marvelous wonders and miracles. How has life come through death? And righteousness through sin? How has a blessing come through a curse? Glory through dishonor? And power through weakness? Before the time of Christ, the heavenly powers knew only the simple and singular wisdom of God, which accordingly enacted the miracles in nature. There was no variety in visible nature that did not have its power in divine nature which provided for all of creation. . . . But this manifold wisdom of God which was constituted by the coupling with the opposites, was clearly taught now by the Church. How is the Logos made flesh? How is life mixed with death? How is our sickness cured by His own suffering? How does he destroy the power of the enemy through the weakness of the Cross?[48]

Through the Mystery of the Incarnation the Mind Learns That the Privations of Christ Became Our Habits and a Paradoxical Healing

Briefly, I must say that in the mystery of the divine economy, the mind learns that the privations of Christ became our habits, as St. Maximos said. That is to say, the Incarnation of the Logos became our theosis. His *kenosis* or self-emptying became our fulfillment; his condescension our exaltation; his passion our dispassion; his death our life. Learning and understanding this the mind rejoices and is glad. In fact, in this mystery of divine economy the mind discovers a marvelous and paradoxical science of healing. The mind realizes that in divine economy we do not overcome our opponents with the opposite forces, as the care of the physicians and the physicists prescribe, but rather our illnesses are healed by similar illnesses. The mind discerns that through the poverty of God the Logos our own poverty was healed; through his death our death and through his *corruption* our own corruption was healed.

When the Son of God Became Incarnate and Died He Came Out of Himself

Finally, is it ever possible for our mind not to be delighted and gladdened when it ponders that the immortal and dispassionate Logos, the Second Person of the Holy Trinity, begotten of the Father before all ages, condescended not only to become incarnate by the Holy Spirit and the Virgin Mary, but also to toil and to hunger, to thirst and to be slandered, to suffer and in the end to die a death on the cross out of love for us? "But God shows his love for us in that while we were yet sinners Christ died for us" (Rom 5:8). I believe therefore that our mind most certainly will not only rejoice but because of the abundant joy will even shed sweetest tears. For the most beloved Son of God, because of his overabundant love for mankind, sinful mankind, came out of himself (to use a daring expression), even though he remained within his Hypostasis as the Logos of God incarnate and it was as such that he suffered and died, and again came to himself through the resurrection. And this is not my own word, but that of St. Gregory of Nyssa.[49] The Church of Christ has taken from this Father the words which are sung on Holy Saturday: "This is the day of rest when the only begotten Son of God rested from all his works; when he kept a sabbath through the economy of death in the flesh, and returned to what he is eternally through the resurrection."

Why on Pascha Day We Read the Theological Gospel: John 1:1ff.

And this is the true reason why on the great Sunday of Pascha, that is on the Day of the Resurrection the Gospel according to St. John is read, which contains the high theology and emphasis on the divinity of the Logos of God. This is to prove that the Son of God in all of the period of his earthly life, especially during the time of his passion, death, and burial, exercised such condescension and such self-emptying of his glory and so humbled himself for the love of mankind that, as St.

Gregory the Theologian noted, he appeared as if he had gone out of himself, that is, out of the authority of his natural divinity. When he was resurrected, he returned—so to speak—to himself and his own former authority of divinity was restored. For the resurrection from the dead is an activity of the almighty power and authority of divinity. This is what St. Paul was indicating when he wrote: "According to the working of his great might, which he accomplished in Christ when he [God the Father] raised him from the dead and made him sit at the right hand in the heavenly places" (Eph 1:19–20). Elsewhere he wrote: "For he was crucified in weakness, but lives by the power of God" (2 Cor 13:4). Through the resurrection the body of the Lord, which was previously susceptible to suffering, transcended suffering; the corruptible became incorruptible. The body that had become through suffering and death without form and comely glory was now brightened and beautiful and glorified with the same glory of divinity hypostatically united with him. "Father, glorify thou me" (as man), asked Jesus the Theanthropos before the resurrection, "glorify thou me in thy presence with the glory which I had with thee [as God], before the world was made" (Jn 17:5).

When the Lord wanted to show that he had received this glory after the resurrection, he said to his disciples when he appeared to them after his resurrection: "All authority in heaven and on earth has been given to me" (Mt 28:18). For the authority he had as God and Creator of all, he received and inherited as man, but not before the resurrection but after it. This is why St. Paul wanted to point out that the divine name was exalted and that Jesus received the name that is above every name not before the passion and the resurrection, but after. Having said before about Jesus, "And being found in human form, he humbled himself and became obedient unto death, even death on a cross," he then added: "Therefore, God has highly exalted him and bestowed on him the name which is above every name" (Phil 2:8–9). And again elsewhere, "But we see Jesus, who for a little while was made lower than the angels, crowned with glory and honor" (Heb 2:9). But when do we see Jesus crowned with glory and honor, O Paul? It is obvious that he was so crowned after the passion and the resurrection. Jesus, himself, confirmed this when he spoke to Cleopas and the other disciple on the way to Emmaus: "Was it not necessary that the Christ should suffer these things and enter into his glory?" (Lk 24:26). This was also revealed by the voices of the angels, the four animals, and of the elders which St. John the Theologian heard in the Book of Revelation: "Worthy is the Lamb who was slain, to receive power and wealth and wisdom and might and honor and glory and blessing!" (Rv 5:12). When was he worthy to receive these? He received these after he was slain and resurrected. Or to put it simply, the body of the Lord became through the resurrection an appropriate vehicle to demonstrate in it and through it the divine attributes, to the extent, of course, that it was receptive of them, including divinity itself and its glory. These could not have been revealed before the resurrection through his body, being susceptible to corruption because of the economy, even though it was from the time of conception deified because of the hypostatic union. This was elsewhere confirmed by St. Gregory of Nyssa: "The God-bearing flesh [of Christ] was from no other but our own nature and it was reunited to the divinity through the resurrection."[50]

The Mystery of the Incarnation Is Incomprehensible

And again to restate briefly, it is impossible for the mind of man not to marvel and wonder and not to receive for itself spiritual joy, when it ponders three aspects of this mystery: (a) The awesome mystery of the divine Incarnation is incomprehensible, not only for all the wise of the world and for those in Christ who are children and imperfect persons, but also for those even who are most high and transcendent and perfected men and great theologians and who are in spiritual gifts truly like the great forerunner and baptist John, the greatest of man born of woman. (b) The mystery of the Incarnation is incomprehensible, not only for the lower orders of angels who are near the earth—Orders, Archangels, and Angels; not only for the middle orders of angels—Lordships, Powers, Authorities; but also for the supreme angelic hierarchy directly in touch with God—Thrones, Cherubim, and Seraphim, and even for those elder and primary minds in this supreme hierarchy. (c) The mystery of the Incarnation is to remain incomprehensible, not only during the present age, but also during all the endless ages of ages. The exact manner and reason of this mystery is to remain always a secret and unrevealed to all the blessed ones both men and angels just as these matters have been confirmed by the truthful words of the Holy Fathers who are moved by the Holy Spirit.

. . . In summing up the incomprehensibility of the mystery of the incarnation, St. Maximos wrote the following: "The great mystery of the Incarnation will always remain a mystery. For those who are saved by it, this mystery will always possess an as yet unseen aspect that is greater than the aspect that is comprehensible. But this revealed aspect still remains completely hidden. God is superessential and as a lover of man becomes truly man out of the human existence but the *how* he becomes man remains always beyond expression and human comprehension. For he becomes man in a way that transcends man."[51] Therefore Augustine was right in theologizing about this sublime mystery and saying (in the first part of his questions) that God, being almighty, can create other more perfect creatures, with the exception of these three which cannot accept any addition or improvement, namely, the humanity of Jesus Christ, the quality of the Virgin Mary as the mother of God, and the glory of the blessed. Oh, mystery of all mysteries the most wonderous! May all be put to shame who do not accept the ever-virgin Mary and mother of God!

Man Must Meditate upon the Mysteries of the Lord

For this reason, dear friend, make it a habit for your mind to meditate at length upon the words of this mystery of the Incarnation of the Logos of God and I assure you that you will never be without matter and reasons for spiritual delights and complete festivals. St. Gregory the Theologian experienced such spiritual delights and was able to write: "How many festivals there are for me in each one of the mysteries of Christ! But of all these, the first is my perfection and recreation and return to the first Adam."[52] Think then of sweetest Jesus, sometimes as a babe lying in the manger; sometimes being held in the arms of Symeon; now being baptized by St. John in the river Jordan and witnessed by the Father; now doing miracles or being transfigured on the mountain and shining brighter than the sun; and now preaching the gospel of salvation. Other times think of him as being mocked and slandered, as suffering and as hanging naked on the cross, and as dead and covered in the tomb. Other times again, think of him as raised from the dead and ascended to heaven and seated at the right hand of God the Father. This is exactly what St. Gregory the Theologian has urged us to do when he wrote: "Walk without blame throughout all the ages and activities of Christ as a dedicated disciple seeking to learn all about Him."[53] St. Isaac too said: "Fix your mind upon all the mysteries of the economy of the Savior so as to meditate upon them."[54]

PROPER DELIGHTS OF THE MIND

It Is Also a Great Delight to Envision the Physical Appearance of Christ

Let me say this too. Even the mere envision of the physical appearance and the beauty of the divine face of Jesus brings inexpressible delight so that you will want to say enthusiastically: "You are all sweetness, O Savior; you are all desire and appeal; you are all insatiate; you are all beauty irresistible." Also you will want to say: "You have attracted me with desire, O Christ, and you have transfigured me with your divine love." Moreover, you will want to say with St. Paul: "Who shall separate us from the love of Christ? Shall tribulation, or distress, or persecution, or famine, or nakedness, or peril, or sword?" (Rom 8:35). Also you will want to ask the question of the bride: "Have you seen him whom my soul loves?" (Sg 3:3). And you will want to say many other similar words of love. Think of those most pure eyes of Jesus, so calm, so sweet; the straightness of his nose; the somewhat chestnut-colored and at the same time golden hair and beard of his; his great and joyous forehead; the blended color of his calm and royal face; his fine, long fingers and his perfectly shaped hands; his moderate stature, and simply all of the other symmetry and grace, which shone in all of his members. Jesus was so beautiful that, as Lentulus, that officer who had seen the Lord with his own eyes in Jerusalem, wrote to the senate in Rome, there has never appeared on earth another person more beautiful than Jesus. Foreseeing this beauty, prophet David wrote: "You are the fairest of the sons of men" (Ps 45:2). Aquila rendered this line: "You were adorned with beauty by the sons of men." Symmachus rendered it: "Among the sons of men you are good in beauty." The bride in the Song speaks lovingly to him: "Behold, you are beautiful, my beloved, truly lovely" (Sg 1:16). This is why the people could not be satisfied when looking upon him, nor did they want to take their attention away from him. St. John Chrysostom, explaining the passage "When Jesus saw great crowds around him" (Mt 8:18), wrote: "The people were really attracted to him and they loved him and marveled at him, desiring always to be looking upon him. Who would want to leave while he was doing these wonderful deeds? Who would not want to simply get a glance of the face and the mouth that was saying such wonderful things? He was not so wonderful only when he was doing miracles, but even when he was just looked upon simply he was just full of grace."[55] This is what the prophet David meant when he said that he was the most beautiful among the sons of man. Now, if the physical body of sweetest Jesus was so beautiful then when he was bearing a corruptible body, how much more beautiful is it now that it has become incorruptible and glorified and his divine face is shining in heaven infinitely more brightly than the sun? This is why St. John Chrysostom has sought with his eloquent homilies to move us to do everything we can so that we may achieve and enjoy the most sweet vision of the glorified and most beautiful and most desired divine face of Jesus. For if one is to be deprived of the vision of that most beautiful and most desired face of Jesus, this is truly a worse calamity than a thousand hells. For as St. Chrysostom wrote: "Even if we experience a thousand hells, none of these will be anything like the experience of seeing the calm face of Jesus and his serene eyes turn away from us as being unable to endure looking upon us."[56]

6. The Attributes of God a Source of Spiritual Delight

The sixth and final source of spiritual delights for the mind is the natural and supernatural vision of the attributes of God. Sacred Scripture calls these the virtues or the glory of God: "My glory I give to no other, nor my virtues [praise] to graven images" (Is 42:8). "His *glory* covered the heavens and the earth was full of his praise" (Hb 3:3). The older theologians and saints called these natural attributes of God also natural and essential powers of God and uncreated energies. St. Dionysios Areopagite in particular called them processions of the cause of all, divine gifts and united theology. The newer theologians prefer the more common term attributes and perfections of God. The mind rises above this earth, cuts through the air, passes beyond the atmosphere, the planets and all the starry expanse of space, and even beyond the angelic and other-worldly powers. The mind thus goes out and beyond all physical and spiritual things and reasons to envision the unconfused Monad and the indivisible Triad, the first and most pure and most simple *Being*, the principle of all principles, the cause of causes; the transcendent and hidden One, the truly one and three, the Triune God. The mind meditates on God, not only relatively as the creative cause of all, but rather directly and absolutely and in himself—as nature and essence that is unmoved, unchanged, infinite, without beginning, simple, unmixed, indivisible, immortal, inapproachable light, ineffable power, limitless size, transcendent glory, desired goodness, and irresistible beauty that is strongly partaken by the contrite heart, but impossible to express with words, as St. Basil wrote.[57] In other words, the mind with its steady, spiritual and incisive eyes looks upon God as a transcendent sun who emanates natural and essential rays, that is, reflects His perfections and innumerable and uncreated qualities and natural attributes.

The mind enters into the reasons and the vision of these natural perfections and attributes of God through faith and the teachings of the Sacred Scriptures and of the holy Fathers. Thus guided, the mind receives not only joy and delight, but, if I may say so, becomes itself all joy and delight and finds itself swimming in an ocean of gladness. On one hand the mind sees the kingdom of God which is not measured in aeons and years, but is without beginning and without end and beyond all aeons and years. "The Lord will reign forever and ever" (Ex 15:18). It is not proper to say that the kingdom of God has a beginning or an end in time, as St. Maximos has noted.[58] On the other hand, the mind meditates on the majesty of God and sees that it is infinite and beyond its comprehension. "Great is the Lord, and greatly to be praised, and his greatness is unsearchable" (Ps 145:3). The mind moreover sees the almighty power of God which creates everything that exists and which can in an instant uphold an infinite number of worlds. The mind also considers the divine wisdom according to which everything is eternally foreknown and in time created by divine fiat. Thus the mind contemplates the divine righteousness which has determined in all beings measures and bounds which they may not transgress. Finally, the mind envisions the comprehensive and perfect goodness of God which is revealed by the divine perfections and all the revelations (progressions) of God who is the cause of all. Out of this goodness as an active cause, God has not only created whatever exists, but through it he also preserves everything. In brief then the mind sees the natural powers and perfections, all being infinite and ineffable in size, all innumerable in number, all incomprehensible to understand, all uncreated in their being, all most beautiful to behold, all without beginning and without end in time. These attributes of God are everywhere present and yet they transcend everything as to space. These attributes of God are thus likened to the nets of the apostles of old when they caught so many fish that they were about to break. Like the nets, the mind is so overwhelmed by the enjoyment of so much joy and delight as a result of the attributes of God that it is in danger of being torn and going out of itself!

PROPER DELIGHTS OF THE MIND

The Ultimate Blessedness Is the Vision of the Divine Perfection of God, Who Essentially Transcends Them

In creation all the creatures partook of these divine attributes, each one according to its material need. But as the theologians tell us, the future blessedness and joy of all the saved—both angels and men—will be the vision of God, not in his essence and nature, but according to the divine attributes and perfections and activities of God. In other words, the future blessedness of the faithful, the whole of paradise, all of the hoped-for blessings will be these most beautiful and most desired natural attributes and activities of God, which will then be more perfectly revealed and understood by the blessed faithful. The blessed Maximos noted: "The Kingdom of God is the communication by grace of the naturally good attributes of God."[59] In all of these the mind rejoices and becomes beside itself for joy when it meditates and realizes that the cause and origin and source of these supremely perfect gifts is the superessential essence of God. Or to put it in another way, the cause of these attributes is the Triune God himself, the Three Hypostases or Persons of the Godhead, who are one and the same God with one essence, three hypostases, and the essential perfections. However, as St. Maximos said, "God in his essence is infinitely transcendent not only of all the creatures that partake of him, but also of the divine energies which are partaken."[60] Similarly, St. Dionysios said: "As those beings that are holy, divine, primary or noble are superior to non-beings so is the incommunicable cause transcendent of all the beings and of all those who partake and of all participation."[61] This is why the mind asks itself questions and is astonished beyond comprehension; the heart leaps and dances in spirit and sings a song of triumph. This is delight itself, this is sweetness, for it discerns that this vision of God and this gladness is the fulfillment of desire, as St. John Chrysostom explained:

> What does it mean to "be glad and exult in thee"? (Ps 9,2). It means that I have such a master that he is my delight and my joy. Whoever knows this delight as it should be known does not feel any other. For this is delight itself, while everything else is only names of delight. This joy causes man to be lifted up; it causes the soul to be free of the body; it flies toward heaven; it raises me beyond the worldly cares; it relieves us from evil.[62]

PROPER DELIGHTS OF THE MIND

The Mind Becomes Like the Object Perceived and the Heart Like the Object Loved

As Aristotle noted, the mind becomes like the object it perceives (not in essence but in action). Now, by seeing these perfections of God, the mind is changed by divine grace to become like them in action. For example, the divine wisdom the mind perceives makes it wise; the divine holiness makes it holy; the divine goodness makes it good; the divine simplicity makes it simple; the divine light makes it light. In the same way, the mind becomes by grace like all the other divine activities. Therefore, how can the mind not rejoice then when it sees itself changed for the better and when among mortals it sees itself becoming rich with the happiness of immortals? How can the mind not rejoice when it sees itself being raised toward the likeness of God? And when it is seized by God or when it seizes God? Since the heart also has the natural attribute to make the heart like the object it loves, how is it possible for one who loves the divine perfections not to be filled with gladness when he sees his heart transfigured to be like his beloved God? How can he not say with St. Paul: "It is no longer I who live, but Christ who lives in me?" (Gal 2:20).

The Doxology of God Comes from the Innumeration of God's Perfections. God Is Both Communicable and Incommunicable

In fact, how is it possible then for the mind not to be full of joy and overflowing with it when it realizes that the more it numbers and observes and studies these natural perfections and attributes of God the more does it want to glorify and praise the very same God who is the natural cause of these perfections? According to St. Basil the glorification of God is a direct result of the innumeration of God's attributes. Briefly then, let me also add that, as you know, God is communicable in his energies and perfections but incommunicable in his essence, as well as in the infinite nature of his divine perfections. The (human) mind of course is by nature a lover of the good and seeks always to understand the best and the highest. It is drawn by the delight of having communication and participation in the divine perfections and so it seeks with all of its power to rise to the highest of these. Now since the mind is finite and therefore cannot contain the infinite, it realizes that that which it was unable to comprehend is much higher and much more delightful than that which it did understand. Thus, it marvels and ponders and does not know what will come of this amazement. In this state the mind is filled with divine love and kindles the soul with strong desires that are the result of a divine love and delight that is in turn provoked by the comprehensible aspect of the incomprehensible God and the ensuing questions that are raised. This divine love purifies the mind; purified, the mind becomes more godlike; becoming godlike by grace the mind remains subsequently in this state, as St. Gregory the Theologian noted:

> It seems to me that the divine attracts the mind to what is communicable to it. What is altogether incommunicable is not even hoped for nor attempted. This incommunicable aspect of God is contemplated in amazement. As it is marveled it is also desired; being desired it purifies the mind (and the soul); and this purification makes the mind to be like God. When human minds are so purified God speaks to them as his own (to use a daring phrase of youth). God is thus united to "gods" and is known as much perhaps as He already knows those who know Him.[63]

The Mind and God Serve as a Type for Each Other. The Mind Therefore Imitates the Divine Perfections

According to the opinion of the theologians, the mind and God are a type one to another, as the mind who loves rises to God who is loved. The mind rises to God through contemplation of his divine perfections, while the beloved God condescends from his height toward the mind that loves him, uniting himself with it, and filling it with grace and deifying it. Thus, in this ascent of God the blessed and supernatural union of God and mind is accomplished: the lover with the beloved; the prototype with the image, or to put it simply, the Creator who is infinitely removed with the infinitely removed by nature creature. And this is what St. Gregory the Theologian said regarding the Holy Spirit coming down on Pentecost in the upper room: "This indicates the ascent of the recipients and the descent of God toward us as was the case with Moses before. It is necessary for us to rise up for this communion with God to take place. As long as each side remains where it is—one in majesty and the other in humility— the goodness and loving kindness [of God] remains incommunicable and there is a great impassable chasm between God and man." St.

Maximos has also noted this important principle: "God, for the love of man, becomes man to the degree that man has deified himself through love of God. Moreover, man is grasped by God according to his mind toward what is known, as much as man has revealed the by nature invisible God through the virtues."[64] What fulness of virtue! What divine graces! What supernatural good things come from the study of the attributes of God! These graces and supernatural good things can be enjoyed more fully and more perfectly by the mind, when it not only envisions these all-beautiful attributes and qualities and perfections of God, but when it also seeks and struggles to imitate them as much as possible through works. For as it is not enough for an artist to only look upon a painting that is precise and perfect according to the rules of the art, but is also necessary for him to be able to imitate it with his own hand if he wishes to receive its shape, so also with the mind, it is not enough to simply contemplate the divine perfections; it is necessary for him to imitate them in practice, if one wants to cultivate himself according to them. Theory alone is without foundation; imitation and practice is everything. Is God by nature primarily good? "No one is good except one, God" (Mt 19:17). And does he have this goodness as a natural perfection and an inseparable quality of his being? (Yes, he does.) Thus, the mind must imitate this goodness of God through practice, as it is written: "You chasten us so that we may meditate upon thy goodness" (Wis 12:22). One must become good by participation and grace, doing good not only to those who do good to us, but even to those who do us harm and are our enemies. We must be like God who "makes his sun rise on the evil and on the good, and sends rain on the just and on the unjust" (Mt 5:45). For in this way one becomes a son of God and is said that he is of God, as it is written: "Love your enemies and pray for those who persecute you, so that you may be sons of your Father who is in heaven" (Mt 5:44–45a). "He who does good is of God" (3 Jn 11). Is God by nature holy and does He possess natural perfection and holiness? Then the mind must also be like that freely, as it is written: "You shall be holy; for I the Lord your God am holy" (Lv 19:2). Also, "he disciplines us for our own good, that we may share his holiness" (Heb 12:10). Is God by nature compassionate and merciful? "The Lord God is merciful and gracious" (Ex 34:6). And does he have this mercy and grace as inseparable perfections? Sacred Scripture confirms this throughout. Thus the mind, too, must struggle to become imitatively merciful and compassionate toward all its brothers and sisters as the Lord has commanded: "Be merciful, even as your Father is merciful"(Lk 6:36).

In other words, in all the virtues and good works which the mind uses, it must keep before itself as an example and an image the natural attributes and the perfections of God. These must be imitated as much as possible and through works one must prove that his mind is cultivated and refined by these perfections. St. Paul has urged all Christians to "be imitators of God, as beloved children" (Eph 5:1). If the mind seeks to imitate these divine perfections, it will not only avoid pride, but will not even raise a simple thought of pride in the heart as if it has achieved or is achieving some particular virtue. This is so because we thus realize very well that all the virtues are eternal and infinite in time and magnitude, as natural perfections of God. And, as St. Maximos said, they are also unattainable by imitation. Therefore, how can anyone be prideful when he sees that he only partakes of these virtues as much as a single drop partakes of a great sea? When our mind seeks to imitate these divine perfections, it will never neglect to walk in the endless way of godly progress and ascent. We will be ever stretching to reach those things that are ahead, and forgetting those things that are left behind, according to St. Paul. He who imitates these divine perfections, that is, he who is naturally in the image of God, will become willingly also in the likeness of God. For St. Gregory of Nyssa said: "You possess the image of God by being rational; you receive the likeness of God by acquiring virtue. In creation I have the image, but I become through the exercise of my free will in the likeness of God."[65] Through this likeness, the mind is united with God; the image is united with the prototype and is deified or, what amounts to the same thing, is saved. For according to St. Dionysios, none can be saved who is not first deified. (This is in truth a very fearful word.) Again, no one can be deified who has not previously become in the likeness of God through the possible imitation of his divine perfections and has thus been united to God. "Salvation is not possible but by the deification of the saved; deification is likeness and union with God."[66]

When the mind imitates the natural perfections of God, it becomes an earthly "God" by imitation and by grace, bearing in itself those exceptional and most beautiful perfections which only God himself possesses essentially and by nature. "You are gods sons of the most High, all of you" (Ps 82:6). Such a transfigured person overshadows and endures without malice in a divine manner the mistakes of his fellow human beings, just as God endures the mistakes of the whole world. This is what happened to the great St. Macarios of Egypt, as it is written in the *Gerontikon*, who attained to that super perfection of God, that is, to a degree possible and receptive by human nature, through participation in that infinite perfection. "You, therefore, must be perfect, as your heavenly Father is perfect" (Mt 5:48). This is the commandment of our Lord Jesus.

Ponder over the *theoria*, but also struggle for the possible imitation of these more-than-beautiful, more-than-marvelous perfections of God and draw ineffable delight. And if you happen to be a bishop and you become like God through the imitation of his moral perfections, then you will be truly adorned and the words of St. Dionysios will apply to you: "The bishop seeks to be likened unto God [as much as possible] for he desires that all men be saved and come to a knowledge of truth."[67] Above all seek to acquire the vision of the divine light, that enlightening and beautifying cause of all. St. Dionysios called God "beauty" because of the beauty and the harmony with which he endows each creature, but he also called him "intelligible light" because of the well-spring and more-than-abundant emanation of light with which he fills the *supracosmic*, the *pericosmic*, and the *encosmic* mind.[68]

The Vision of the Divine Light and the Divine Beauty Is the Sweetest of All the Attributes of God

Of all the physical and visible creations, light is the sweetest and the most desirable. "Light is sweet, and it is pleasant for the eyes to behold the sun" (Eccl 11:7). The beauty of bodies both living and nonliving attracts the heart more than any other organ to love it. "The eye desires grace and beauty" (Sir 40:22). Thus, the vision of the divine light and the divine beauty, both the one granted to us from the outside and the one we acquire through our efforts,[69] is more sweet and more desirable than all the other attributes and perfections of God. Similarly the heart of the lover is pierced and wounded by the arrows of strong desire for God, of almighty eros and divine love. The reason for this is the fact that as the physical light of the sun provides the brightness to the physical eyes and makes it possible for them to distinguish the visible creations in the physical world, so also is the spiritual light of the superessential sun which grants illumination and clarity to the eyes of the soul the means by which they can discern through it all the

220

blessed visions in the spiritual world and all the mysteries of the future age.[70]

What the Sun Is to Physical Things, God Is to Spiritual Things

St. Gregory the Theologian said succinctly and wisely something which he borrowed from Plato:

> What the sun is to physical things, God is to spiritual things. For the one gives light to the visible world and the other to the invisible world. The one makes the bodily visions to be like the sun, and the other makes the spiritual natures to be like God. Moreover, the sun makes it possible for those who see to see and for those that are seen to be seen, and of the objects that are seen the sun is the best. So, also with God. To those who think and to those who are thought about, God makes it possible for the thinkers to think and for those thought about to be thought about. And of those realities thought about, God is the ultimate reality, where every appeal ends since there is nothing beyond God.[71]

"In the sun he has set his tabernacle . . ." (Ps 18:4 LXX). That is, God has set in the sun an image and a likeness of his divinity. This is why certain holy teachers have properly referred to the sun as a sort of *hieroglyphic* of God. (This seems to me to be the simplest and natural interpretation of this verse, even though others interpret it differently.)

Do you want to be convinced how the vision of the divine light and the divine beauty is the sweetest and most desirable vision of all the other perfections of God? Listen to those theologians who have experienced it. So that if you are not touched and moved by anyone else toward the love of God, you may perhaps be moved by these truly enthusiastic teachings. St. Basil wrote about the divine light and beauty in this manner:

> What is more marvelous than divine beauty? What thought is more gracious and delightful than the thought of God's majesty? Which desire of the soul is so strong and unbearable as the desire brought about by God to the soul that is purified of every evil and can truly say that it is wounded by love? The lightning rods of God's divine beauty are altogether ineffable

221

and inexpressible. No word can suffice; no sound is acceptable. Even if one speaks about the morning star, the brightness of the moon, the light of the sun—all these are useless in helping us to conjecture that divine glory. They fall so short in comparison with the true light as a deep darkness and a gloomy moonless night cannot compare with the brightness of the noon day. This divine beauty is invisible to the eyes of the flesh; it is only perceived by the soul and the mind alone. And even when it illumined some of the saints, the sting of this divine desire became unbearable for them.[72]

Again, St. Basil wrote: "True beauty that is most lovely and visible only to the purified mind is around the divine and blessed nature. He who looks upon flashings of light and rays receives something of this light—just as a tinge of a bright color brought close to us is reflected on our face. When Moses was speaking to God his face was glorified by participation in the divine beauty of God that emanated from His glory."[73]

The brother of St. Basil, St. Gregory of Nyssa, also noted in agreement with his brother: "If one has an eye capable of seeing for an hour, how can he remain unmoved by love for such divine beauty? The perceived beauty is great, but infinitely greater is the invisible beauty that is conjectured by meditating on what is visible."[74] Again he wrote: "To compare a small drop of water with the great abysses, or a small spark with the great rays of the sun, is to compare all that men marvel as good with that beauty that is considered the ultimate good that transcends every good."[75]

St. Kallistos also spoke about the spiritual delight of the mind.

The mind having inexplicably risen to the One beyond understanding is in a sense enamored by him, for a beauty that is ineffable and inconceivable emanates from him as from an almighty source. When the mind finds itself in the condition of receiving divine illumination, it is like the fishnet filled beyond endurance and in danger of breaking because of the many fish. The mind stands in wonder before this divine beauty; it is inebriated as if by wine, and ecstatic as if senseless. Unable to contain the vision of this extraordinary beauty beyond beauty, the mind suffers an ecstasy beyond comprehension. Therefore, it is bound by the bonds of love and burning with a thirst for God.[76]

The words of the blessed Augustine about the divine light and beauty are also most enthusiastic and can stir the heart to such love. Here is what he has written about the divine light:

O true light, marvelous light, light beyond praise, light that illumines the eyes of the angels! Behold, I see! I thank you! Behold, I see the light of heaven. A ray from the light of your face illumines from above the eyes of my understanding and makes my whole being rejoice. Increase this light, I pray, O Provider of Light. Increase the light shining in me: Make this light broader; make it more abundant, I pray. What is this fire that is burning my heart? What is this that I am feeling? What is this light that is illumining my heart? O light ever burning and unwaning, light me! O light ever shining and unwaning, illumine me! It is an advantage to be lit by you! O holy light, how do you burn with sweetness? How do you shine inexplicably? How do you create the desire in us to be enflamed? Alas, for those who are not lit by you! Alas, for those who are not illumined by you! O true light, you enlighten the whole world, your light fills the world. Alas, for the blind eyes that do not see you! O sun, you enlighten both heaven and earth. Alas, for the foggy eyes that are incapable of seeing you. . . . For the eyes that have become accustomed to darkness cannot look upon the rays of your utter truth. Nor are they who dwell in darkness capable of understanding anything about this light. They see only darkness; they love only darkness; they align themselves with the darkness. Going from darkness to darkness, they do not know where they are falling. They are miserable, not knowing in what way they are harmed. They are most miserable when, even though they do know, they nevertheless allow themselves to fall with their eyes open.[77]

As for the divine beauty, the blessed Augustine had this to say:

This God of ours, there can be no other besides him. This is what I seek when I seek my God. This is what I love when I love my God. After a long time, I have come to love you. You were within and I was outside, and I was seeking for you, the one without form, there among the forms which you have created. You were with me, but I was not with you. . . . O light, you enlightened me, and I saw you and I loved you. For no one loves you except he who has seen you. And no one sees you except he who does love you. Lately have I come to love you thus, O ancient beauty! I have loved you late; shame on that time when I did not love you.[78]

Similarly on Mt. Thabor St. Peter was illumined, mind and body, by the bright rays of the divine light, and his heart was deeply moved by that sweetest and extraordinary vision of the more-than-beauty beauty of the divinity of the transfigured Jesus. Because of this, he did not want to be removed from this most delightful vision. Enthusiastically and ecstatically he said: "Lord, it is good that we are here; if you wish, I will make three booths here, one for you and one for Moses and one for Elijah" (Mt 17:4). Macarios of Philadelphia, interpreting this passage in his homily on the Transfiguration, said this:

What is more beautiful than to be with Christ? What is more desirable than his divine glory? Nothing is sweeter than that light which illumines the entire order of men and angels. Nothing is more beloved than that life [of God] in which we all live and move and have our being. There is nothing sweeter than the ever-living beauty, nothing more pleasant than the unceasing gladness. There is nothing more desirable than eternal joy and blessedness, about which no word can suffice to explain or thought to comprehend its sublimity and infinity. For how indeed can one speak about what is essentially an inexpressible beauty? Or how can one measure and describe what is essentially indescribable? This is the supreme object of hope and the revelry of desire. This is also the end and the zenith of all the blessings and promises and gifts of God bestowed upon us supernaturally. It is the enjoyment of a Christlike blessedness. It is the election of seeing in a pure vision the theophany of the Lord. It is the fulfilment of his revelation in a pouring out of his light in bright flashing rays. It is the imposition of those supernatural rays of divine light. It is participation in divine brightness. . . . When St.

Peter was made worthy to look upon this most glorious end, he did not want even for an instant to be separated from it. For he had tasted the delight of the future age and had immediately removed from his soul everything for the sake of that delight and joy which had entered into his being with that vision of the divine light of the transfigured Christ.

These passages should suffice to confirm the point which has been made.

Notes

1. Letter to Olympias, ch. 1.
2. Ecclesiastical Hierarchies, ch. 1.
3. Preamble to the Broad Monastic Rules.
4. Commentary on Matthew, ch. 11.
5. On the Nativity, Homily 20.
6. On the Statues, 16.
7. Address to the Young Men.
8. Homily 4, On Ephesians.
9. Those Who Think They are Justified by Works, ch. 29.
10. Commentary on the fourth chapter of the *Ladder*.
11. Theological Chapters, I Century, ch. 50.
12. Homily on Epiphany.
13. Homily 1.
14. Homily 26, On Discretion.
15. On Matthew, ch. 11.
16. Epistle 56 to Heron the Monk.
17. Epistle 57 to Hyphelios the Grammarian.
18. Homily 1, On Romans.
19. Homily 5, On Anna.
20. On the Spiritual Law, ch. 48.
21. Homily 46.
22. Homily 65.
23. Homily on Epiphany.
24. Homily 58.
25. Homily In the Beginning Was the Word.
26. Homily on Hail.
27. Commentary on Psalm 1.
28. On the Spiritual Law, ch. 6.

29. Ibid.
30. Homily on Hail.
31. Letter to Antiochians.
32. Ecclesiastical Hierarchies, ch. 1.
33. Ibid., ch. 5.
34. Epistle 151 to Eusebius the Bishop.
35. Commentary on Romans.
36. On the Holy Spirit, ch. 5.
37. Homily 1, On the Song of Songs.
38. Mystical Theology, ch. 3.
39. Divine Names, ch. 1.
40. Homily on Pascha.
41. On Theology, Homily 2.
42. Ibid.
43. Theological Chapters, 4th Century, ch. 85.
44. Encheiridion, ch. 21, ch. 26.
45. On the Holy Spirit, ch. 50.
46. Homily 60.
47. Homily on the Resurrection.
48. Homily 8, On the Song of Songs.
49. Homily 1, On the Resurrection.
50. Catechetical Oration, ch. 32.
51. Theological Chapters, III, ch. 12.
52. Homily on the Nativity.
53. Ibid.
54. Epistle 4.
55. Commentary on Matthew.
56. Homily 24, On Matthew.
57. Homily on Faith.
58. Theological Chapters, II, ch. 86.
59. Ibid., I, ch. 20.
60. Ibid., I, ch. 44.
61. Divine Names.
62. Commentary on Psalm 9.
63. Homily on the Nativity.
64. Theological Chapters, IV, ch. 74.
65. On Let Us Create Man in Our Image.
66. Ecclesiastical Hierarchies, ch. 1.
67. Ibid., ch. 2.
68. Divine Names, ch. 4.

69. The so-called vision received from the outside differs from the vision acquired by effort as heaven differs from earth and the soul from the body, according to Kallistos Xanthopoulos. The one is initiated through the direct action of God himself and received passively by those who have been purified by a divine illumination of the heart. The other vision is initiated actively by the self and is dependent upon the external analogies of nature. And yet, even the *acquired vision* of the divine light and beauty creates much joy for those who do not also have the *received* vision from God.

70. There is a natural reason why the eyes are attracted by the physical light and the mind by the spiritual light; it is the principle of similarity and relationship which one has toward these objects. The physical eyes are so composed to be recipients of light, so that they love to have the light which is similar to their nature. God also created the mind to be an intelligible light and accordingly to love the spiritual light. For, as the saying goes, similarity is amiability. This still holds true even though the mind has been darkened and has fallen into an unnatural condition, and of course, it requires supernatural power and grace to overcome this darkness and to see the supernatural light of God. . .

71. Homily on St. Athanasios the Great.

72. Broad Monastic Rules, 2.

73. Commentary on Psalms 29 (30).

74. Homily 1, On the Song of Songs.

75. On Virginity, ch. 1.

76. Philokalia, ch. 24.

77. Questionibus 35.

78. Ibid., 32.

CHAPTER TWELVE

An Epilogue
on the Spiritual Delights

The Enjoyment of Spiritual Pleasures of the Mind Excludes the Physical Passions

There, with the help of God, I have commented for you what are the spiritual and natural pleasures or delights of the mind. Revel in them therefore and enjoy them as much as possible. There is no one to criticize or obstruct you; rather, there are many to praise you and to prompt you. On the contrary, avoid as much as possible the bodily and physical pleasures for which there are many critics who would obstruct you, but certainly no one to praise you and to prompt you. Let me say to you, therefore, that if you become accustomed to enjoying these spiritual and true pleasures, you will surely little by little come to hate the physical and false and painful pleasures. This is confirmed by St. Basil, who said: "When the psalmist received the insight of the flashing brightness coming from the beautiful messiah, he was touched in the heart by this beauty and proceeded to love that spiritual beauty, which once it was revealed to the human soul, everything else previously esteemed appeared worthless and objectionable."[1] This is why when St. Paul came to know the risen Lord, he considered everything else worthless so that he might win Christ. Do you hear? When the spiritual beauty is revealed to the soul and when it tastes the spiritual delights, then the formerly desirable pleasures of the body are hated and rejected. The whole reason why the physical pleasures are loved is the fact that the mind has not yet attained a vision and has not tasted a more sublime delight than the physical ones. In this case, one suffers like the person who thinks the bread made with acorn or millet or corn bran is the sweetest and most tasteful because he has never tasted the bread made from wheat and the finest wheat flour. St. John Climacus has put it well. "He who has tasted the heavenly things can readily disdain earthly things, while he who has no such experience is readily pleased with temporal things."[2] St. Thalassios also said: "An indication that the mind is truly preoccupied with spiritual matters is the disdain of all those things which fawn upon the senses." The wise Theodore of Jerusalem said: "The mind that is always preoccupied with these worldly matters cannot possibly desire to know what is truly good. For if the mind turns to a matter foreign to it, it will certainly more readily turn to something that is kindred. And when the soul comes to know and love such a kindred [spiritual] matter, how can the lover endure to be with earthly matters? Will he not consider the carnal life as an obstruction of good things?"[3] And again: "The spiritual good things are so many and so superior that even a brief outpouring and slight revelation of that infinite divine beauty is sufficient to convince the mind to reject everything that is earthly and to be concerned only with spiritual matters, and to be unwilling to ever separate itself from these delights."[4]

The Enjoyment of Spiritual Delights Makes the Physical Senses Dormant

Why do I say only that these physical senses are hated? Even the five senses and even the passionate aspect of the soul are made inactive and dormant when the mind enjoys the spiritual and true pleasures. Thus St. Gregory of Nyssa has confirmed this:

> For the sake of the vision of the truly good things the bodily eyes become inactive. The perfected soul is not attracted by anything that these bodily eyes may project and prefers to see through the mind only the spiritual reality that lies beyond the visible. The sense of hearing is thus similarly dormant and inactive when the soul is involved with matters transcending reason. As for the other more physical senses, it is unnecessary even to mention. . . . All these senses, as if in a state of sleep, lie dormant while the pure activity of the heart goes on to consider spiritual matters untroubled and unclouded by physical activities.[5]

AN EPILOGUE

There are of course many references in the Fathers on this subject. Let me add just one more from St. Isaac, who made the same affirmation: "Life in God is the cessation of the senses; when the heart lives the senses cease."[6]

The Senses and the Body Can Also Enjoy the Spiritual Pleasures Both Now and in the Future Life

Shall I say a still greater thing? When the spiritual realities are being enjoyed by the mind, the physical and painful pleasures are not only hated; the senses are not only dormant and inactive, but, as we said in the beginning, they accordingly participate together with the mind in the enjoyment of those spiritual delights. According to the holy Fathers, the body by necessity participates according to its nature, together with the senses, in the divine and blessed passions, both in this present life and in the future as well. According to St. Gregory Palamas "the mind mediates between the divine grace and the thickness of the body, transmitting the divine things to its attached body."[7] Therefore, even the physical eyes see the divine light and the spiritual beauty, and the physical hearing hears the spiritual sounds of heaven. The same is true of all the senses when they are touched by the grace of God and transfigured. Therefore, St. Gregory Sinaite said boldly: "He who does not see and hear and feel spiritually is dead."[8] This is why St. Maximos declared that the senses become organs of virtue when rationality prevails. St. Kallistos, too, has written at length to show that God out of love for mankind can be revealed and received through every intelligible and spiritual sense.

Through the enjoyment of these spiritual pleasures of the mind, in which the senses partake, the whole body internally and externally is refined, enhanced, beautified, strengthened, and transfigured to be more spiritual. For this reason, it does not need bodily food to be nourished, nor sleep to rest, nor does it feel any weariness. The body is thus nourished and rested and renewed by a divine nourishment and rest and enjoyment. We have thousands of such examples in the Old Testament and in the New Testament of grace. Thus, Moses spent forty days and forty nights on Mt. Sinai (in prayer) without food, drink, sleep, and without rest. Similarly, Elijah, with the help of the food provided for him by the angel, spent forty days and forty nights on the mountain. The great Saint Paisios, that beloved friend of God, and St. Meletios the Confessor spent many forty-day periods in absolute abstinence. Also, St. John Chrysostom spent three whole months without eating any physical food. St. Symeon the Stylite spent years without any earthly food. And there are many, many more that even to mention their names alone is a difficult task. All of these (men and women of God) by enjoying the divine and spiritual delights of the mind received from this life in part as an earnest that blessedness and happiness which they will enjoy in the future age when the body will be glorified and free of bodily needs. For then, God will be both food and drink and garment and light and anything else so that, as St. Paul said, "God may be everything to everyone" (1 Cor 15:28 . . .).

This manual of spiritual counsel introduces and teaches an evangelical, a Christian, and, therefore, an eternal blessedness and happiness. It teaches the mind not only to meditate upon divine matters, but also to do the virtues commanded by God. It teaches not only to examine the things of God and his divine perfections, but also to love God with our whole heart and through love to keep his commandments and to imitate his perfections. Knowledge, alone, makes one vain, but love edifies. Knowledge comes from nature, while love comes from faith. The former is simply knowledge and, therefore, uncertain; the latter is experience and union with God and, therefore, certain and true. Knowledge belongs to the philosophers and to those outside; faith belongs to the Christians and the faithful. Or to put it in another way: The philosophers can possess knowledge but they are incapable of faith.

Finally, this manual teaches an eternal blessedness. A true, rational, evangelical, a Christian blessedness is also by nature an eternal blessedness. He who possesses in his heart the ultimate and most blessed Good, God himself, through faith and love, can endure all the sufferings that may come his way and consider them as beneficial to his spiritual well-being. Even though pain may come to the members of the body so that it suffers according to its very nature, blessedness is to be found in the soul and, for this reason, the believer can rejoice and be glad in the hope of such eternal blessedness. For he who possesses such blessedness in God from now cannot lose it even in death, but will continue to enjoy such blessedness more fully and more perfectly in heaven.

Dearly beloved and respected bishop, I have written to you about these spiritual matters which you may consider to be counsels and admonitions, but which I consider to be only a reminder. And if you should be pleased by these poorly expressed words, it is certainly because of God who provides all grace and because of your effective prayers which have beseeched God. Through your prayers God has now deigned to open my mouth who am impure, as he opened the mouth of that dumb animal and made it speak. I mean the donkey of Balaam. I have thus reminded you of what has been forgotten and what is beyond my power. St. Dionysios the Areopagite wrote to his fellow bishop Timothy as follows: "If what has been said is correct, it must be attributed to him who is the Cause of all good things and who grants both the ability to speak at all and the ability to speak well."[9] But, if your soul does not look favorably upon these words, which I hope is not the case, then who is to blame? I, my bishop, I am the first to blame, for I say and do not practice. And he who teaches and does not practice is, according to St. Paphnoutios, like the unsalted bread that is without taste and badly digested. "Can that which is tasteless be eaten without salt, or is there any taste in empty words?" (Jb 6:6 LXX). I have done this, therefore, in obedience to St. Neilos, who said: "It is necessary even for him who does not do good things to say good things so that he may be shamed by the words." Again he said, "Formulate virtue in such a way so as not to deceive but to benefit those who see it." The second reason why I am to blame is that I did not keep within my means, but extended myself beyond my reach. I, the least and lacking monk seeking maturity, who should have been reminded and guided toward greater things and perfected by Your Grace, dared on the contrary to remind and guide you. For, did not St. Paul confirm this very principle? "It is beyond dispute that the inferior is blessed by the superior" (Heb 7:7). And did not the great son of Zacharias say to the Lord: "I need to be baptized by you, and you come to me?" (Mt 3:14).

But, alas, what am I to do? I have become like a flintstone and you as a fiery iron. You knocked hard once, you knocked harder two and three times, seeking from him who needs advice to receive letters of counsel. What was I to do with such requests? I drew out these few sparks from the cold stone of my understanding for my own sake, as St. Mark noted: "A man is presented to his neighbor according to what he is, and it is God who will act on the hearer according to what he has believed."[10] It is therefore up to you from here on to take these few sparks and to light the fire of zeal and commitment in your heart, and with it to consume from your senses those passions harmful to the soul and the evil images from your imagination; it is up to you now to be warmed by the spiritual prayer of the heart and to be enlightened in your understanding, so that you can guard both your mind and heart from the passions and the evil thoughts and be able to enjoy the true and spiritual delights of your mind. These spiritual delights, after all, are the central focus of this effort. It is hoped that through all this spiritual growth you will be able to become a type and an example of every good and every virtue for the flock which has been entrusted to you by God. Moreover, it is hoped that you will also move those who look upon you to glorify the Arch-Shepherd Christ for having granted to them such a Christ-imitating shepherd. This is what St. Paul wrote to Timothy and to Titus, his co-workers in the Church: "Let no one despise your youth, but set the believers an example in speech and conduct, in love, in faith, in purity" (1 Tm 4:12). And to Titus he said: "Show yourself in all respects a model of good deeds, and in your teaching, show integrity, gravity, and sound speech that cannot be censured, so that an opponent may be put to shame, having nothing evil to say of us" (Ti 2:7–8). St. Isidore Pylousiotes also wrote: "God lights a priest as a lamp and places him on the lampstand of his light-bearing cathedra for the purpose of emanating light to the Church as well as doctrines and deeds devoid of darkness, so that when the people see the rays of this living lamp, they will direct themselves toward it and glorify God the Father of lights."[11]

As you receive spiritual benefit from these writings, [my dear bishop,] please remember me last of all in your prayers to the Lord, so that I may not only say and remind. For this is quite easy for all, according to the wise man who was asked: "What is easy?" And he answered: "To teach others." Pray, therefore, for me that I may also practice whatever I say and remind to others, for this is the truly difficult thing to do. St. Gregory the Theologian certainly summed it up when he said: "Grace is given not to those who speak [their faith] but to those who live their faith."

Notes

1. Commentary on Psalm 45.
2. Homily 16, ch. 15.
3. Philokalia.
4. Ibid.
5. Homily on the Song of Songs, I.
6. Homily 73.

AN EPILOGUE

7. Homily on Xeni.
8. Ch. 8.
9. Divine Names, ch. 13.
10. On the Spiritual Law, ch. 78
11. Epistle 22 to Dositheos.

"GLORY BE TO HIM WHO PROVIDES
BOTH THE BEGINNING AND THE END."

Indexes

Index to Preface and Introduction

INDEXES

INDEXES

Origen, 20
Otranto, 26
Ottoman Empire, 1, 18
Oxford, 9

Paissy, 14
Palmer, G.E.H., 21, 22, 26
Papadopoulos, Theodore, 9
Parios, Athanasios, 40
Paris, 9
Parthenios, St., 15
Path to Paradise, The (Scupoli), 26
Patmos, 8
Patriarchs, 7
Paul's Fourteen Epistles Interpreted by Theophylaktos, Archbishop of Bulgaria (Nicodemos), 32–33
Paul, St., 32–33, 36
Paulopoulos, Nicodemos, 52
Pedalion (Nicodemos), 3, 43. *See also: Rudder, The*
Phanar, 7
Phanariots, 6–7
Philokalia (Nicodemos), 2–3, 13, 20–24, 27, 37
Photios, St., 32
Pinamonti, 28
Pisa, 9
Plato, 9, 29
Prayer of the Heart (Kallistos), 37
Pythagoras, 29

Recaut, P., 8
Repentance, 43
Roman Catholics, 26
Rome, 9
Rudder, The (Nicodemos), 41, 43–47
Runciman, Steven, 8–9
Russians, 11

Scupoli, Lorenzo, 26–27
Sherrard, Philip, 22
Silvestros of Caesarea, 13
Skyropoula, 14, 47
Smyrna, 9, 10, 33
Sophronios, Patriarch of Jerusalem, 12
Spinoza, 52
Spiritual Exercises (Nicodemos), 3, 17, 28–30
Spiritual world, 33

St. Anne, the skete of, 12
Stefanides, Vasilios, 7
Symeon the New Theologian, St., 3, 30, 37, 38
Symvoulevtikon Encheiridion (Nicodemos), 3–4
Synaxaristes (Nicodemos), 17–18

Ten Commandments, 42
Terpos, Nectarios, 18
Thassos, 14
Theocracy, Byzantine vs. Islamic, 6
Theodore the Studite, St., 30, 34
Theodoretos, 28, 32, 44
Theodosios II, Patriarch, 12
Theophan the Recluse, 21, 26, 27
Thephrastos, 29
Theophylaktos, 32, 33
Thessalonike, 9
Toynbee, Arnold, 7
Trebizond, 9
Tsesme, 11
Turkish State, 4–6, 11, 18–19

University of Athens, 7
Unseen Warfare (Nicodemos), 3, 17, 26–28, 48

Vaporis, Nomikos M., 18
Vardis, Anthimos, 11
Velichkovsii, Paissy, 21
Venice, 9, 26
Vienna, 40
Virgin Mary, 24, 35, 36, 48
Voltaire, 52
Voulismas, Ierotheos, 10–11

Ware, Kallistos, 22
Ware, Timothy, 7
Western Church, 6
Western Enlightenment, 52
Wheler, George, 7
Woodhouse, C.M., 9
Writings From the Philokalia on Prayer of the Heart (trans. Kadloubovsky and Palmer), 21

Zagoraios, Dionysios, 37
Zante, 9
Zygabenos, 32

Index to Texts

Abraham, 143, 189
Ache, 93

Adam, 76, 81, 150–151
Adultery, 157

237

INDEXES

Agamemnon, 94
Agathon, 114
Alexander the Great, 91, 103, 144, 200
Alexander the Macedonian, 99
Amos the Prophet, 102, 111, 131
Angels, 143, 145, 194, 207, 210
Anger, 149
Anthony, St., 130
Apophatic theology, 197
Aquila, 212
Araspus, 95*n*13
Archilohos, 145
Aristotle: on controlling the breath, 160; on games of chance, 133; on the imagination, 146; on the mind, 216; on the mind and senses, 139, 140
Armenopoulos, 133
Artemis, 92
Athanasios, St, 124, 130
Atheism, 203
Augustine, St.: on creation, 74; on divine light and beauty, 223–24; on the Incarnation, 204, 211
Aurelious, Marcus, 101
Avradatus, 91

Balaam, 113, 232
Balthasar, 111
Baptism, 68
Basil the Great, St.: on acquiring the virtues, 183; on the attributes of God, 213–14, 216; on beauty, 222; on bribery, 122; on clothing, 124–25, 128, 129; on the commandments, 174, 176; on counselors, 181–82; on creation, 71, 202; on delights of the mind, 228; on divine light, 221; on eating, 109, 112, 116*n*3, 117–18*n*7; on the eyes, 86–87; on faith, 184; on God the Creator, 196; on the heart, 154, 167; on the imagination, 148, 152; on the Incarnation, 204; on laughter, 114–16; on life, 125; on living in the world, 138; on meditation, 158; on melodies, 97; on prayer, 170; on purity of mind, 139–40, 157; on reading Scripture, 187, 188–89, 192, 195; on reasons for creation, 74; on slander, 99; on suffering, 143; on temperance, 110; on the tongue, 114; on the virtues, 177; on vision, 91
Baths, 132–33
Bathsheba, 91
Beds, 131–32
Blachia, 170
Body, 68–69, 74, 230–31
Book of Revelation, 209
Books, 190
Breath, controlling the, 160

Caesar, 98
Cambysis, 91
Canon of Polycheitus, 106*n*4
Cataphatic theology, 197
Catherine, Queen of France, 103
Chastity, 184
Chedorlaomer, King, 143
Chilon, 188
Christ Jesus: blessed others, 118*n*10; will crown the victors, 143; did not laugh, 115–16; did not have vain imaginations, 150–51; Name of, 168–69; New Adam, 82; physical appearance of, 212; responds, 143; resurrection of, 208–09
Chrysostom, St. John: on acquiring the virtues, 183; on the body, 121; on clothing, 123–24, 129; on the eyes, 88; fasted three months, 231; on games of chance, 133; gladness in God, 215; on the heart, 157; on the Holy Scripture, 187, 188, 192, 194; on laughing, 119*n*13; on the mind, 68; on the physical appearance of Christ, 212–13; on the pleasures, 82; on prayer, 170; on revenge, 182; on tears, 116; on the virtues, 177, 182; on the will of God, 175
Church Fathers, on physical pleasures, 78
Clement of Alexandria, 129
Cleon, 134*n*5
Cleopas, 209
Climacus, St. John: on absence of malice, 180; on clothing, 128; on prayer, 162, 163–65; on reading of Scripture, 192; on the senses, 80; on silence, 168; on spiritual delights, 229; on the touch, 121; regarding women, 92
Clothing, 123–29
Conscience, 175–76
Contrition, 162
Courage, 184
Creation, praises God, 200–01
Curses, 113–14
Cyril of Alexandria, St., 116*n*3
Cyrus, 91

Daedalos, 151
David, 91, 123, 125, 137, 175, 179, 189, 212
Death, comes quickly, 125
Delagazis, Ioannis, 106*n*3
Delight, spiritual, 173–74
Democritos, 67, 119*n*16
Desire, 149
Devil: in the heart, 156–57; and the imagination, 149–50; and passions, 141–42; and prayer, 171; and the sense of touch, 120–21; and the senses, 78
Diadochos, St., 133, 140, 156, 162, 165, 171

INDEXES

INDEXES

INDEXES